EXPATRIATE
TAX AND INVESTMENT
HANDBOOK

EXPATRIATE
TAX AND INVESTMENT
HANDBOOK

Fifth Edition

Nigel Eastaway and David Phillips

© Allied Dunbar Assurance plc 1995

ISBN 0 75200 166 3

Published by

Pearson Professional Limited
Maple House, 149 Tottenham Court Road
London W1P 9LL

Associated Offices

**Australia, Belgium, Canada, Hong Kong, India, Japan,
Luxembourg, Singapore, Spain, USA**

A CIP catalogue record for this book is available from the British
Library.

Printed in Great Britain by
Mackays of Chatham plc, Chatham, Kent

Abbreviations

CGT	capital gains tax
CGTA 1979	Capital Gains Tax Act 1979
ESC	Extra-Statutory Concession
EU	European Union
FA	Finance Act
FSA 1986	Financial Services Act 1986
IHT	inheritance tax
IHTA 1984	Inheritance Tax Act 1984
para	paragraph (of a Schedule to an Act)
s	section (of an Act)
Sched	Schedule (to an Act)
TA 1988	Income and Corporation Taxes Act 1988
TCGA 1992	Taxation of Chargeable Gains Act 1992
TMA	Taxes Management Act 1970
VAT	value added tax
VATA 1983	Value Added Tax Act 1983

Acknowledgements

The central chapters of this new edition of the Handbook, with their updated exposition of United Kingdom tax legislation as it affects British expatriates, were provided by *Moores Rowland*, Chartered Accountants, and in particular by Nigel Eastaway, FCA, FCIS, FTII, partner in that firm. The special chapter on tax aspects of property in the United Kingdom owned by expatriates was written by P A Goodman, MA, ACI, ATII of *Wilkins Kennedy*, Chartered Accountants. The chapter on pensions contributed to the previous edition by Debbie Harrison, BA, author of several books on UK and European pensions published by the *Financial Times*, has been extensively revised for this edition. There is also a new chapter on offshore financial centres, written by Peter Gartland, editor of *Offshore Alert*. The chapter on investment originally written by Richard Sayer with contributions from other colleagues of his at *Allied Dunbar*, has been specially revised for this edition by Peter Ashton of *Allied Dunbar International Assurance Limited*.

David Phillips, MA, DPhil
Editor
Former editor, *Resident Abroad*
(The *Financial Times* magazine for British expatriates)

Contents

Abbreviations   **v**

Acknowledgements   **vi**

Introduction   **xiii**

1   Key terms and concepts in the expatriate world   **1**

1.1   Introduction   1
1.2   Key terms and rules   2

2   Categories of expatriate   **13**

2.1   Introduction   13
2.2   Short-term working abroad: the expatriate who
       remains UK resident   13
2.3   Long absences   14
2.4   Foreign emoluments   18
2.5   Other reliefs for resident expatriates   19
2.6   Long-term working abroad: the non-resident   21
2.7   The short-term self-employed expatriate   22
2.8   The long-term self-employed expatriate   23
2.9   Categories of expatriate   24
2.10   The expatriate family   26
2.11   Expatriates retiring abroad or permanently emigrating   27

3   Guide to domicile and residence: the tax consequences   **29**

3.1   Introduction   29
3.2   Using the guide   29
3.3   Domicile chart   34
3.4   Residence charts   36
3.5   UK taxation chart   42
3.6   UK taxation—effect on investments chart   44

4 Income arising in the United Kingdom **47**

4.1 Introduction 47
4.2 The UK schedular system of income tax 48
4.3 Interest from bank and building society deposits 49
4.4 Interest from government, local authority and corporate stocks 51
4.5 Life assurance policies 54
4.6 National Savings 56
4.7 Pensions 56
4.8 Employments 57
4.9 Trades and professions 58
4.10 Royalties and patents 61
4.11 Maintenance payments 61
4.12 Trust and estate income 62
4.13 Avoidance of higher rate liability 63
4.14 Lloyd's Underwriters 64
4.15 Non-resident's entitlement to UK personal allowances 65

5 Tax aspects of UK property **67**

5.1 Rental income 67
5.2 Loan interest 68
5.3 Administration and collection of tax 70
5.4 Self-assessment 71
5.5 Furnished holiday lettings 71
5.6 Mortgage interest relief at source (MIRAS) 72
5.7 Capital gains tax: principal private residence 74
5.8 Inheritance tax 76

6 Capital gains tax **77**

6.1 Residence 77
6.2 Husband and wife 77
6.3 Emigration 78
6.4 Property 78
6.5 Business gains 78
6.6 Reinvestment relief 82
6.7 Foreign taxes 83
6.8 Trusts 83
6.9 Offshore funds 83
6.10 Gifts from non-residents 84
6.11 Non-sterling bank accounts 84
6.12 UK investment managers 85

7 Inheritance tax **87**

7.1   Chargeable transfers   88
7.2   Exemptions and reliefs   89
7.3   Potentially exempt transfers   89
7.4   Transfers between spouses   89
7.5   Annual allowances   89
7.6   Normal expenditure out of income   90
7.7   Gifts in consideration of marriage   90
7.8   Dispositions for maintenance of family   91
7.9   Other exempt transfers   91
7.10   Business property relief   91
7.11   Agricultural property relief   92
7.12   Potentially exempt lifetime transfers of agricultural and
       business property   93
7.13   Persons not domiciled in the United Kingdom   93
7.14   Location of assets   94
7.15   The non-UK domiciled spouse   94
7.16   Settled property   95
7.17   Inheritance tax planning   96
7.18   Insurance policies   97
7.19   The family home   98

8 Wills, settlements and trusts **101**

8.1   Wills and assets in more than one jurisdiction   101
8.2   Will trusts   102
8.3   Incidence of inheritance tax   103
8.4   Written variations   103
8.5   Trusts   104

9 Other UK taxes **117**

9.1   Value added tax   117
9.2   Cars   119
9.3   Excise duties   119
9.4   Personal belongings   119
9.5   Stamp duty   120

**10 The taxpayer's rights and obligations in his country of
    residence** **123**

10.1   Taxpayers' rights   123
10.2   Taxpayers' obligations   125

11 Double taxation agreements | 137

11.1	Fiscal residence	137
11.2	Dividends	138
11.3	Interest	139
11.4	Royalties	139
11.5	Income from real property	140
11.6	Businesses	140
11.7	Capital gains	141
11.8	Independent personal services	141
11.9	Dependent personal services	141
11.10	Entertainers and sportsmen	142
11.11	Students and teachers	142
11.12	Pensions	142
11.13	Other income	144
11.14	Non-discrimination	144
11.15	Mutual agreement procedure	144
11.16	Exchange of information	144
11.17	Inheritance tax	145
11.18	Unilateral relief	146
11.19	Treaty shopping	146

12 The returning expatriate | 147

12.1	Tax liabilities on return	147
12.2	Capital gains tax	152
12.3	Dangers of evasion	153
12.4	Miscellaneous investments	154
12.5	Unremittable overseas income	155
12.6	National Insurance	155
12.7	Other matters	155

13 Constructing an investment portfolio
by Peter Ashton | 157

13.1	Introduction	157
13.2	Establishing objectives	157
13.3	Risks and rewards	159
13.4	Constructing a portfolio	162

14 Bank and building society deposits | 165

| 14.1 | Banking services for expatriates | 165 |
| 14.2 | Bank and building society deposits | 166 |

15   Fixed-interest securities   **169**

15.1   British government stocks   169
15.2   Bulldog bonds   170
15.3   Eurobonds   170
15.4   Corporate bonds   172

16   Direct investment in equities   **173**

16.1   Useful publications   173
16.2   Individual investors: risks and potential advantages   174

17   Collective investment vehicles
       by Pauline Skypala   **177**

17.1   Introduction   177
17.2   UK investment and unit trusts   177
17.3   Offshore funds   179

18   Life assurance
       by Peter Ashton   **185**

18.1   Introduction   185
18.2   Three types of contract   186
18.3   Offshore single premium bonds   187
18.4   Portfolio bonds   187
18.5   The UK taxation of offshore single premium bonds   188

19   Pensions
       by Debbie Harrison   **191**

19.1   Employees   191
19.2   State pensions   192
19.3   EU Multilateral Agreement   194
19.4   Occupational pensions   195
19.5   Retention in home scheme   195
19.6   Final salary   195
19.7   Money purchase   196
19.8   Personal pensions   196
19.9   Pension options abroad   197
19.10 Offshore pensions   198
19.11 Transfers   200
19.12 Retiring abroad   201
19.13 Useful addresses   203

20   Coping with exchange rate movements
     by Howard Flight   **207**

20.1   Exchange rates and cash: managed currency funds   207
20.2   Exchange rates and bonds   208
20.3   Exchange rates and equity investment   209
20.4   Exchange rates and day-to-day living expenses   210

21   Offshore financial centres
     by Peter Gartland   **211**

21.1   Introduction   211
21.2   The Channel Islands and the Isle of Man   212
21.3   Luxembourg and Dublin   214

Appendix I   Checklists of dos and don'ts   217

Appendix II   Tax tables   221

Appendix III   Useful addresses   223

Index   225

Introduction

To be forewarned is to be forearmed, and nowhere is this maxim more apposite than in the fields of tax and investment. It is for this reason, that in preparing this new edition of the Handbook, we have gone into some detail about some important future changes over the next few years in the UK tax system, when all income liable to UK tax will be taxed on a current year basis and self-assessment regulations will come into force. Here, as in the rest of the book, the specific relevance of these changes to British expatriates is the focus of the exposition, which is aimed primarily at professional advisers, but which some individual expatriates with no professional background in these matters will also find useful.

The intention of the Handbook is to help British citizens living overseas, whether working or in retirement, to manage their financial affairs to their greatest possible advantage. To do this, it considers both current and future income, from whatever source; and assets, whether already acquired, likely to be acquired in future, or destined to be passed on to the owner's heirs. The objective is, of course, a practical one, and for this reason we have ignored some possible changes in the various areas of expatriate concern that are still only possibilities of one degree or another. Examples are the indexation of social security pensions for expatriates and the introduction of single pricing and disclosure of charges for unit trusts. These are matters subject to debate and consultation processes which could go on for months, but might just as well go on for years. As soon as anything substantive arises, it will be covered in future editions of this Handbook.

Even as far as UK taxation is concerned, it is impossible in a book of this size to cover the subject exhaustively. Here we have tried to concentrate on the areas that we feel are likely to be of prime importance to the expatriate. For a more detailed explanation of UK tax legislation, the reader is referred in the first instance to the *Allied Dunbar Tax Handbook* and the *Allied Dunbar Pensions Handbook*; and in the field of investment to the *Allied Dunbar Investment and Savings Handbook.*

United Kingdom taxation is a complicated matter, not least when it concerns British expatriates. The main reason for the complexity is that the whole present system of taxation has evolved over nearly two centuries in a piecemeal fashion, with several distinct powers, Parliament, the Treasury, the law courts, and the Inland Revenue, taking part in the process.

There is a further source of complexity as far as expatriates are concerned. The various Taxes Acts and annual Finance Acts are drawn up with the habitually resident population in mind. Provisions specifically affecting expatriates are, so to speak, usually incidental to the main thrust of fiscal legislation. Case law relevant to expatriates can be cited as early as 1824, but by their very definition cases are also incidental, and proverbial wisdom has it that they are altered by circumstances. It follows that there is no systematic treatment of expatriates in what can be described only by an indulgent use of the word as the British tax *system.*

That system, such as it is, is what the Inland Revenue, tax lawyers, chartered accountants, and other professional advisers have to interpret and implement. But expatriates themselves are more likely to have a different perspective altogether. For them it is more natural to consider the whole matter of tax and investment from the point of view of their own particular function—whether, in other words, they are working or retired and, if working, whether they are on a short-term contract or a more lasting arrangement, whether they are in the service of the Crown, employed by a company or a non-commercial international organisation, whether they are self-employed, and so on.

In this new edition of the Handbook we approach the subject from both these main angles: from the various categories of expatriate according to function; and from the tax system itself. But even before this can be done, there are various key terms and concepts that keep cropping up in any discussion of expatriate financial matters which are by no means self-explanatory.

So we begin the Handbook with an explanation of these fundamental terms. We follow this with the two ways of classifying expatriates just mentioned. We then conclude these introductory chapters with an outline of the tax implications for expatriates, whether they are resident or non-resident in the eyes of the Inland Revenue.

Chapters 4 to 11, which follow, treat these tax matters in much greater detail, with a view to laying the foundations of sound tax planning. The tax treatment of any income an expatriate may have in the United Kingdom is first explained, a separate chapter is devoted to income from property in the United Kingdom, and further chapters deal with capital gains tax, inheritance tax, and other UK taxes. The important and highly complex subject of trusts is taken up in another chapter.

At no point in expatriate life is it more important to plan and act in advance, where tax and investment are concerned, than in the period immediately before returning to the United Kingdom, and advice on these matters is contained in a separate chapter.

The next ten chapters deal with the management of an expatriate's personal finances, and among other topics cover the construction of an investment portfolio, an explanation of the various investment media available, and the role of life assurance. Special chapters are devoted, respectively, to investment funds (including offshore funds) and to pensions for expatriates. The offshore theme is developed further in a new chapter on offshore financial centres.

Finally, a certain amount of reference material has been put into the appendices to the Handbook, including tax tables, and a list of useful addresses.

1 Key terms and concepts in the expatriate world

1.1 Introduction

Table 1.1 Terms and rules explained in this chapter

	page		page
United Kingdom	2	Domicile of choice	5
UK Finance		Deemed domicile	6
Acts and Taxes Acts	2	Residence	7
Extra-statutory		Dual residence	7
concessions	2	The six-month rule	8
UK tax year	3	The three-month rule	9
Expatriate	3	Available accommodation	9
Offshore	3	Working abroad	9
Domicile	3	Emigration	10
Domicile of origin	4	Ordinary residence	10
Domicile of dependence	5		

This chapter is addressed in the first place to the reader new to the subject, but it may also be useful for reference purposes to more experienced expatriates or their professional advisers.

Any person leaving the United Kingdom to spend a prolonged period overseas will soon be obliged to add a whole battery of new terms to his or her vocabulary, or at the very least, new meanings to familiar expressions. Some of these terms crop up frequently in the context of tax and investment, where they are not only specially defined but tend to have specific legal implications.

As these terms are fundamental to an understanding of the topics covered by this book, we review them at the outset. Inextricably bound up with these terms, and indeed often forming a decisive part of their definition, are a number of rules applied in practice by the Inland Revenue to determine the tax status of UK expatriates. Here we also review some of the more far-reaching of these rules.

1.2   Key terms and rules

1.2.1   United Kingdom ('The United Kingdom of Great Britain and Northern Ireland')

The United Kingdom was originally established by the Union of Great Britain and Ireland in 1801, and took its present form in 1921 when the Irish Free State (since 1949, the Republic of Ireland) was created.

The United Kingdom now consists of England, Wales and Scotland (which make up Great Britain), and Northern Ireland (Ulster). It does not include the Channel Islands or the Isle of Man, which have their own legislative assemblies and their own tax laws.

1.2.2   UK Finance Acts and Taxes Acts

The Finance Act is the annual enactment of a Bill put before Parliament by the government of the day concerning the raising of finance by taxation. It incorporates the measures proposed by the Chancellor of the Exchequer in his Budget, after they have been considered in close detail in committee.

Taxes Acts either introduce a new tax, such as inheritance tax (IHT) in 1984, or consolidate previous enactments relating to a particular tax or taxes—a recent example is the Income and Corporation Taxes Act 1988 (TA 1988).

The Financial Services Act 1986 (FSA 1986) is an act of a different kind. Its purpose was to regulate the carrying on of investment business, and to make provisions concerning insurance and stock market dealings. The Act is of interest to expatriates not only because it establishes the framework of investor protection in the United Kingdom, but because it also contains provision for the recognition by the Secretary of State of collective investment schemes (unitised funds) in member states of the European Union and in other states recognised as 'designated countries or territories'.

1.2.3   Extra-statutory concessions

These are detailed modifications to the various taxing statutes applied in general practice by the Inland Revenue. The concessions were last revised and consolidated in June 1994 as booklet IR 1. Details may be obtained from HMSO Publications Centre, 51 Nine Elms Lane, London SW8 5DR, any tax inquiry centre, tax office or the Public Enquiry Room, West Wing, Somerset House, Strand, London WC2R 1LB.

1.2.4   UK tax year

As a consequence of the reform of the calendar in 1752, the tax year in the United Kingdom runs from April 6 one year to April 5 the next. British expatriates should be aware, however, that the tax year in their host country will be on a different basis—usually coinciding with the calendar year.

1.2.5   Expatriate

The word 'expatriate' means simply a person living away from his or her native country. It in no way refers, as is often mistakenly implied, to a person's former situation or state (there is no such thing as a 'patriate', anyway), and it is incorrect to spell the word with a hyphen.

'Expatriate' is not a legally defined term, and it is not part of the Tax Inspector's vocabulary. Instead, the Inland Revenue uses the words 'resident' and 'non-resident' (discussed below). In this book we shall henceforth follow the style of Inland Revenue leaflets by referring to individuals most often as 'he', rather than 'he or she', but only for the sake of brevity and simplicity.

1.2.6   Offshore

An asset, such as a bank deposit or shares in an investment fund, or a liability such as a bank loan is said to be offshore when it is in a jurisdiction at least one remove from that of the individual holding the asset or incurring the liability. In spite of its legal implications, however, the term is not a legal term as such, but simply one of ordinary discourse. It usually refers to a jurisdiction which, from the investor's (or borrower's) point of view, offers opportunities to mitigate tax liabilities.

1.2.7   Domicile

In 1987 the Law Commission and the Scottish Law Commission presented a report to Parliament recommending changes in the present laws concerning domicile. As far as British expatriates are concerned the proposed changes could be important, in so far as they would make it easier to establish a domicile of choice (see **1.2.10**). Interest in the Law Commission's recommendations was rekindled towards the end of 1991, when in reply to a parliamentary question the Attorney General said that the government had accepted the recommendations and would introduce legislation when a suitable opportunity arose. For a number of reasons, however, it is unlikely that such legislation will be enacted in the near future and on 26 May 1993 the Prime Minister confirmed that the government had no immediate plans to introduce legislation on this subject.

What follows immediately below sets out the rules in force at the time of this Handbook's publication.

Domicile is a long-established concept rooted in English common law. It is the fundamental concept determining an individual's rights and duties. It can be defined as the legal relationship between an individual and a territory subject to a distinctive legal system. Strictly speaking, therefore, a person has a domicile in, for example, England and Wales, Scotland or Northern Ireland rather than the United Kingdom but for most purposes the term UK domicile is used. The courts of that territory may then invoke that system as the individual's personal law (relevant, for instance, to marriage and divorce, and what lawyers refer to as 'succession'—inheritance, in another word). The point about the courts is important, because many expatriates are under the misapprehension that they individually, and not the courts, are able to determine their domicile.

Put more practically, if somewhat less accurately, domicile refers to the country to which an individual belongs, the country which is his natural home in which he resides and intends to remain permanently or indefinitely. Important as it is in UK law, domicile is not a universal concept of private international law. Outside the British Commonwealth, only the United States, Denmark, Norway and Brazil use domicile as the connecting link between an individual and the system of law to which he is subject. Most European countries use nationality as the test determining personal law.

For British expatriates, the question of domicile is significant for reasons of tax. It is particularly important in regard to IHT, but it can also have a bearing on an individual's liability to other taxes, as we explain in later chapters.

1.2.8   Domicile of origin

While it is perfectly possible for an individual to be without a fiscal residence at any time, he cannot be without a domicile. A domicile of origin is established at birth. For legitimate children this is the domicile of the father. An illegitimate child, or a legitimate child whose father dies before his birth, takes the domicile of the mother at the time of birth unless the child is adopted in which case the domicile of origin becomes that of the adoptive father. The parent's domicile will prevail regardless of where the child is born, despite any effect the place of birth may have on the child's nationality or citizenship. A child will retain this domicile of origin until he can establish an independent domicile of choice or until his father (or mother in the case of illegitimate children) himself acquires a new domicile of choice. In the latter case the child will also acquire the new domicile but this will be a domicile of dependence, not a domicile of choice.

1.2.9 Domicile of dependence

Dependency on the domicile of the parent will continue until the child reaches the age of 16 or marries, whichever is earlier (Domicile and Matrimonial Proceedings Act 1973). This does not, however, apply in Scotland where a boy can acquire an independent domicile at age 14 and a girl at age 12. Where the parents of a child under 16 (or the respective ages in Scotland) are living apart, the child's dependent domicile is that of his mother if he lives with her and does not have a home with his father.

Until 1973, a woman acquired her husband's domicile on marriage. Any woman married before 1 January 1974 will therefore have had a domicile of dependence, but she will now (following the Act of 1973 just quoted) be considered to have that domicile as one of choice if it is not also her domicile of origin. Since the beginning of 1974, a married woman has been treated as an independent person in matters of domicile and will retain her domicile of origin on marriage on or after 1 January 1974 unless she establishes her own new domicile of choice.

1.2.10 Domicile of choice

The third form of domicile, the domicile of choice, is the one which can be of greatest interest to expatriates and which can cause the most problems. It can be very difficult to convince the courts that a new domicile has been acquired. The basic requirements are that the person should reside in the new country and that he should intend to stay there for an unlimited period. The residence part can be simply established; the length of that residence is not necessarily material, so that if, for example, a person dies shortly after arrival, he may none the less have satisfied the test of residence. Providing evidence of the intention to remain is more complex.

Some of the indicators of intent which will be considered on the advancement of any claim to a change of domicile include the following:

(1)   a period of residence in the new country;
(2)   purchase of a home there;
(3)   disposal of property in the old country;
(4)   development of business, social, religious and political interests in the new country;
(5)   burial arrangements there;

(6)   local education of children;
(7)   the making of a new will according to local laws;
(8)   application for citizenship of the new country;
(9)   severance of all formal ties with the old country.

It is invariably impossible to prove an intention; the best that can be hoped for is that the circumstantial evidence will be sufficient for the authorities to be convinced.

If a domicile of choice is abandoned then the domicile of origin revives until such time as a new domicile of choice is acquired. It would be open to the authorities to claim that on the facts of the abandonment of a purported new domicile, it did not exist. This can have serious effects for IHT if the revived domicile of origin is considered as never having been lost.

1.2.11   Deemed domicile

The 'deemed domicile' provisions contained in Inheritance Tax Act 1984 (IHTA 1984), s 267 have no counterpart in the income tax or capital gains tax legislation. The effect of this section is to treat as UK domiciled anyone who emigrates from the United Kingdom having been previously domiciled there or who had been a long-term resident. This deeming provision endures for a period of at least three years following departure.

The section treats an individual as domiciled in the United Kingdom if:

(1)   he was domiciled in the United Kingdom within the three years immediately preceding the relevant time; or
(2)   he was resident in the United Kingdom in not less than 17 out of the 20 income tax years ending with the income tax year in which the relevant time falls.

The 'relevant time' referred to above is the time at which a transfer of value takes place.

For the person domiciled initially within the United Kingdom, item (1) means there is a period of at least three calendar years from the acquisition of a new domicile during which time liability for IHT remains. For the long-term UK resident who is not domiciled here, there must be an absence of three complete income tax years before he can be free of IHT. Double taxation agreements which cover IHT may affect this provision: see Chapter 11 and Chapter 7.

1.2.12 Residence

Whatever meanings may be given to the words 'residence' and 'resident' in everyday discourse, we are concerned here only with their use in the context of UK taxation. In that context, the expressions 'ordinarily resident', 'dual residence' and 'non-resident' are also frequently used, and are defined below. None of these terms is explicitly defined in the various Taxes Acts, and the Inland Revenue states that it uses the terms 'resident' and 'ordinarily resident' in their everyday sense without giving them any special or technical meaning.

Nevertheless, the terms have been explained in a number of court decisions, going back at least as far as 1875; and the Inland Revenue in practice applies a number of rules to their application, which are set out in some detail in its booklet IR 20: *Residents and Non-residents—Liability to Tax in the United Kingdom* last revised in November 1993. Most, if not all of these rules are subject to exceptions; some (but not all) of them have statutory force; while others embody certain concessions that are allowed in practice by the Inland Revenue, although not specified in the Taxes Acts. These are the so-called extra-statutory concessions (see **1.2.3**).

The booklet IR 20 points out that the terms 'resident' and 'ordinarily resident', while not defined in the UK Taxes Acts, are always used to describe a situation arising in a tax year (ie from 6 April to 5 April in the following year), and not in relation to some longer or shorter period. The question that generally has to be decided is whether or not a person is resident (or ordinarily resident) in the United Kingdom in a particular tax year.

The residence of a married woman is determined independently from that of her spouse. The income of a married woman has been taxed independently from her spouse since 1990/91.

1.2.13 Dual residence

An individual who is resident for tax purposes in the United Kingdom is not precluded from also being resident elsewhere, and a claim to non-residence cannot be sustained simply on the grounds of being resident in another state. A person may be resident in two or more states in the same tax year or, indeed, resident in none. Where dual residence gives rise to a double charge to tax then special provisions may exist in a tax treaty between the states which can overrule the purely domestic regulations on residence. See Chapter 11.

Finally, before going on to a discussion of the current practice, it should also be pointed out that *force majeure* will be ignored in any decision as to whether or not an individual is resident in the United Kingdom under the six-month rule. Illness, military service, or even, in borderline cases, the cancellation of a flight, can sufficiently extend a stay so as to render the otherwise non-resident person resident for a particular tax year. However, for the three-month rule any days spent in the United Kingdom because of exceptional circumstances beyond the taxpayer's control, for example, illness of the taxpayer or a member of his family, are not normally counted.

1.2.14   Physical presence: the six-month rule

If an individual is to be regarded as resident in the United Kingdom for a given tax year he must normally be physically present in the country for at least part of that year. *He will always be resident if he is in the United Kingdom for six months or more in the tax year.* **There are no exceptions to this rule** (the Inland Revenue's use of bold type), although a double taxation treaty may treat the taxpayer as non-resident for income and gains covered by the treaty. Six months is regarded as equivalent to 183 days. For this purpose a count is made of the total number of days spent in the United Kingdom during the year, whether the stay consists of one period only or a succession of visits. Under present Inland Revenue practice days of arrival and days of departure are normally ignored.

In spite of the words in bold type in the previous paragraph, the rule it refers to is subject to qualification in the case of an individual leaving the United Kingdom permanently, or leaving to take up full-time employment abroad for a period which includes one complete tax year. Such an individual, or his spouse, may be treated as non-resident and not ordinarily resident (see below for an explanation of this expression) from the day following his departure. This treatment can be applied regardless of when during the tax year the individual leaves. If, for example, he leaves on 5 January, he will have been resident for nine months, but will be treated as non-resident for the three remaining months. This treatment is purely concessionary, but is an Inland Revenue practice of some long standing.

The converse of the six-month rule does not generally apply. That is to say that an individual who is not physically present in the United Kingdom for six months is not necessarily to be treated as non-resident for tax purposes.

An individual's residence is what lawyers call 'a question of fact'. That is to say, a question of actual circumstances. But a permanent or semi-permanent abode is not necessary to establish residence. In various court cases, a yacht, a shooting lodge and a hunting box have been held as establishing that their occupants were resident in the United Kingdom. But in other cases, living in hotels or with friends in the United Kingdom was not enough to render the individuals concerned resident for tax purposes. If an individual is physically present in the United Kingdom for less than six months, the Inland Revenue's decision as to whether or not he is resident for tax purposes depends on other circumstances.

A final point to be made about physical presence is that under TA 1988, s 334, a British subject or a citizen of the Republic of Ireland whose ordinary residence (see below) is in the United Kingdom will continue to be taxed as resident if he is abroad for the purpose of occasional residence only.

1.2.15 The three-month rule

Under this rule a person may become resident if he makes regular lengthy visits to the United Kingdom. Where the visits are made every year for four consecutive years, and the average length of stay over those four years is 91 days or more a year, then the visitor will be considered as resident in the United Kingdom. Where the pattern of visits is irregular or cannot be foreseen then the residence status will apply after the fourth year. If, on the other hand, the pattern is known and admitted then residence will start from the original date of arrival.

When calculating the number of days, days of arrival or departure would normally not be counted, however frequent the visits. It would, however, seem prudent if this rule jeopardises non-resident status to keep visits to no more than 90 days per annum on average.

1.2.16 Available accommodation

If a person goes abroad permanently but has accommodation (eg, a house or apartment) available for his use in the United Kingdom, he was, prior to 1993/94 regarded as resident here for any tax year in which he visited the United Kingdom, however short the visits were. From 1993/94 available accommodation in the United Kingdom is ignored in the case of a short-term visitor to the United Kingdom, ie a person who does not intend to stay more than three months a year in the United Kingdom.

1.2.17 Working abroad

A person who leaves the United Kingdom to work full-time abroad under a contract of employment is treated as not resident and not ordinarily resident from the day following departure if the absence will last for at least a complete tax year and any visits to the United Kingdom do not breach the six-month or three-month rules described above. UK residence would be acquired on the day of arrival in the United Kingdom following the end of the employment.

An Inland Revenue booklet IR58 'Going to Work Abroad' answers many of the questions asked about tax where a UK resident works abroad as an employee. The Department of Social Security Leaflet NI132 gives information about National Insurance Contributions.

1.2.18   Emigration

A person who leaves the United Kingdom permanently is provisionally treated as not resident and not ordinarily resident from the day following departure if he can provide evidence that his emigration is permanent. Normally this provisional ruling is confirmed after the taxpayer has lived abroad for a whole tax year, provided that the six-month or three-month rules are not breached. In the absence of such evidence the taxpayer remains provisionally resident in the United Kingdom for up to three years. If on a final analysis the six-month or three-month rules have not been broken the taxpayer is reclassified as not resident from the day of departure and his tax liabilities adjusted accordingly.

Table 1.2   Residence summary

A person who is resident in the United Kingdom will usually have a liability for UK income tax on his worldwide income and would also be liable for capital gains on any chargeable gains.

In essence, a person will be considered resident in the United Kingdom if:

(1)   he is physically present in the United Kingdom for six months or more in the tax year, given that six months are equivalent to 183 days and days of arrival and departure are ignored; or

(2)   he makes substantial and habitual visits to the United Kingdom; 'substantial' is taken to mean an average of three months or more each year and visits are considered 'habitual' after four consecutive years; or

(3)   being a British subject (or citizen of the Republic of Ireland) he has left the United Kingdom for the purpose only of occasional residence abroad (TA 1988, s 334).

1.2.19 Ordinary residence

Whereas the term 'residence' is mainly concerned with individual tax years, the term 'ordinary residence' (more often encountered in the adjectival form 'ordinarily resident') implies a greater degree of continuity. Again the term is not defined in any statute, but in some relevant cases the courts have held ordinary residence to be the converse of occasional or casual residence. The Inland Revenue booklet IR 20 states that 'ordinarily resident is broadly equivalent to habitually resident. If a person is resident in the United Kingdom year after year, he is ordinarily resident here'.

An individual who becomes resident in the United Kingdom under the three-month rule (see **1.2.15**) will also be considered ordinarily resident.

2   Categories of expatriate

2.1   Introduction

Statistically speaking, British expatriates are a fairly representative sample of the UK population at large, except that for obvious reasons their age distribution is different. In ordinary commonsense terms, therefore, expatriates come in all forms and guises, and it is a mistake to think that they conform to any kind of stereotype. So in this chapter when speaking of categories of expatriate, we mean to refer only to their various situations or functions that determine their tax status in the eyes of the Inland Revenue. This, we believe, is to adopt the individual's own point of view. Because in seeking a thread to guide him through the ghastly British tax labyrinth, the individual expatriate is likely to begin by defining his own situation in terms of his functional reasons for being overseas in the first place—whether, that is to say, he is working abroad and, if so, for how long and under what terms and conditions; whether he has retired abroad; whether he intends to return to the United Kingdom, and, if he does, when; or whether he has decided (or more or less decided) to emigrate permanently.

From this point on, our Handbook inevitably becomes more technical, and in particular we are obliged to resort to the use of abbreviations when referring to the various Taxes Acts and Finance Acts, not to mention the occasional Inland Revenue statement of practice or its extra-statutory concessions. For an explanation of these abbreviations the reader is referred to the list on page v.

2.2   Short-term working abroad: the expatriate who remains UK resident

The previous chapter explained the terms 'resident' and 'non-resident' and it was pointed out that most working expatriates would achieve non-resident status if their overseas work was for a period that included at least one complete tax year. There are, however, many people who, although abroad for more than 12 months, are not in fact overseas from 6 April to the following 5 April and who do not, therefore, qualify for non-resident treatment.

Although the expression is, literally, a contradiction in terms, we refer here to persons in this category as 'resident' (ie not non-resident) expatriates. A person in this category might, for example, have an 18-month contract commencing in June 1995; his return in December 1996 means that he has spent part of two tax years abroad but not one complete year. Then there is the case of the person whose UK job entails much foreign travel, perhaps for months on end, but whose duties in the United Kingdom cannot be described as merely incidental to his duties abroad. This category might include seamen whose voyages start or finish in the United Kingdom but who travel the world in between times. Finally, among the group of people who are abroad often but either not often enough, or not for long enough to qualify as non-resident for UK tax purposes, are the travelling salesmen, consultants, airline pilots and the like.

What all of these 'semi-expatriates' have in common is that they cannot obtain the tax benefits of the non-resident expatriate proper. They remain liable for UK income tax on their worldwide income. In the 'export or die' atmosphere of the 1970s, the importance of the semi-expatriate to the country's economic well-being was recognised and new legislation was introduced to counter the disincentive effect of domestic taxation for these people. The legislation, mainly contained in TA 1988, s 193, Sched 12, is complex and not without ambiguity. In essence, this Schedule provides for total exemption from UK income tax for earnings from work done overseas provided that certain conditions are satisfied.

2.3   Long absences

Relief under this category may be obtained against earnings from an employment the duties of which are performed wholly or partly outside the United Kingdom. Any duties performed abroad which are merely incidental to those performed at home will be treated as being performed in the United Kingdom and will not be taken into account for the purposes of this relief. In order to qualify for relief as a long absentee, a person must perform the duties of his employment in the course of a qualifying period of at least 365 qualifying days. A qualifying period is not restricted by tax years and may span two or more years. For example, a qualifying period may run from September 1995 to December 1996. In that case the

Schedule E assessments for 1995/96 and 1996/97 would take account of the emoluments for that part of the qualifying period in each year of assessment and grant the relief accordingly. A period of non-residence does not count as part of a qualifying period from 6 April 1992. Therefore pay for terminal leave spent in the United Kingdom following a period of non-residence would be taxable (Inland Revenue Statement of Practice SP 18/91).

A qualifying period consists either of days of absence from the United Kingdom or partly of such days and partly of days in the United Kingdom. In the former case, the situation is quite straightforward. The person performing the duties of his employment wholly abroad for at least 365 days will obtain the relief. Given that the legislation refers to 'in the course of a qualifying period' there does not seem to be a requirement that the employment must subsist for the whole period. Therefore, an absence of 365 days made up of six months' work interspersed with six months' overseas holiday would still be a qualifying period but not six months' work followed by six months' holiday (*Robins v Durkin* [1988] STC 588). A day will be considered as a day of absence if the person is outside the United Kingdom at the end of the day, ie at midnight (*Hoye v Forsdyke* [1981] STC 711).

The alternative definition of a qualifying period, ie where there are some days spent in the United Kingdom, contains stringent restrictions on the length of time which can be spent in the United Kingdom. Between any two periods of absence, the time spent in the United Kingdom must not exceed 62 consecutive days. Thus a person abroad for two periods of 155 days with a 60-day break between them will achieve a qualifying period of 370 days and qualify for the relief. In addition, the number of intervening days in the United Kingdom must not exceed one-sixth of the total number of days in the period under consideration. In the marginal case of a person abroad for 365 days apart from a 62-day return to the United Kingdom, although he does not break the 62-day rule, the period fails to achieve qualifying status because of the one-sixth rule. For seafarers, from 6 April 1991 the limits are relaxed to 183 consecutive days and a total of one-half (TA 1988, Sched 12, para 3 (2A)).

2.3.1 Qualifying periods—illustrative example

Going on from the simple case of the single return visit, qualifying periods may be built up from a series of overseas spells interspersed by returns to the United Kingdom. But what is vital with this regime is to keep a close check on the length of each stay both at home and overseas.

This build-up of qualifying periods to a length sufficient to entitle the employee to obtain the tax relief is best illustrated by an example.

Example: Qualifying periods

Mr Smith is a consulting engineer who has always worked in the United Kingdom. In May 1994 he is recruited by A Ltd, an international consultancy, and is appointed to one of their projects in Nigeria for a period of 18 months. His movements over that time are given below.

Period	In Nigeria	In UK	Total
A	20	—	20
B	—	12	32
C	38	—	70 (38) ⅙th=11.7
D	—	5	43
E	95	—	138 ⅙th=23
F	—	15	153
G	65	—	218 ⅙th=36.3
H	—	40	258
I	120	—	378 ⅙th=63
J	—	10	388
K	60	—	448 ⅙th=74.7
L	—	25	473
M	70	—	543 ⅙th=90.5
N	—	90	
O	40	—	40

In this example, periods A, C, E, G, I, K, M, O are all qualifying periods as they are periods of absence from the United Kingdom. None of them individually gives rise to the 100 per cent tax relief because they are each less than 365 days. Period A–C might be a qualifying period if the intervening days do not break either the 62 days or ⅙th rules. Period B, the intervening days in the United Kingdom does, however, break the ⅙th rule so A–C is not a qualifying period. As a result, periods A and B fall out of the reckoning. A new accumulation process begins with period C. C–E is a qualifying period, so too are C–G and C–I but C–I also exceeds 365 days so the 100 per cent tax relief is due. The qualifying period ceases after period M since period N is more than 62 days. A new progression can commence with period O.

What the example illustrates is that the qualifying period tests have to be applied after every overseas period. An expatriate in this situation must keep a very close watch on his visits to the United Kingdom. If Mr Smith had left the United Kingdom one day earlier in period B or stayed abroad two days longer in period C, then period A–C would have qualified.

Holidays taken abroad during a spell of overseas duty or at the end of such a spell will be included in the qualifying period. Holiday or terminal payments at the end of a qualifying period but within the same tax year will generally also qualify for tax exemption notwithstanding that the employee might spend his terminal leave in the United Kingdom, provided that the period of absence from the United Kingdom amounted to 365 days or more, but the taxpayer had not ceased to be UK resident (SP 18/91).

2.3.2 Apportionment of emoluments

The earnings or emoluments which qualify for relief are those which are attributable to the period of overseas work. Thus someone who works solely abroad may obtain exemption for all his emoluments. Where a person works partly abroad and partly in the United Kingdom (where the UK duties are not merely incidental to the overseas duties) then there is provision for the emoluments to be apportioned between the respective duties (TA 1988, Sched 12, para 2). Inland Revenue practice, however, permits relief against the whole of the emoluments unless there is some question of artificiality about the employee's arrangements with the employer (Inland Revenue letter dated 12 February 1980, reproduced in *Moores Rowland's Yellow Tax Guide*).

The occasion on which apportionment is more likely to be a consideration is where the individual has two or more associated employments, one in the United Kingdom and others overseas. If, for instance Mr Jones, a colleague of Mr Smith, was employed both by A Ltd and A (Nigeria) Ltd, a subsidiary of the British company, and unlike Mr Smith, Mr Jones spent one year in the United Kingdom and one year in Nigeria, then if Mr Jones received a UK salary of £5,000 per annum and a Nigerian salary of £50,000 per annum he would have some difficulty in persuading the Inland Revenue that this was not an artificial tax avoidance ploy.

In any negotiations over apportionment, the amount which can be relieved is that which can be shown to be reasonable having regard to the nature of, and the time devoted to, the overseas duties in relation to the duties performed in the United Kingdom, and to all other circumstances. Returning to Mr Jones' position, he might be able to claim that his overseas duties were substantially more onerous, involved longer hours and greater responsibility than his UK duties, that local taxes and the cost of living were far higher than in the United Kingdom and that, all things considered, £50,000 per annum was a fair rate for the job. Such a claim might well succeed. But if Mr Jones, as is not unlikely, were provided with company accommodation, car, servants and the general panoply of expatriate benefits, and received only £10,000 per annum in Nigeria with the balance paid into his UK or tax haven bank account, then his claim would be resisted with a degree of righteous cynicism.

Apportionment apart, relievable emoluments include salaries, bonuses and allowances, benefits in kind and so on. When one considers the nature of the average expatriate remuneration package with its medical cover, possible school fee payments, and other benefits as well as those mentioned earlier, the value of the tax relief becomes apparent. This, perhaps more than anything else, should ensure that the employee keeps a careful eye on his return visits.

One final point to consider about this relief is the timing of the absence itself.

For employees of companies based in the United Kingdom which operate PAYE, the relief is normally obtained by the issue of a 'No Tax' code if it is clear that the 100 per cent relief will be due.

2.4   Foreign emoluments

This term is used to describe the emoluments of a person *not domiciled in the United Kingdom* from an employment with a person or concern which is resident outside the United Kingdom. Thus, for example, an American working for an American corporation would be in receipt of foreign emoluments. Whether, and to what extent, foreign emoluments are taxable in the United Kingdom depends both on the residence position of the individual and the place in which he carries out the duties of his employment.

Duties performed in the United Kingdom are chargeable on the arising basis regardless of the residence status of the individual concerned. Where the duties are performed abroad the individual's residence is crucial. If he is non-resident then there is no liability for emoluments earned outside the United Kingdom. If he is resident but not ordinarily resident in the United Kingdom, then foreign emoluments for duties performed abroad will be chargeable on the remittance basis. If he is both resident and ordinarily resident in the United Kingdom, then the emoluments will be charged on the arising basis unless the duties of the employment are carried out wholly abroad. In this latter case the remittance basis is applied.

2.5 Other reliefs for resident expatriates

The normal rules which apply to relief for expenses, ie that they are incurred wholly, exclusively and necessarily in the performance of the duties of the employment, apply to duties which extend overseas and to the emoluments therefrom. In the usual way the expenses would be deductible from the gross emoluments and the special relief of 100 per cent would be calculated on the net amount. However, for employments which involve working overseas, certain expenses are allowable which would not be so in purely domestic circumstances. In addition, certain benefits which would be taxable in the UK employment are available with no tax penalty for overseas work.

It has already been mentioned that emoluments cover all benefits in kind and that these often form a significant part of an expatriate remuneration package. It follows, therefore, that the 100 per cent relief can cover the benefits so provided. In addition to the generality of this, there are special rules relating to travel costs, board and lodging of the overseas worker and to travel costs of the employee or his family during his spell abroad.

These rules are contained in TA 1988, ss 193, 194 and cover the following situations. In each case the employee is resident and ordinarily resident in the United Kingdom and his emoluments are not foreign emoluments:

(1)   If the duties of the employment are performed wholly outside the United Kingdom then travelling expenses incurred by the employee to take up the employment and to return at the end of that employment are allowable as a deduction.

(2)   If the cost of board and lodging is provided or reimbursed by the employer this will not be assessable in the case of wholly overseas employment.

(3)   Where there are two or more employments and at least one of them is performed wholly or partly outside the United Kingdom, then travelling expenses incurred by the employee getting from one place of employment to another, where either or both places are outside the United Kingdom, are deductible against the emoluments of the second employment.

    Where the expenses described above are not incurred wholly in the performance of the duties of the employment(s), they may be apportioned with relief restricted to that part related to the employment.

(4)   Travel expenses for an unlimited number of outward and return journeys to the United Kingdom by the employee are to be allowed tax free in the hands of the employee if paid for by the employer.

Table 2.1

Employees Not in Receipt of Foreign Emoluments

UK Residence Status	Employment Performed Wholly or Partly in UK		Employment Performed *Wholly Abroad*
	UK Duties	Overseas Duties	
Resident and Ordinarily Resident	*Case I* Earnings arising (less 100% deduction where appropriate)	*Case I* Earnings arising (less 100% deduction where appropriate)	*Case I* Earnings arising (less 100% deduction where appropriate)
Resident but Not Ordinarily Resident	*Case II* Earnings arising	*Case III* Earnings remitted to or received in UK	*Case III* Earnings remitted to or received in UK
Not Resident	*Case II* Earnings arising	Exempt	Exempt

Foreign-domiciled Employees Working for Foreign Employers

UK Residence Status	Employment Performed Wholly or Partly in UK		Employment Performed *Wholly Abroad*
	UK Duties	Overseas Duties	
Resident and Ordinarily Resident	*Case I* Earnings arising (less 100% deduction where appropriate)	*Case I* Earnings arising (less 100% deduction where appropriate)	*Case III* Earnings remitted to or received in UK
Resident but Not Ordinarily Resident	*Case II* Earnings arising	*Case III* Earnings remitted to or received in UK	*Case III* Earnings remitted to or received in UK
Not Resident	*Case II* Earnings arising	Exempt	Exempt

(5)   Where an employee is absent from the United Kingdom for a continuous period of 60 days or more, certain travel facilities will not attract any UK tax liability. These facilities are for travel by the employee's spouse and/or children under the age of 18 between the United Kingdom and the place where the duties are performed and include any accompanying journey at the beginning of the period, or an interim visit; and any return journey. These travel facilities

will be tax-exempt for up to two outward and return journeys by any person in any one tax year if provided by the employer or reimbursed by him.

Several points must be noted about the reliefs described above. First, in the case of board and lodgings and the family travel facilities, the relief extends only to cases where the cost is met directly or by reimbursement by the employer. There is no relief available for the employee against his emoluments if he bears these costs himself. Secondly, the relief for travel facilities is restricted to travel to and from the place where the duties are actually performed. There is no allowance, for example, for a family reunion at any halfway house. Thus Mr Green who is working in Australia for three months could not obtain relief for a trip for himself and his family to meet up in Singapore, say. Neither his travel nor that of his family would qualify.

2.6 Long-term working abroad: the non-resident

In our discussion of the terms 'resident' and 'ordinarily resident' in Chapter 1, we pointed out that these terms are not explicitly defined in any of the Taxes Acts, but that the Inland Revenue claims to use them in an everyday, non-technical sense. Chapter 1 also indicated, however, that the way the Inland Revenue applies these categories in practice depends on rather complex rules.

For all that, the rules applying to the expatriate who has gone abroad to work as an employee for an extended period are to some extent simpler than those concerning other categories of expatriate. Perhaps the definition of 'long-term' is the most arbitrary part of it, because it means not simply longer than a year, but covering a complete tax year (6 April one year to 5 April the following year).

We can therefore repeat from Chapter 1 our designation of the expatriate who leaves the United Kingdom to work full-time abroad under a contract of employment, and which will last for a period including at least one complete tax year, as a person who will normally be treated by the Inland Revenue as not resident and not ordinarily resident from the day following his departure. This treatment remains provisional until the individual in question has actually remained abroad for a full tax year and, in that tax year, has not infringed any of the other residence rules explained in Chapter 1.

Although the treatment is provisional it does not normally prevent the Inland Revenue from making a tax repayment on departure if, for example, only part of the individual's personal allowances have been granted under PAYE. Where the year is split in this way into a resident part and a non-resident part, full allowances are due. There is no apportionment. The expatriate should obtain the tax repayment claim form P 85 and submit it shortly before departure. An accompanying spouse is normally given similar treatment under Extra-Statutory Concession A78.

The main tax consequences of having the status of not resident and not ordinarily resident in the United Kingdom concern UK income tax and CGT, and are explained in detail later on in this Handbook. But broadly speaking, as far as income tax is concerned, the non-resident whose earnings arise from trade or employment carried on wholly overseas will have no UK liability on those earnings.

2.7   The short-term self-employed expatriate

The rules governing self-employed expatriates are not so straightforward as those applying to expatriates under a full-time contract to an overseas employer. But here again we can usefully distinguish between those who remain UK resident under the rules and those who succeed in acquiring non-resident status.

Where the individual remains UK resident and carries on a trade or profession wholly overseas, his profits from that trade or profession are subject to UK income tax under Schedule D, Case V (see Chapter 4 for an explanation of the schedular system).

The profits of a trade or profession carried out partly in the United Kingdom and partly overseas by a UK resident are assessable under Case I or Case II in the same way as those of a purely domestic business.

Where an individual carries on a trade, profession or vocation wholly or partly outside the United Kingdom, he will be taxed on a change of residence as if the trade, profession or vocation had permanently discontinued and immediately recommenced. This not only allows overlap and loss relief to apply as for a real cessation but enables the non-resident to be taxed only on his UK income and the resident on his worldwide income. Losses before the change may be carried forward and set against profits or gains arising after the change. For these purposes there is a change of residence when a non-resident becomes resident in the UK, or where a UK resident ceases to be resident.

These provisions apply from 1997–98 except where a trade, profession or vocation commenced after 5 April 1994, in which case the change may apply for 1995/96 and 1996/97. The object is to tax a resident individual on his worldwide income, but a non-resident only on income arising in the United Kingdom. There is no deemed cessation on becoming non-resident before 6 April 1997 where the business has existed prior to 6 April 1994.

Extra-Statutory Concession A11 which splits a fiscal year for tax purposes where the individual becomes resident or non-resident during that year will continue to apply. The strict position is that an individual resident for part of a fiscal year is resident for the entire year (*Neubergh v IRC* [1958] STC 181; *Gubay v Kington* [1984] STC 99). If the taxpayer wished to claim the strict legal position, the deemed cessation and commencement would take place on 6 April in the year in which the non-resident became UK resident on 5 April in the year in which a UK resident ceased to be so resident. This could be important where losses arose which it was desired to set against other income under TA 1988, s 380. It could also be relevant for a non-resident becoming UK resident if losses were to be claimed under TA 1988, s 381 for the first four years of the trade following the deemed commencement.

Self-employed expatriates also receive travel and subsistence reliefs comparable to those for UK resident employees working abroad.

2.7.1   Claims for relief

The reliefs available under Schedule E may be claimed within the normal six-year time limits, although in most cases involving substantial overseas working, the relief may be initiated by the company's PAYE office with reference to its PAYE tax office.

Relief under Schedule D must be claimed within two years of the end of the year of assessment to which the claim relates.

2.8   The long-term self-employed expatriate

In the case of expatriates who leave with no employment arranged overseas or with the intention of establishing themselves in self-employment overseas in the full sense, the Inland Revenue in effect takes a 'wait and see' attitude for up to three years. During that time a provisional status of ordinarily resident is maintained and at the end of the period, again assuming no breaking of the residence rules in the meantime, the status of not resident and not ordinarily resident may be granted and backdated to the day following departure. Any tax collected in the interim which would not have been payable by a non-resident can be repaid.

The treatment as non-resident from the day following the day of departure is concessionary (Extra-Statutory Concessions A11 and D2), and the Inland Revenue reserves the right not to apply it in certain cases, such as where a large capital gain is made immediately after departure (see Chapter 6). Wherever a concession gives rise to a significant loss of tax to the Revenue, its application is in doubt.

2.9   Categories of expatriate

2.9.1   Expatriates with a special status

There are certain classes of expatriates who, although actually working overseas, may be deemed to be performing their duties in the United Kingdom. These include Crown servants and the armed forces, seafarers and airmen, and persons employed in exploration or exploitation activities in a designated area under the Continental Shelf Act 1964, s 1(7). The special circumstances of these individuals are described below.

2.9.2   Crown servants

The duties of an office or employment under the Crown are deemed to be duties performed in the United Kingdom irrespective of where they are, in fact, performed. The effect of this is to render the emoluments from such an employment liable to UK income tax under Case II of Schedule E if the employee is not resident and under Case I, but without any of the special reliefs, if the employee is resident. It must be stressed that this deeming provision (TA 1988, s 132(4)(a)) does not, of itself, affect the individual's residence position. If the Crown servant can otherwise satisfy the conditions for non-residence then the other advantages, such as no liability on overseas investment income or to CGT, will still accrue. In addition, certain allowances which are certified as representing compensation for the extra costs involved in living overseas are payable tax free. Under TA 1988, s 278 certain classes of non-resident, including Crown servants, are entitled to some or all of the normal UK personal allowances (for full details see Chapter 4—Income arising in the United Kingdom). In practice, the Crown servant will be taxed under PAYE with an appropriate code for the personal allowances.

One exception to the UK tax liability of Crown servants concerns locally recruited staff overseas. If they are unestablished staff who are not UK resident and the maximum pay for their grade is less than that of an executive officer in the United Kingdom on the Inner London rate, then no tax will be payable (Extra-Statutory Concession A25).

2.9.3 Armed forces

In general terms, members of the armed forces on overseas duty are treated in the same way as other Crown servants. There is, however, one special relief available to members of the armed forces or their spouses. Such individuals will be treated as resident in the United Kingdom for the purpose of obtaining relief on qualifying life assurance premiums or policies issued before 13 March 1984.

2.9.4 Seafarers and airmen

Duties by seafarers and members of aircraft crews are deemed to be performed in the United Kingdom if the voyage does not extend to a port outside the United Kingdom or if the person concerned is a resident of the United Kingdom and part of the voyage or flight begins or ends here (TA 1988, s 132(4)(*b*)). This provision is now subject to TA 1988, Sched 12, para 5. This latter provision provides that seamen and aircrew engaged on voyages outside the United Kingdom are entitled to the special 100 per cent deduction for long absences (see page 14) in respect of the proportion of voyages or flights spent outside the United Kingdom. From 6 April 1991 the conditions for seafarers are more favourable: the limits on intervening days are 183 consecutive days and one-half in total instead of 62 consecutive days and one-sixth (TA 1988, Sched 12, para 3(2A)). The legislation covers two types of voyage or flight: one which begins or ends outside the United Kingdom, and any part beginning or ending outside the United Kingdom of a journey which begins and ends in the United Kingdom.

In a letter dated 22 July 1980, reproduced in *Moores Rowland's Yellow Tax Guide*, the Inland Revenue expanded on the meaning of this provision, by quoting an example concerning the following voyages. A voyage from Tilbury to Antwerp would qualify as being carried out overseas; a voyage from Newcastle to Tilbury to Antwerp would qualify for the Tilbury–Antwerp portion; a round trip Tilbury–Antwerp–Tilbury would also qualify and that portion of a Newcastle–Tilbury–Antwerp–Tilbury–Newcastle trip would likewise be considered as overseas working. The Inland Revenue practice is that a voyage containing a scheduled call at an overseas port will have an overseas portion, but if there is no such scheduled call, then the voyage will not qualify as constituting overseas working. For the purposes of calculating the number of qualifying days for the 100 per cent relief, a person will be considered as leaving the United Kingdom when a ship leaves its berth for a foreign port or when an aircraft takes off.

2.9.5   Oil rig workers

For tax purposes, the territorial sea of the United Kingdom is deemed to be part of the United Kingdom under FA 1973, s 38. This area is further extended in the case of employments in designated areas concerned with exploration or exploitation activities. Generally this means that persons employed in the British sectors of the North and Celtic Seas will be treated as working in the United Kingdom. 'Designated areas' are those designated by Order in Council under the Continental Shelf Act 1964, s 1(7). Apart from the rig workers themselves, this extension of the United Kingdom is also of interest to the crews of ships and aircraft servicing the offshore installations. Flights or voyages to the installations will not constitute overseas working.

2.10   The expatriate family

Many aspects of UK tax law treat the family effectively as a single unit. Thus, children's income inasmuch as it derives from a parental gift or settlement is treated as the income of the parent. This unified treatment ceases in the questions of residence and domicile. Not only is it the case that the residence or domicile of one spouse does not affect the residence or domicile of the other, but children are capable of having a residence status quite independent of their parents once they are no longer minors.

Because each member of a family is considered individually there is some scope for intra-family tax planning. There can also be some pitfalls if this is not done properly.

It is not unknown for the husband (in the majority of cases) to be treated as not resident in the United Kingdom from the day following departure on account of his full-time overseas employment, but his accompanying wife remains classified as a UK resident because of breaching the three-monthly rule on return visits to the United Kingdom.

It is not uncommon for an expatriate wife to have part-time employment abroad and in the United Kingdom this is taxable, if she remains resident for tax purposes.

The expatriate wife with no income of her own, either earnings or investment, is unaffected by her residence status. But if her husband has investment income arising in the United Kingdom which is liable to tax, for example, income from letting the family home, there is scope for transferring that income to the wife. It should be noted that the resident wife of a non-resident husband is entitled to the single personal allowance. This means that her allowance can be used to offset investment income, resulting perhaps in a repayment of tax credit or of income tax deducted at source. It is important, however, that income-producing assets should be held in one name only if the income would be exempt in the husband's case. A joint bank deposit account where one of the parties is resident will produce interest all of which is liable to UK tax, whereas a sole account held by the non-resident party would escape tax under FA 1995, s 128 (see also Chapter 14).

The general rule is that UK assets producing taxable income should be held by the resident spouse and UK assets producing an income exempt in the hands of a non-resident and non-UK assets should be held by the non-resident spouse.

Independent taxation means that spouses are also treated separately for capital gains tax (CGT), each having an annual exemption (£6,000 for 1995/96).

Children who remain resident in the United Kingdom, perhaps staying at a boarding school, are also entitled to a personal allowance. Where the parents are resident in the United Kingdom this personal allowance of the children is rarely of significant benefit unless the child has a substantial income from a non-parental source. Gifts from parents to children are treated as settlements and any income arising therefrom is treated as if it were the parent's income (TA 1988, s 660B).

2.11 Expatriates retiring abroad or permanently emigrating

The Inland Revenue treatment of persons retiring abroad or otherwise permanently emigrating is very much the same as that given to a temporary expatriate taking up overseas employment and the non-resident status remains conditional until a complete tax year has been spent abroad and any visits have been kept within the limits described in Chapter 1. Confirmation of the non-resident status is rarely, in fact, given, unless the emigrant has cause to continue to complete UK tax returns because of continuing UK income sources. Although an enquiry might be made of the emigrant to determine whether or not he remains non-resident after the first tax year, as often as not this is a futile enquiry and his tax office file will eventually become a dead file. The Inland Revenue does, however, have remarkable powers of recovering files, if not the individuals they relate to, from limbo. The dead file will normally be traced should the emigrant decide to return to the United Kingdom.

It would be normal for most people leaving permanently to sell their home in the United Kingdom and this is considered as quite firm evidence of intent by the Inland Revenue. It is by no means crucial for the emigrant who has employment arranged in his new country, because he will in any case be treated as any other overseas employed expatriate.

2.11.1   The retired expatriate

But in the case of a retired emigrant or one who is self-employed, failure to divest himself of his property in this country will mean that he will continue to be regarded provisionally as resident and ordinarily resident for up to three years after departure. A decision on his resident status will be made retrospectively in the light of what has actually happened in the meantime. During the three intervening years, his tax liability will be provisionally computed on the basis that he remains resident in the United Kingdom. Such a person will also have a provisional entitlement to personal allowances (since he is provisionally resident) and these will be reflected in any PAYE code operated, for example, against a company pension, or may form the basis of a tax repayment claim if tax is deducted, or effectively deducted in the form of tax credits, from interest, dividends, or other sources of income.

If after three years the emigrant has not broken the rules, then his non-resident, non-ordinarily resident status will normally be backdated to the day following his departure. Any tax paid in the meantime because of his provisionally resident treatment which would not have been payable in the case of a non-resident will then be repaid.

3 Guide to domicile and residence: the tax consequences

3.1 Introduction

Based on the concepts of domicile and residence explained in the two preceding chapters, this chapter is intended as a schematic guide to the tax and investment planning chapters that follow it. It is intended, therefore, as a bridge between the definitions and categories established in the previous chapters and the detailed exposition of tax matters, particularly, in the subsequent chapters of this book. In the tabular form in which it is presented, the guide leads only to general conclusions and strategies. **It is not a rule-book**, but is simply intended to point in the right direction. In using this guide, it is important **to check the status of each spouse separately**, in order to identify the relevant category.

3.2 Using the guide

Step 1: establish domicile

Use Domicile Chart as guide.

For IHT purposes **only**, it is possible for the Revenue to **deem** an individual UK domiciled (such action does not disturb the legal domicile).

Step 2: establish where resident for tax purposes

Use:

Residence Chart 1 for non-UK domiciled individuals
Residence Chart 2 for working UK expatriates
Residence Chart 3 for non-working UK expatriates.

Step 3: check tax and investment considerations

Having decided domicile and residence category, use:

(1)   UK Taxation Chart to check planned actions for tax effectiveness
(2)   UK Taxation—Effect on Investment, to check overall financial strategy*.

The symbols on this latter chart can be regarded as:

    Usually harmless, or even good!

    May well be harmless, but take care to double check

    Check—there could be disadvantages

    Check carefully—there will usually be major disadvantages

*Ensure no conflict with sensible tax and investment planning.

Category: A

Applies to:
Non-UK Domicile
Non-UK Resident
Non-UK Ordinarily Resident.

Basic strategy:
Can invest in the United Kingdom provided local legal and exchange controls permit. To minimise risk of IHT on UK assets, should:

(1)   restrict UK assets below IHT zero-rated band;
(2)   take advantage of UK government exempt stocks;
(3)   ensure any 'portable' assets are held outside the United Kingdom.

Also, should take advantage of investments offered by offshore subsidiaries of UK institutions, which can offer investments free of UK taxation other than that deducted at source. A similar effect can be achieved through a non-UK private investment company.

Category: B

Applies to:
Non-UK Domicile
UK Resident
UK Ordinarily Resident.

Basic strategy:
To minimise UK tax liabilities should keep all assets and accumulated gains/income outside the United Kingdom, remitting to the United Kingdom **only** the absolute minimum. If remittance, to cover living expenses, is unavoidable, individuals should create separate accounts to contain and identify:

(1) income arising outside the United Kingdom;
(2) gain-laden capital from asset disposal; and
(3) capital untainted by income or gain.

Remittance could be from (2) up to limit of CGT exemptions in any one year; if more cash is required, remittance could be made from (3). Only when absolutely necessary should cash be remitted from (1).

Category: C

Applies to:
UK Domicile
Non-UK Resident
Non-UK Ordinarily Resident.

Basic strategy:
Invest in offshore subsidiaries of UK institutions, to retain investment qualities without unnecessary UK tax implications. Ensure spare capital is working for capital growth as well as income, and realise all accumulated capital gains while still non-UK ordinarily resident. Still liable to UK IHT on worldwide assets, check local estate or gift taxes rules.

Take care to maintain a realistic level of health insurance and life cover and keep equal cover for a spouse running the UK family base, if appropriate.

If one spouse remains UK resident, take care to avoid **joint** assets, as the income/gain on the asset will be assessable to UK taxes.

Category: D

Applies to:
UK Domicile (but claiming new domicile of choice)
Non-UK Resident
Non-UK Ordinarily Resident.

Basic strategy:
As part of the exercise to replace UK domicile with new domicile of choice, the individual concerned must show that all formal ties with the United Kingdom have been severed. Single ties, eg a banking service, an investment in a UK equity, etc, will not individually prevent a successful claim to non-UK domicile, but together could convince the UK authorities that the individual retains British roots.

The individual should, therefore, move everything possible offshore and use UK facilities only if quite sure it will not damage non-domicile claim.

It may be a wise precaution to plan for eventual IHT liability, on the assumption that the claim may eventually fail.

Note:
A UK expatriate will be treated as deemed domiciled (for IHT purposes only) for first three years following departure.

Domicile and residence charts start on page 34.

3.3 Domicile Chart

UK Domiciled or Non-UK Domiciled?

Note: If 'domicile of choice' is not **actively** established, domicile will be either 'domicile of origin' or 'domicile of dependence'.

Note*: If parents were married (to each other!) at time of birth, take father as relevant parent: otherwise, take mother as relevant parent.

Note*: Except in Scotland, where the relevant age is 14 for males and 12 for females.

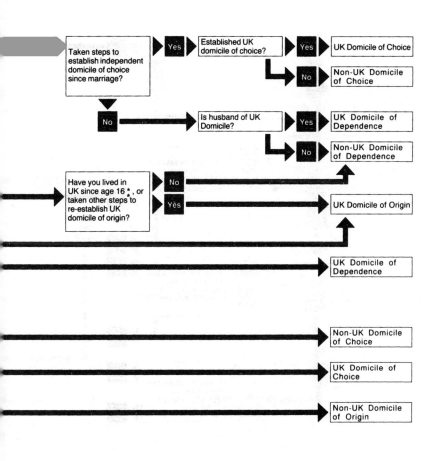

3.4   Residence Charts

Residence Chart 1 (Non-UK Domicile)

Non-UK Domiciled

ie roots, parentage etc outside UK

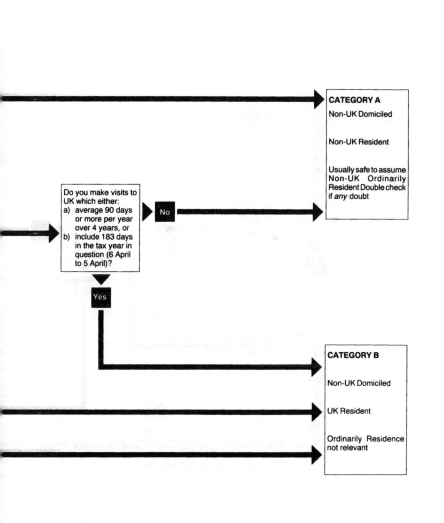

Do you make visits to UK which either:
a) average 90 days or more per year over 4 years, or
b) include 183 days in the tax year in question (6 April to 5 April)?

No

Yes

CATEGORY A

Non-UK Domiciled

Non-UK Resident

Usually safe to assume Non-UK Ordinarily Resident Double check if *any* doubt

CATEGORY B

Non-UK Domiciled

UK Resident

Ordinarily Residence not relevant

Residence Chart 2 (UK Domicile—employed)

UK Domiciled working abroad

ie roots, parentage etc (domicile) in UK, and in
full-time gainful occupation outside UK.

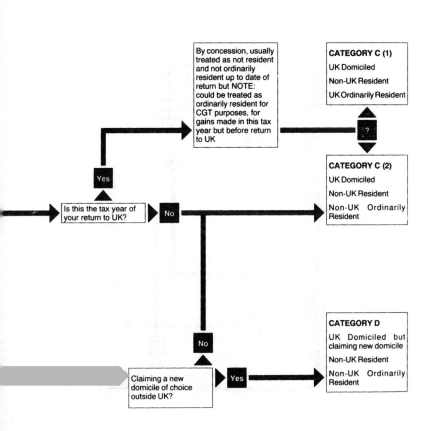

By concession, usually treated as not resident and not ordinarily resident up to date of return but NOTE: could be treated as ordinarily resident for CGT purposes, for gains made in this tax year but before return to UK

CATEGORY C (1)

UK Domiciled

Non-UK Resident

UK Ordinarily Resident

?

CATEGORY C (2)

UK Domiciled

Non-UK Resident

Non-UK Ordinarily Resident

Yes

Is this the tax year of your return to UK?

No

No

Claiming a new domicile of choice outside UK?

Yes

CATEGORY D

UK Domiciled but claiming new domicile

Non-UK Resident

Non-UK Ordinarily Resident

Residence Chart 3 (UK Domicile—not employed)

UK Domiciled living abroad

ie roots, parentage etc (domicile) in UK, living
outside UK, but not in full-time gainful occupation.

3.5   UK Taxation Chart

UK Taxation Chart		
Client Category	**UK Income Tax**	
	Income arising in UK	Income arising Abroad
A Non-UK Domicile Non-UK Resident Non-UK Ordinarily Resident	- UK withholding tax deducted on dividends etc arising in UK - Overseas dividends collected in UK can be passed on gross of UK tax to non-residents - Some UK Government Stocks (exempt Gilts): interest and Bank and Building Society interest can be paid gross if non-UK ordinarily resident - UK personal reliefs and allowances may be available depending on citizenship and or status	No liability, but may be subject to local taxes
B Non-UK Domicile UK Resident UK Ordinarily Resident	Liable on all income arising in UK Able to claim normal UK Personal reliefs and exemptions	Liable on any income remitted to the UK (Income arising and retained outside UK is not assessed unless and until remitted to UK)
C1 UK Domicile Non-UK Resident UK Ordinarily Resident	**As for Category A** (but gilt exemptions do not apply while still ordinarily resident in UK Bank and Building Society interest liable to deduction of Basic Rate Tax)	No liability, but may be subject to local taxes
C2 UK Domicile Non-UK Resident Non-UK Ordinarily Resident	As for Category A	No liability, but may be subject to local taxes
D Claiming Non-UK Domicile of Choice Non-UK Resident Non-UK Ordinarily Resident	As for Category A	No liability, but may be subject to local taxes

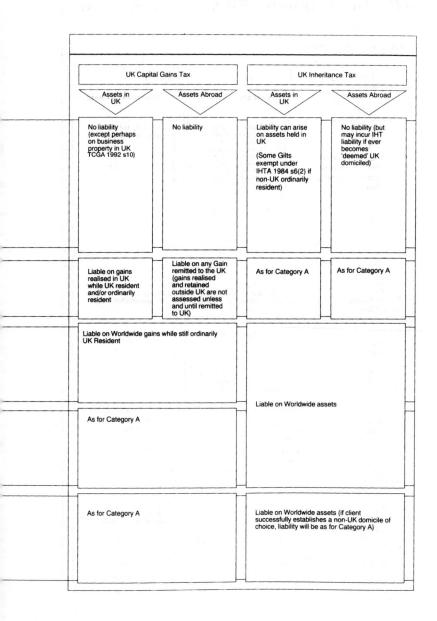

	UK Capital Gains Tax		UK Inheritance Tax	
	Assets in UK	Assets Abroad	Assets in UK	Assets Abroad
	No liability (except perhaps on business property in UK TCGA 1992 s10)	No liability	Liability can arise on assets held in UK (Some Gilts exempt under IHTA 1984 s6(2) if non-UK ordinarily resident)	No liability (but may incur IHT liability if ever becomes 'deemed' UK domiciled)
	Liable on gains realised in UK while UK resident and/or ordinarily resident	Liable on any Gain remitted to the UK (gains realised and retained outside UK are not assessed unless and until remitted to UK)	As for Category A	As for Category A
	Liable on Worldwide gains while still ordinarily UK Resident		Liable on Worldwide assets	
	As for Category A			
	As for Category A		Liable on Worldwide assets (if client successfully establishes a non-UK domicile of choice, liability will be as for Category A)	

3.6   UK Taxation—Effect On Investments Chart

UK Taxation - Effect on Investments			
Client Category	**UK Equities UK Loan Stocks UK Unit Trusts etc**	**UK exempt Government Stocks**	**Other UK Government Stocks (excluding exempt Gilts)**
A Non-UK Domicile Non-UK Resident Non-UK Ordinarily Resident	⚠️ Beware IHT and UK withholding tax - although investment advantages may outweigh tax disadvantages	☺ Can claim interest gross of UK withholding tax, and asset is exempt from IHT	⚠️ Beware IHT and UK withholding tax - prefer UK Exempt Government Stocks if possible
B Non-UK Domicile UK Resident UK Ordinarily Resident	⚠️ Beware IHT and CGT, plus: Income will be paid in UK net of withholding tax or basic rate tax Prefer offshore alternatives, with income paid gross, and assets outside UK for CGT and IHT purposes Income remitted to the UK is taxable		
C1 UK Domicile Non-UK Resident UK Ordinarily Resident	⚠️ Beware UK withholding tax - prefer offshore alternatives with less, or no, withholding taxes on Income distribution (Offshore funds are usually cheaper to invest in than dealing directly with foreign markets)	❓ Strictly, cannot claim interest gross of UK withholding tax until no longer ordinarily UK resident (will receive any income net in interim)	⚠️ Beware UK withholding tax - prefer offshore alternatives with similar security: for example Allied Dunbar Sterling Fixed Interest Fund
C2 UK Domicile Non-UK Resident Non-UK Ordinarily Resident		☺ Can claim interest gross of UK basic rate tax as not ordinarily UK resident (CARE if making claim to UK personal reliefs under TA 1988, s 278)	
D Claiming Non-UK Domicile of Choice Non-UK Resident Non-UK Ordinarily Resident	⚠️ Apart from the tax disadvantages as described in C above the investment will form a UK connection which may damage the domicile claim - prefer offshore alternatives	❓ If non-UK domicile is established, will be as for A above but in the interim a UK asset and a UK connection	⚠️ The same considerations apply as for UK equities for D prefer offshore alternatives eg Allied Dunbar Sterling Fixed Interest Fund

UK Taxation - effect on investments		UK Taxation - effect on money movement		
UK Bank and Building Society Deposits	Joint holdings with spouse who is UK resident for tax purposes	Overseas Income remitted to UK	Capital Gains arising in UK	Overseas Capital Gains remitted to UK
Can request interest paid gross of basic rate tax if non-ordinarily resident - but beware IHT	Could expose income and gains to UK tax liability	No tax implications to prevent free movement of money into UK (CARE if increasing UK assets - Beware IHT)		
This Box is a continuation of page 44	No immediate disadvantage while both UK resident	Will incur UK income tax if remitted to UK - Retain offshore	Delay realisation of any UK gains until tax year after leaving UK if possible. Gains realised while resident will incur CGT	Will incur CGT if remitted Retain offshore and only remit to limit of annual CGT exemption
Cannot claim interest gross of UK basic rate tax until no longer ordinarily UK resident (will receive any income net in interim)	Any assets held jointly with resident spouse are assessable to UK taxes. (Each spouse should maintain separate bank account, investments and other assets in own sole name)	Remitting to UK will not incur a tax liability in itself - but it usually makes more practical sense to send all 'spare' income direct to offshore investment to save time, postage and paper	Will incur CGT liability if realised while still ordinarily UK resident whether remitted to UK or not - delay until not ordinarily resident	Will incur CGT liability if realised while still ordinarily UK resident whether remitted to UK or not - delay until not ordinarily resident
Can claim interest gross of UK basic rate tax as not ordinarily UK resident. Care if making claim to UK personal reliefs under TA 1988, s 278 - prefer offshore alternatives			An ideal time to ensure that all UK gains already accrued are realised do not delay until after return to UK!	An ideal time to ensure that all UK gains already accrued are realised do not delay until after return to UK!
UK Banking could be regarded as a strong remaining tie with UK and taken together with other UK links, invalidate non-domicile claim - prefer offshore Bank Services	Non-domicile claim would be rare if spouse remains in UK - joint assets with resident spouse would almost certainly defeat any non-UK domicile claim	Remittance of Income to UK may serve to reinforce UK links and increase UK assets	This would mark a disposal of UK assets and therefore severing of UK ties. Helpful in decreasing UK assets in event of non-domicile claim being successful	Remittance of capital to UK may serve to reinforce UK links and increase UK assets

4 Income arising in the United Kingdom

4.1 Introduction

In this and the following five chapters we look in more detail at the impact of UK taxes of various kinds on the British expatriate, and in the two subsequent chapters we describe some of the principles determining his liability to tax in another jurisdiction, particularly that of his overseas residence. The UK tax system is so complex that the use of the expression 'tax planning' indicates undue optimism in most individual cases. Nevertheless, to be forewarned is the only way to be forearmed in one's dealings with the tax administration in any country; and to act as far as possible in advance will in many cases save not only a great deal of time and trouble but considerable amounts of money as well.

Tax legislation is complex because it tries by means of general measures to apply equity to numberless individual instances. Anyone who deals professionally with the tax matters of expatriates soon becomes aware of the enormous variableness of their individual circumstances: in fact at times it seems that no two sets of circumstances are exactly alike. For this reason, if for no other, a Handbook of this kind cannot provide all the answers. To obtain a complete picture, the expatriate must in any case consider any local taxation which applies in his country of residence and the provisions of any double taxation agreement between that country and the United Kingdom. But even when this has been done, in many cases the complications are such and the sums of money potentially involved so large that it is essential to seek individual professional advice.

For most British expatriates the source of their actual earnings will be outside the United Kingdom. But many will receive an income from one source or another in the United Kingdom itself. Many who were previously resident will already have investments in the United Kingdom, and many more will wish to invest there. It may also be the case that an expatriate will receive earnings from UK business or draw a pension from an earlier employment.

In any of these circumstances, a UK source of income will have a tax consequence, but the British tax system is such that the tax consequence may be different for every type of income. Earnings from employment are treated differently from pensions, which in turn are treated differently from business profits. Earned income is treated in a different manner from investment income, and different types of investment give rise to different methods of taxation.

This chapter looks in some detail at the taxation consequences attaching to the major types of income originating in the United Kingdom, so far as UK tax is concerned. Income from letting UK property is considered separately in Chapter 5, and further chapters deal with capital gains tax and inheritance tax.

4.2   The UK schedular system of income tax

An unusual feature of the UK income tax system is that different sources of income are assessed separately, with varying rules for computing the income, relief for losses, and due dates for payment of tax.

The tax schedules, as they are known, corresponding to each distinct source of income, originated in Addington's Act of 1803 which, by taxing each source separately with deduction of tax at source where possible, avoided the need for a return of total income. No UK taxpayer had to make such a return until Lloyd George introduced supertax on incomes over £3,000 in his 1909 'people's Budget'.

The sources of income covered by each of the Schedules are broadly as follows:

Schedule A:	rents from land
Schedule C:	interest on government securities
Schedule D:	
Case I:	profits from trades and businesses (self-employment)
II:	profits from professions and vocations (self-employment)
III:	interest on investments
IV:	interest on overseas securities
V:	income from overseas possessions
VI:	other annual profits or gains

Schedule E: income from employment and pension
Schedule F: income from dividends and distributions paid by UK
               companies and unit trusts
Schedule B: (annual value of commercial woodlands) was abolished in
               1988.

A UK taxpayer with several sources of income may have to deal with several tax offices. As a general rule, Schedule E income is dealt with by the tax office for the area where the salary or pension is paid, and Schedule D, Cases I and II profits are dealt with by the tax office covering the business address. Other income is dealt with by the tax office covering the taxpayer's home address if the taxpayer is UK resident.

4.3   Interest from bank and building society deposits

Income accruing to a UK deposit account was strictly speaking taxable on income arising in the United Kingdom under Schedule D, Case III, up to 5 April 1995.

However, where the beneficial owner of the account was not resident in the United Kingdom and certain other conditions were fulfilled, then under Extra-Statutory Concession B13 no action was taken to pursue that tax charge on bank deposits or building society interest or from certificates of deposit, deep gain securities, or client account deposits. From 6 April 1995, FA 1995, s 128 limits UK tax on such income to any tax deducted at source.

The provisions relating to deduction of tax at source on bank interest do not apply to a non-resident, provided that he has declared in writing to the deposit taker liable to pay interest that at the time of the declaration he is beneficially entitled to the interest and is not ordinarily resident in the United Kingdom. The declaration contains an undertaking that if the depositor becomes ordinarily resident in the United Kingdom he will notify the deposit taker accordingly and must be in the form prescribed by the Board of Inland Revenue and contain such information as they may reasonably require (TA 1988, ss 481(5)(*k*), 482(2)).

Where, exceptionally, a declaration does not incorporate the address of the person making it, it needs to be supported by a certificate from the deposit taker. In such a case, the deposit taker needs to certify that, to the best of his knowledge and belief, the persons to whom the declaration relates are not ordinarily resident in the United Kingdom; that the person making the declaration has undertaken to notify him of a relevant change in residence status; and that if he receives information indicating that any of the persons concerned are ordinarily resident in the United Kingdom, he will deduct tax. In addition the Revenue is empowered to prescribe or authorise the form of the declarations and certificates under SI 1992 No 14.

4.3.1   Excluded income

From 6 April 1995 the UK tax liability of a non-resident is limited except in the case of income from a trade or profession carried on through a branch or agent, or under Schedule A, to the tax deducted at source if any. This is achieved by taking out of charge the excluded income and also ignoring the personal allowances given under a double taxation treaty or to Commonwealth citizens or citizens of the Republic of Ireland and certain others under TA 1988, s 278. Effectively, the personal allowances are set against the excluded investment income, although any balance of allowances in excess of this income could then be claimed against chargeable income assessed on a UK representative or under Schedule A. In essence, Extra-Statutory Concession B13 is enacted.

Excluded income is defined in FA 1995, s 128, but does not include income charged on a UK representative as a trade or profession carried on through a branch or agent in the United Kingdom.

The excluded income, which is only subject to UK tax in the hands of a non-resident if, and to the extent that, it is subject to deduction of tax at source, is—

(1)   income from government securities taxable under Schedule C, deposit interest and other income taxable under Schedule D, Case III and dividends taxable under Schedule F, ie investment income other than from land in the United Kingdom;

(2)   transactions in deposits taxable under Schedule D, Case VI under TA 1988, s 56;

(3)   social security benefits taxable under Schedule E under TA 1988, s 150 or 617 and incapacity benefits taxable under FA 1994, s 139;

(4)   income received through a broker or investment manager that meets the requisite conditions for exemption in FA 1995, cl 114, other than underwriting profits of a Lloyd's name, currently excluded by Extra-Statutory Concession B40; and

(5)   any other income that may be designated by the Treasury by statutory instrument.

Excluded income taxed at source includes income where tax is deducted or treated as deducted, which is paid or treated as paid, or in respect of which there is a tax credit. The amount of tax is the amount deducted, paid or credited as appropriate.

A non-resident trust does not qualify for exemption where there is a UK ordinarily resident individual or UK resident company as a relevant beneficiary, which mirrors the exclusion in Extra-Statutory Concession B13 and for authorised unit trusts under SI 1994 No 2318. A relevant beneficiary is defined by reference to entitlement to income, current or prospective.

Joint accounts, where one party is resident and the other is non-resident, as is often the case with married expatriates, are wholly taxable (regardless of whether the account is with a UK bank or offshore) because the interest is generally not apportioned between the two individuals but accrues to them jointly and can be drawn by either of them. This is a point missed by many expatriates.

In general, UK bank and building society deposit accounts are to be avoided. If it is desired to maintain a deposit account with a British bank, it should be made with an offshore branch or subsidiary of the bank, for example, in the Isle of Man. In that way it will be beyond the reach of the UK legislation and attract no UK tax.

4.4 Interest from government, local authority and corporate stocks

Government stocks
In the main, British government stocks are subject to UK income tax and the majority have tax deducted at source. But interest from certain stocks is exempt from tax if they are beneficially owned by a person not ordinarily resident in the United Kingdom. The stocks which are currently exempt are listed below.

9%	Conversion Stock 2000	3.3.2000
9%	Conversion Stock 2011	12.7.2011
9½%	Conversion Stock 2001	12.7.2001
9¾%	Conversion Stock 2003	7.5.2003
13¼%	Exchequer Stock 1966	15.5.1996
	Floating Rate Treasury Stock 1999	09.03.1999

2½%	Index Linked Treasury Stock 2024	Not later than 17.7.2024
4⅜%	Index Linked Treasury Stock 2030	22.7.2030
4⅜%	Index Linked Treasury Stock 2004	21.10.2004
4⅝%	Index Linked Treasury Stock 1998	27.4.1998
5½%	Treasury Stock 2008/12	10.9.2008 to 10.9.2012
6%	Treasury Stock 1999	10.8.1999
6¼%	Treasury Stock 2010	25.11.2010
6¾%	Treasury Loan 1995/98	1.5.1995 to 1.5.1998
6¾%	Treasury Loan 2004	26.11.2004
7%	Treasury Convertible Stock 1997	06.08.1997
7%	Treasury Stock 2001	6.11.2001
7¼%	Treasury Stock 1998	30.3.98
7¾%	Treasury Stock 2006	8.9.2006
7¾%	Treasury Loan 2012/15	26.1.2012 to 26.1.2015
8%	Treasury Stock 2000	7.12.2000
8%	Treasury Loan 2002/06	5.10.2002 to 5.10.2006
8%	Treasury Stock 2003	10.6.2003
8%	Treasury Stock 2013	27.9.2013
8½%	Treasury Loan 2000	28.1.2000
8½%	Treasury Stock 2005	7.12.2005
8½%	Treasury Loan 2007	16.7.2007
8¾%	Treasury Loan 1997	1.9.1997
8¾%	Treasury Loan 2017	25.8.2017
9%	Treasury Loan 1994	17.11.1994
9%	Treasury Loan 1992/96	28.1.93 (last repayment)
9%	Treasury Loan 2008	13.10.2008
9%	Treasury Stock 2012	6.8.2012
9½%	Treasury Loan 1999	15.1.1999
12¼%	Treasury Loan 1995	15.11.1995
13¼%	Treasury Loan 1997	22.1.1997
15¼%	Treasury Loan 1996	3.5.1996
15½%	Treasury Loan 1998	30.9.1998
3½%	War Loan	

Since the majority of stocks suffer tax at source, the non-resident stock-holder must apply for the gross payment of exempt stocks. Application should be made to The Financial Intermediaries and Claims Office, St John's House, Merton Road, Bootle, Merseyside L69 9BB.

Stocks normally paid without deduction of tax include 3½ per cent War Loan, and registered stocks and bonds on the National Savings Stock Register.

Exempt stocks have long been a mainstay for the appropriate portion of the British expatriate investor's portfolio because of their competitive yield and high security. They also form the basis of a large offshore gilt fund industry and both direct and fund investment can form part of a sound investment portfolio.

Local authority stocks
Interest from local authority stocks is generally paid after deduction of tax. The only exception to this is where the stock was issued for borrowing in a foreign currency. In that case, and subject to Treasury direction, the interest may be paid gross and be exempt from income tax if the stockholder is not resident in the United Kingdom.

Corporate stocks—debentures, etc
These, too, are generally paid effectively net of income tax at the basic rate, although arrangements can be made for interest to be paid gross under a double taxation agreement (see Chapter 11).

Any other interest
Subject to the exceptions described above and to the specific provisions of double taxation treaties (see below) all interest payments made to non-residents should be paid net of UK income tax at the basic rate.

Double taxation agreements
Where there is a double taxation treaty in force between the United Kingdom and the country of residence of the recipient, then the treatment of interest may be covered therein. It is normal in these cases for interest to be payable gross and tax to be payable in the country of residence. Many agreements, however, have provision for a withholding tax in the country of origin. The appropriate agreement must be checked.

4.4.1 Dividends

Dividends paid by UK companies are technically paid gross, ie, there is no income tax deducted at source. However, alongside the dividend there is an associated tax credit currently equal to one-quarter of the net dividend. So far as the payer is concerned, this tax credit is accounted for and paid to the Inland Revenue as advance corporation tax (ACT). This ACT can be used to offset the payer's final or mainstream corporation tax liability in due course. So far as the payee is concerned the tax credit can be treated as analogous to income tax deducted at source. For the UK resident non-taxpayer, the credit can be repaid, but for the non-resident taxpayer, the dividend counts as excluded income from 6 April 1995, and there is no further UK tax charge. Previously the quantum of dividend income on which any higher rate tax was calculated was the sum of the dividend plus tax credit, TA 1988, s 207A.

Thus, where a person received a dividend of £400, there would have been a tax credit associated with the dividend of £100. For the non-taxpayer, this £100 could and still can be repaid. If the recipient of the dividend had a marginal tax rate of 40 per cent, however, then there would have been additional tax of £100 due on his dividend income:

Dividend	£400
Tax Credit	100
	£500
Tax @ 40%	200
Less: tax credit	100
Additional tax due	£100

This tax treatment applies to dividends and other distributions from UK companies, investment trusts, and unit trusts.

In general terms, the non-resident is not able to reclaim the tax credit. However, under certain double taxation agreements payment of the tax credit can be made subject to a UK withholding tax. This withholding tax is 15 per cent of the sum of the dividend plus tax credit, therefore allowing 25 per cent of the tax credit to be paid.

Where an expatriate is entitled to personal allowances under TA 1988, s 278 then the tax credit can be repaid up to the amount of allowances due: see **4.15**.

4.5   Life assurance policies

The benefits payable under UK Life Assurance Policies are liable to UK tax for non-residents and residents alike. For tax purposes, policies are classified as 'qualifying' or 'non-qualifying'. A qualifying policy must be held for ten years, or three-quarters of the original term agreed, and the premiums must be paid regularly, at least once a year, and must be spread evenly throughout the duration of the policy. For a qualifying policy normally there will be no tax liability where the proceeds are payable to the original policyholder or to somebody to whom the policy has been given. In the case of a non-qualifying policy, tax may be payable on the proceeds. (For a single premium bond, for example, the permitted annual withdrawal is a cumulative 5 per cent per annum, which, if taken, could be for a maximum period of up to 20 years.) Tax is payable only by higher rate taxpayers—which includes those who are moved into the higher rate when any gain on total surrender or excess withdrawal is added to their annual taxable income—and is charged at the difference between the basic and the higher rate of tax (15 per cent for the 1995/96 tax year). For non-UK residents without other significant amounts of UK income, this will generally mean that there is no tax due.

It is important to bear in mind though, that this seemingly beneficial tax treatment is granted to take into account the tax that is paid by UK Life Assurance Companies on the profits and gains within policy funds. Currently, franked income (that from UK equities and gilt edged securities) is taxed at 25 per cent, all other income (from foreign equities and Eurobonds, for example) and capital gains are taxed at 33 per cent but of course the allowance available to individuals to offset the first of £6,000 of gain, is not applicable. For non-UK residents 'offshore policies' may prove to be a better investment. An 'offshore policy' is one issued by a life assurance company resident in a tax haven where policy funds pay little or no tax on income and gains and the policy proceeds are similarly free of tax.

Expatriates returning to the United Kingdom should note that the proceeds of policies effected after 17 November 1983 may be fully liable to tax on the accrued profits, ie without the benefit of the basic rate tax credit, although the profit will be apportioned in direct relation to the periods of residence and non-residence during the policy term and only that portion relating to the period of UK residence will be subject to tax. (The proceeds of offshore policies taken out before 18 November 1983 continue to be free of liability to UK taxation.)

These comments refer only to UK taxation and non-UK residents must also take account of any local tax liability that may be due on policy proceeds.

Where life assurance premium relief is available (for a qualifying policy issued on or before 13 March 1984) the premiums may be paid net of the relief—currently 12½ per cent of the premium. The policyholder is eligible for relief if the policy is written on his life or that of his spouse, if either of them pays the premiums, and if the person paying is resident in the United Kingdom for tax purposes. Where the policyholder and his spouse will both be non-resident for the whole of a tax year the premiums must be paid gross, but net payments may be resumed when they again take up UK residence.

4.6   National Savings

Most of the investments offered by the Department for National Savings are tax free both for residents and non-residents. But the yield from these investments largely reflects this, in that greater yields can often be obtained elsewhere. As with other 'tax-free' investments there is no guarantee that the proceeds will remain so overseas.

The main taxable National Savings investments are the National Savings Bank investment account, income bonds and capital bonds which usually offer very competitive interest returns. Interest on all of these is always paid without deduction of income tax.

4.7   Pensions

Many expatriates will, whether now or later, receive pension income from the United Kingdom and for tax purposes this income may be divided into three separate groups:

(1)   State pensions—these include Old Age Pension and the State Earnings Related Pension Scheme.
(2)   Private pensions—such as an occupational pension payable by a UK employer or self-employed and personal pensions (including Personal Pension Plans which became available from 1 July 1988).
(3)   Government pensions—pensions arising from UK government service: eg an armed services pension, an NHS pension, a teacher's pension etc.

State pensions are always paid gross and can be paid in any country. The pensioner is liable for tax in the country where he is resident, but where he receives any other pension taxable in the United Kingdom (see below), the State Retirement Pension will usually be taxed alongside that other pension. This is carried out either by a reduction of allowances or by the use of the higher rate of taxation in addition to the basic rate.

Private pensions continue to be liable to tax in the United Kingdom— they are likely also to be liable for tax in the country in which the expatriate is resident. Fortunately the United Kingdom has double taxation treaties with more than 90 countries, including those where expatriate Britons are most commonly to be found. Most of these treaties include an article covering private pensions and provide for the pension to be paid gross in the United Kingdom and taxable only in the country of residence.

Government pensions are always taxable in the United Kingdom and, like private pensions, they are likely also to be liable for tax in the country of residence. Once again, relief is available where there is a double taxation agreement in force—this will normally provide for government pensions to be taxable only in the United Kingdom. (More information on double taxation agreements may be found in Chapter 11.)

Non-residents in receipt of a UK pension will often qualify for UK personal allowances (TA 1988, s 278) and these allowances should be claimed.

4.8 Employments

The taxation treatment of employments which are carried on partly within and partly outside the United Kingdom is fully described in Chapter 2. Some non-residents do, however, have employments which are carried on wholly in the United Kingdom. Commonly, these are directorships where the non-resident does not work full-time in the employment but attends board meetings, etc, in the United Kingdom. The whole of the remuneration from an entirely domestic employment is liable to UK income tax. Taxable too are benefits in kind and travelling expenses from the overseas home to the United Kingdom received or incurred in the performance of such employments, unless they are wholly, exclusively and necessarily incurred in the performance of the duties; TA 1988, s 198, *Taylor v Provan* [1974] STC 168.

Where a non-UK domiciled individual comes to work in the United Kingdom and was not resident in the United Kingdom during either of the two preceding tax years or was not present in the United Kingdom at any time during the two years up to the date of his arrival, he is entitled to relief for travel between the United Kingdom and his normal place of abode abroad for a period of five years, so long as the cost is borne or reimbursed by the employer. The journey includes travel from the home in the United Kingdom to the home overseas. Where the employee is in the United Kingdom for a continuous period of 60 days or more, he is entitled to relief for two visits a year by his spouse and minor children so long as the expenses are paid for or reimbursed by the employer. Apportionment is possible in cases of duality of purpose. There are provisions to prevent double allowances.

Where it can be shown that some part of the duties of the employment are carried out overseas then part of the remuneration should be exempt from tax.

4.9   Trades and professions

Where a non-resident has trading or professional income arising in the United Kingdom this will normally be liable to UK income tax under Schedule D, Cases I, II or V. It is important, however, to consider the nature of the trade, where it is actually carried on, and whether or not an agent is involved.

A trade *with* the United Kingdom should not be confused with a trade *within* the United Kingdom. The latter is certainly taxable but the former may not be. A non-resident trader may have a representative office or an advertising department within the United Kingdom, he may even have a sales agent in the United Kingdom, without incurring any income tax liability. But care must be taken with agents, as discussed below. An advertising or representative office will not be trading in the United Kingdom if, for example, the contracts for the sale of goods, or for services, are in fact made overseas directly with the trader. This would constitute trading *with* the United Kingdom. But if the overseas trade was represented by a UK sales office, for example, where orders were taken and paid for locally, then this would constitute trading *within* the United Kingdom.

In the simple cases of sale of goods and services, the position is fairly clear-cut, but if the trade involves both manufacturing and selling in different countries then the situation becomes more complex. The introduction of self-assessment in the United Kingdom from 1996/97 will require changes in the taxation of non-residents trading in the United Kingdom up until 5 April 1996, where only selling takes place in the United Kingdom, the profit assessed may be limited to the merchanting profit under the Taxes Management Act 1970 (TMA 1970), s 81. Where UK branch profits do not appear to show the true profit, a proportion of the total worldwide profit may be charged in the United Kingdom based on the turnover in the United Kingdom, under TMA 1970, s 80. Such a situation allows for tax avoidance by arranging for profits to be realised in the least onerous fiscal regime. Needless to say, this is counteracted by anti-avoidance legislation such as the transfer pricing rules contained in TA 1988, ss 770–773.

Where a non-resident trades within the United Kingdom he will be liable to tax, but collecting that tax is another matter, given that courts will not normally enforce foreign tax debts. TMA 1970, ss 78 and 79 attempt to get around this by providing that a non-resident trading in the United Kingdom will be chargeable in the name of any branch or agent in the United Kingdom. Thus the UK sales office mentioned above would be a taxable or chargeable entity in that case. The only exception to this is where the agent is an independent broker or general commission agent carrying on a *bona fide* brokerage or commission agency.

Up until 1995/96 trades and professions have been assessed on a preceding year basis of assessment, on the adjusted profits of the accounting year ending in the preceding fiscal year. From 1997/98 (or 1994/95 for new businesses commenced after 6 April 1994) the assessment will be on the adjusted profits of the accounting year ended in the fiscal year (the current year basis). The financial year 1996/97 is a transitional year normally based on the average adjusted profits for the two accounting years ending in 1996/97. There are complex provisions for commencement and cessation and on a change of accounting date as well as the inevitable anti-avoidance provisions.

The provisions in FA 1995, s 126, which apply from 6 April 1996, relating to income from trading in the United Kingdom through a branch or agent, seek to replace and clarify the provisions of Part VIII of the Taxes Management Act 1970, ss 78–85, and re-enact the legislation for self-assessment without intending to change the established practice any more than is necessary. The Revenue has decided not to introduce legislation on the basic principles which have been established through case law and practice over many years. It is clear that the profits of a trade carried on wholly or partly in the United Kingdom are assessable under Schedule D, Case I (*Ogilvie v Kitton* (1908) 5 TC 538; *Spiers v MacKinnon* (1929) 14 TC 386; *San Paulo (Brazilian) Railway Co Ltd v Carter* (1985) 3 TC 407; *Denver Hotel Co Ltd v Andrews* (1895) 3 TC 356; *Grove v Elliots & Parkinson* (1896) 3 TC 481; *London Bank of Mexico v Apthorpe* (1891) 3 TC 143). Where the trade is carried on wholly abroad the profits are assessable under Schedule D, Case V (*Colquhoun v Brooks* (1889) 2 TC 490; *Trustees of Ferguson Deceased v Donovan* [1929] IR 489), which is assessable on similar lines to Schedule D, Cases I and II.

Trading in the United Kingdom, broadly means that economic activities from which the profits are derived are carried on in the United Kingdom. This has been established by a series of cases, including: *Erichsen v Last* (1881) 1 TC 351; *Tischler v Apthorpe* (1885) 2 TC 89; *Pommery & Greno v Apthorpe* (1886) 2 TC 182; *Werle & Co v Colquhoun* (1888) 2 TC 402; *Grainger & Son v Gough* (1896) 3 TC 311; *Sulley v Attorney General* (1860) 2 TC 149; *Smidth & Co v Greenwood* (1992) 8 TC 193; *Firestone*

Tyre & Rubber Co Ltd (as agents for Firestone Co of USA) v Lewellin (1957) 37 TC 111.

Where a non-resident carries on a trade partly in the United Kingdom and partly outside the United Kingdom, the charge is limited to the profits from the part of the trade carried on in the United Kingdom (*Pommery & Greno v Apthorpe* (1886) 2 TC 182 at 189).

In order to arrive at the measure of profits chargeable in such circumstances, the Revenue will adopt the internationally accepted arm's length principle set out in Art 7(2) and (3) of the OECD model double taxation convention. Trades carried on in the UK but not through a branch or agency rarely occur and present no special problems in determining the profits, which would be subject to taxation in the United Kingdom, unless exempted under a double tax treaty.

The Revenue intends to confirm its understanding of trading in and with the United Kingdom and the arm's length principle for determining UK profits in an issue of *Tax Bulletin* in due course.

A branch or agent in the United Kingdom through which a non-resident carries on, whether solely or in partnership, any trade, profession or vocation, is made the non-resident's UK representative for income and corporation tax purposes in relation to.

(1)   the income from the trade, profession or vocation arising directly or indirectly from the branch or agency;

(2)   income from property or rights such as patents copyright etc which are used by or held by the branch or agency; and

(3)   capital gains on assets situated in the United Kingdom used for the purpose of a trade, profession or vocation or by the branch or agency within TCGA 1992, s 10.

The non-resident's UK representative remains the representative for the income or capital gains which he has received even though he ceases to be the branch or agent and is treated as a separate and distinct person from the non-resident, which allows notices to be served on him and tax collected from him etc.

Where the non-resident is carrying on the trade or profession through a branch or agency in the United Kingdom as a partner in a partnership, the trade or profession carried on through the branch or agency includes the deemed trade or profession arising from the non-resident's share in the partnership under TA 1988, ss 111–114.

Where the non-resident is carrying on a trade in the United Kingdom through a partnership where there is a UK resident partner, the partnership is treated as the branch or agent of each non-resident partner in respect of his share in the partnership profit. The effect is to make any partners present or resident in the United Kingdom jointly liable for tax on the non-resident's share of partnership profits, which overcomes the difficulty of collecting tax from a non-resident partner. It also has the effect of retaining the current liability of partners for the tax liabilities of non-resident partners, even though the joint liability will no longer apply under self-assessment for a UK resident partner in respect of the tax liabilities of his partners, in view of substituted TA 1988, s 111.

4.10 Royalties and patents

Copyright and UK patent royalties paid to non-residents normally have income tax deducted at source by the payer (see, however, Chapter 11). The payer is assessable even if he fails to deduct the tax. The sale of a patent in the United Kingdom by a non-resident vendor involves the deduction of basic rate tax by the purchaser from the consideration paid, under TA 1988, s 524(3).

Where copyright royalties are paid through a third party that party may be liable on the net sum, ie the royalty less commission, TA 1988, s 536(3), (4).

4.11 Maintenance payments

Maintenance payments under a pre-15 March 1988 UK court order were, until 5 April 1989, paid subject to deduction of tax at source unless within the small payment limits of TA 1988, s 351.

For payments after 5 April 1989 under pre-15 March 1988 arrangements:

(1) the payer gets tax relief on payments up to the level for which he got relief for 1988/89; and

(2) an amount equal to that received in 1988/89 is treated as part of the recipient's total income;

(3) however, the difference between the married person's allowance and the single person's allowance (for the relevant year of assessment) is exempt from tax in the recipient's hands.

All payments of maintenance are paid gross—without tax deducted by the payer.

Payers under the old rules may, if they prefer, switch to the current rules mentioned below. These rules will then apply to the recipient as well. An election, which will apply for a whole tax year, can be made at any time during the year and up to 12 months after. An election may be beneficial if payments increase, and the limit for relief 'pegged' at the 1988/89 level is below the maximum amount of relief available under the new rules.

For court orders and maintenance agreements made on or after 15 March 1988:

(1)   the recipient is not liable to tax on any payments received;

(2)   where one divorced or separated spouse is required to make payments to the other, the payer qualifies for tax relief (20% for 1994/95 and 15% for 1995/96) for payments up to a limit equal to the difference between the single and married person's allowances (£1,720 for 1995–96) until the recipient remarries;

(3)   there is no tax relief for other new maintenance or alimony payments; and

(4)   payments are made gross (ie without deduction of tax).

4.12   Trust and estate income

Tax on income received by a non-resident from an estate in the course of administration in the United Kingdom was, before 5 April 1995 initially charged on income distributed in the year of receipt and ultimately the total income was reallocated over the administration period on a day-to-day basis unless he had an absolute interest in the residue, or a share of it (TA 1988, s 695). The personal representatives would deduct tax at the basic rate and issue a tax certificate on form R 185 E for the tax deducted. The income was then treated in the same way as any other UK taxed income and a repayment claim could be made or a higher rate liability could arise.

Where the non-resident had an absolute interest in residue the income was again subject to basic rate tax being withheld by the personal representatives but in this case the income under TA 1988, s 696 was allocated on an arising basis and not on a day-to-day apportionment over the whole administration period. Relief from higher rate tax was available where IHT had been paid on accrued income at the date of death (TA 1988, s 699).

Where the administration of an estate is completed after 5 April 1995, under TA 1988, s 695 as amended by FA 1995, Sched 18, any amount which remains payable to a beneficiary with a limited interest in the residue of the estate on completion, ie one who is entitled only to the income, is deemed for tax purposes to have been paid out as an income distribution in the year of assessment in which the administration period ends. Where the interest ceased, for example on the death of the beneficiary before the end of the administration, any final payment is deemed to be paid for the last year of assessment in which the limited interest existed, for example the year of the beneficiary's death.

Where a person is entitled to a limited interest in the residue of a deceased's estate he is taxed on the grossed-up equivalent of any actual payments made as income distributions in the administration period. The personal representatives should issue a form R 185 to the beneficiaries in respect of income distributions. Each payment has to be grossed up for tax purposes at the applicable rate, ie the basic rate in respect of income other than dividends and the lower rate in respect of dividends, in accordance with TA 1988, s 701.

Where a taxpayer has an absolute interest in the residue of a deceased's estate, ie he is entitled to both the income and capital of the residue, he is, in the first instance, taxed on the grossed-up equivalent at the basic rate, or if dividends, the lower rate of amounts paid to him as income of the year of assessment in which it is paid.

In the case of trust income a life tenant of a UK trust would receive income subject to tax at the basic rate, whereas the beneficiary of a discretionary UK trust would receive his share of income less UK tax at both the basic rate and an additional 10 per cent surcharge, ie currently 35 per cent, under TA 1988, s 687. Again, any overpayment of UK tax may be recovered and any underpayment of higher rate liability remains payable.

4.13 Avoidance of higher rate liability

Where UK investment income received before 5 April 1995 was sufficient, the non-resident could find that he had an individual liability to higher rate taxation in addition to any basic rate tax that may have been withheld at source. In many cases the tax charge could be limited to the basic rate by transferring investments to an overseas holding company in an appropriate tax haven. For example, if investments were held by an investment company in the Isle of Man with directors in, say, Hong Kong, it would be a non-resident company subject, in the Isle of Man, to a flat rate of tax of only £500. As a non-resident company, the liability to tax on its UK investment income would be limited under TA 1988, s 1 to basic rate only. As UK investment income other than Schedule A income from property is likely to be included income as explained at **4.3.1.** it is unlikely in most cases that such companies will be necessary for income tax purposes but they could still have advantages for IHT as the shares would be non-UK property and excluded property in the hands of a non-UK domiciled person.

Despite the obvious attractions, expatriates considering this route should first indulge in some careful consideration. The costs involved in establishing and running an offshore company can be sizeable and nowadays the savings to be made are much less than in previous years, the maximum income tax saving is now 15 per cent. Transferring the ownership of assets into an offshore company can also be a costly business especially where there is stamp duty to be taken into account: share transfers are charged at ½ per cent and conveyances of land and buildings are charged at 1 per cent.

Where it is calculated that the tax saving is likely to outweigh the costs involved, there are still a couple of factors to be borne in mind before proceeding. First, in view of the anti-avoidance provisions of TA 1988, s 739 the offshore investment company route should only be considered by individuals not ordinarily resident in the United Kingdom and the company should be wound up before UK residence is resumed.

This means that the procedure is only suitable as a means of tax limitation for the long-term non-resident, who has or has acquired a non-UK domicile.

Secondly, however, care is required because, as in all tax matters, if there is first, a pre-ordained series of transactions and steps inserted which have no business purpose apart from avoidance of tax, the inserted steps will be ignored for tax purposes: see *Craven v White* [1988] STC 476.

4.14   Lloyd's Underwriters

The taxation of Lloyd's Underwriters is a specialist subject and the comments here are confined to areas of particular interest to non-resident names.

Lloyd's income arises in the United Kingdom and is classified as a trade carried on in the United Kingdom subject to UK tax. It is normally desirable for Lloyd's deposits to be arranged by way of letter of credit or bank guarantee as, for example, exempt gilts held as part of Lloyd's deposits or reserves remain UK taxable as connected with a business carried on in the United Kingdom (*Owen v Sassoon* (1950) 32 TC101) (apart from 3½ per cent War Loan). The CGT and IHT exemptions, however, continue to apply.

The basis of assessment for Lloyd's investment income may not be followed by the overseas Revenue which might, for example, assess the investment income as it arises even though it is not distributed until the account is closed. United States tax paid which would be refunded to a UK resident is treated as an expense so far as a non-resident is concerned and merely reduces the gross income. Transfers to a special reserve fund would not normally have any effect for foreign tax purposes, although they would affect the UK tax payable and therefore the amount available for credit. Where the UK tax is fully relieved overseas there is no advantage in a transfer to the special reserve fund, although care has to be taken to ensure that foreign tax credits are not inadvertently lost.

There are special rules in certain countries for Lloyd's Names, in particular the United States and Canada.

4.15   Non-resident's entitlement to UK personal allowances

Certain classes of non-residents may obtain relief against UK assessable income through entitlement to the normal personal allowances under TA 1988, s 278.

The classes of individuals to which the relief applies include the following:

(1)   Commonwealth citizens and citizens of the Republic of Ireland;
(2)   persons who are or who have been in the service of the Crown;
(3)   missionaries;
(4)   servants of British Protectorates;
(5)   residents of the Isle of Man or Channel Islands;
(6)   persons abroad for health reasons after residence in the United Kingdom;
(7)   widows of Crown servants; and
(8)   residents of countries where relief is given under a double taxation treaty.

In addition, double taxation agreements with many countries provide that the relief applies to residents of that country.

This tax relief is useful where the non-resident has a significant income taxable in the United Kingdom. Where the UK income is small, it may not be worth the trouble of claiming on an annual basis but possibly every few years (the time limit for the claim is six years).

5 Tax aspects of UK property

Peter Goodman MA, FCA, ATII of Wilkins Kennedy, Chartered Accountants

Expatriates often retain property in the United Kingdom which is let during the period of absence overseas. The retention of such property ensures that the expatriate has a place to live in the United Kingdom on the completion of his overseas work, and may be a protection against rises in house prices during the period of absence.

Before entering into letting arrangements, the expatriate needs to give careful consideration to the proposed tenancy arrangements, with particular attention being given to rights of possession. Standard tenancy arrangements may create difficulties at a future date, and consequently advice should be sought from experienced professional advisers in relation to UK landlord and tenant law.

5.1 Rental income

Taxation matters in connection with lettings also need careful review. Income from UK property, being income arising from a source in the United Kingdom, is chargeable to UK tax at lower, basic and, where applicable, higher rates. For fiscal years up to and including 1994/95 assessment to tax was under either Schedule A (Unfurnished Lettings) or Schedule D, Case VI (Furnished Lettings). With effect from 6 April 1995, all income from property (furnished or unfurnished) is pooled and taxed as Schedule A. Expatriates resident in a country which has a double tax treaty with the United Kingdom will find that it is normally the case that the treaty provides for rental income to be taxed by the country in which the property is situated.

In preparing the statement of letting income for Inland Revenue purposes it is useful to give details of the property address, the UK letting agents, and in whose beneficial ownership the property vests. The statement should, for 1995/96 onwards, be prepared in accordance with normal commercial accounting practice, matching income with expenditure in the chargeable period, and making provision for accruals and prepayments.

Expenses associated with letting may include:

(1)   water rates;
(2)   agents' commission;
(3)   building and contents insurance, and valuation fees for insurance purposes;
(4)   service charges and ground rent;
(5)   repairs and maintenance (but not capital expenditure, eg central heating/double glazing installation);
(6)   professional charges for preparing the letting statement;
(7)   advertising;
(8)   wear and tear allowance (for furnished lettings only—being 10 per cent of gross rent receivable less rates paid by the landlord: Inland Revenue Press Release, 13 October 1977);
(9)   cleaning;
(10) garden upkeep;
(11) inventory check-in/check-out costs;
(12) tenancy agreement charges;
(13) interest (see **5.2**).

The statement of letting income is normally prepared and submitted to the Inland Revenue by the property owner(s) direct or by their taxation agents. Additionally, personal allowances should be specifically claimed. Losses incurred in a fiscal year are available to be carried forward to be set off against future income from property. On the cessation of the letting activity, unused losses will not be available for future carry forward.

5.2   Loan interest

For fiscal years 1995/96 onwards loan interest payable is an allowable expense in arriving at net rental income, whereas before 6 April 1995, interest was allowed as a deduction in arriving at assessable letting income. Overdraft interest is not an allowable expense or deduction for tax purposes. A loan taken to replace an overdraft used to finance property acquisition or improvement will generally not qualify for tax relief (*Lawson (Inspector of Taxes) v Brooks* [1992] STC 76).

The conditions to be met to obtain tax relief on interest have changed significantly over the past few years. Before 6 April 1994, the interest had to be in respect of a loan to acquire or improve property and payable in the United Kingdom on an advance from a bank carrying on a *bona fide* banking business in the United Kingdom, or had to be annual interest chargeable to tax under Schedule D, Case III. Additionally, the property in the United Kingdom had to be let at a commercial rent for at least 26 weeks in a 52-week period, and when not so let must have been either available for letting at such a rent or undergoing works of construction or repair. Lettings at below the market rate, taking into account maintenance and repairing liabilities, resulted in loan interest relief being disallowed.

The interest relief rules were simplified in two ways. With effect from 6 April 1994, interest payable on all forms of loans, and in particular loans taken overseas, qualifies for tax relief. This reform opened up a wide range of new tax-efficient financing arrangements, using overseas individual and bank funding, for UK property investment. With effect from 6 April 1995, the rules relating to commercial letting (26 weeks in a 52-week period) were repealed. The overall effect of these changes is that from 6 April 1995, any payment of loan interest is capable of qualifying for tax relief, whether taken from a bank or individual in the United Kingdom or elsewhere, providing the loan was advanced to purchase or improve the UK property.

For loans taken from an overseas lender, care needs to be taken in relation to the legislation covering withholding of tax at source from interest payments. The relevant provisions state that interest paid on a UK-source loan to a person whose place of abode is outside the United Kingdom must be under deduction of basic rate income tax (25 per cent). However, certain double tax treaties provide exemption from this rule.

In November 1993 the Inland Revenue published in their Tax Bulletin the following factors which they regard as most important in determining the source of a loan:

(1)   the residence of the debtor, ie the place in which the debt will be enforced;
(2)   the source from which the interest is paid;
(3)   where the interest is paid; and
(4)   the nature and location of the security for the debt.

If all of these are located in the United Kingdom, then it is likely that the interest will have a UK source. In addition, the Inland Revenue has commented that the precise tax treatment in each case will depend on 'all the factors and on exactly how the transactions are in fact carried out'.

5.3   Administration and collection of tax

This is a complex area which can create a great deal of confusion for the expatriate. Where rents are paid direct by the tenant to the expatriate whose usual place of abode is outside the United Kingdom, then basic rate tax must be deducted from gross rents and paid to the Inland Revenue by the tenant (TA 1988, s 43). Payment of rent into a UK bank account held by the expatriate does not avoid the obligation of the tenant to deduct tax at source. It is important to note that, even if basic rate tax has been deducted by the tenant in these circumstances, it is still necessary to provide the Inland Revenue with a statement of rental income for each tax year in order that the correct income tax liability can be calculated.

Where the property is let through an agent, the provisions of TMA 1970, s 78 apply. This provides that the non-resident owner is assessed and charged to income tax in the name of the agent in the same manner as the non-resident person would have been assessed and charged had he been resident in the United Kingdom. The practical effect of this is that the Inland Revenue assesses the agent on the net rental income of the expatriate and the agent then discharges the income tax liability. There is no legal obligation on the agent, therefore, to deduct basic rate tax at source from rents remitted to the expatriate but, given the agent's responsibilities laid down in TMA 1970, s 78, the agent will ensure that sufficient tax is withheld from rents to satisfy the expected tax liability.

A statutory right of indemnity from the tenant in respect of tax charged (not interest or penalties which may arise from late payment of tax or failure to make the necessary returns) is contained within TMA 1970, s 83(2). In the event that the agent has made an excessive retention in relation to the tax liability arising, such retention should be repaid to the expatriate once the lettings statement and liability to tax have been agreed with the Inland Revenue.

The agent may, in the interim, place the tax reserve in a gross interest yielding account. Gross bank deposit interest is normally not taxable on the expatriate by virtue of Extra-Statutory Concession B13, provided the appropriate certificate of non-residence is signed and the expatriate is not assessable in the name of an agent in the United Kingdom. The presence of a letting agent will not generally prevent the application of the concession, provided that the interest arising is beneficially owned by the expatriate, the deposit is not excessive in relation to rent arising, and the agent's authority is restricted to the withdrawal of funds solely for the purpose of discharging the income tax liability arising on the rents.

For years up to and including 1995/96 tax on lettings income is normally payable on 1 January in the year of assessment.

5.4   Self-assessment

The Inland Revenue has announced certain administrative changes relating to the assessment and collection of tax on property income to take effect from 6 April 1996. These changes are part of the move to self-assessment in the United Kingdom. The main points are as follows:

*   income from property in the United Kingdom will be taxed through deduction at source by the agent for the property or, where there is no agent, the tenant with a final settling up with the non-resident;
*   but where the non-resident chooses, by agreement with the Inland Revenue, to include tax on income from property in payments on account made by the non-resident under self-assessment, no deduction will be required at source.

This opens the way for rent to be paid gross to the non-resident landlord. But this will only apply if the landlord produces to the agent/tenant an appropriate certificate from the Inland Revenue. Certificates will be given by the Inland Revenue on application where:

*   the landlord is likely to have no net tax liability; or
*   the landlord keeps his affairs fully up to date and chooses to pay any income tax that may be due wholly through self-assessment.

Regulations will outline the administrative arrangements that will operate in relation to non-resident property owners. If the non-resident landlord chooses to enter the self-assessment regime, income tax will be payable principally in two instalments. The first payment will be due on 31 January in the year of assessment, and the second on the following 31 July. Any balancing payment that may be payable will be due on the next 31 January.

5.5   Furnished holiday lettings

Letting furnished property as holiday accommodation within the terms of the legislation may secure a beneficial tax treatment of expatriates with other UK-source income. Furnished holiday lettings are treated as a trade if the following conditions are met:

(1)   the accommodation must be in the United Kingdom and let fur-
       nished on a commercial basis with a reasonable expectation of
       making a profit;
(2)   it must be available for letting to the public at large for at least 140
       days in any tax year;
(3)   actual lettings must be at least 70 days in the tax year (although in
       the first and last years in which the trade is carried on the rules are
       modified);
(4)   in a seven-month period, including the months that the property is
       let, no single let should normally be longer than 31 days.

The main income tax benefit to derive from the treatment of the activity
as a trade is the ability to relieve losses against other UK income. There
is no change to the administration and collection of income tax as
described above. For CGT purposes expatriates may, in certain circumstances, and especially if a spouse remains resident and has an interest in
the property, derive a benefit from the availability of roll-over relief and
retirement relief relating to business assets.

5.6   Mortgage interest relief at source (MIRAS)

MIRAS was introduced in April 1983, enabling UK interest payments to
be made net of income tax relief to qualifying lenders. The loan on which
interest payments arise must have been taken out for the purchase (or
improvement, before 6 April 1988) of a property in the United Kingdom
which is used wholly or to a substantial extent as the only or main residence of the borrower, his spouse (or before April 1988 a dependent relative or a former or separated spouse). MIRAS applies only to the first
£30,000 of a loan which satisfies these conditions, and expatriates are
not, as a class, excluded from MIRAS relief. Tax relief is at the rate of 15
per cent for 1995/96 (20 per cent for 1994/95). Qualifying lenders include
most UK building societies, banks, insurance companies and specialised
mortgage funding schemes.

5.6.1   Expatriates who do not let their property while overseas

An expatriate working full-time overseas may be unable to satisfy the
conditions that any UK property retained is used 'wholly or to a substantial extent' as his only or main residence. 'Substantial' is not defined
in the tax legislation, but it is understood that the Inland Revenue regards
this as six months or more in the year. If the expatriate's spouse and

family continue to live in the UK property, then the conditions may be satisfied. Additionally, Extra-Statutory Concession A27 allows temporary absences of up to a year to be ignored in determining whether a property is used as an only or main residence.

In the event that the above conditions cannot be satisfied, MIRAS relief may continue by the application of Extra-Statutory Concession A27. This principally applies when a person is required by reason of his employment to move from his home to another place overseas for a period not expected to exceed four years. MIRAS will continue to apply to mortgage interest payments in respect of a loan for the purchase of a property used as an only or main residence before working overseas, provided this property can reasonably be expected to be used again as such on his return. Relief is not given beyond a period of four years, but if there is a further temporary absence after the property has been reoccupied for a minimum period of three months, the four-year test will apply to the new absence without regard to the previous absence. It should be noted that if arrangements are entered into to take advantage of the concession for tax-avoidance purposes, it is likely that the Inland Revenue will deny the application of the concession (*R v IRC, ex p Fulford Dobson* [1987] STC 344).

If an expatriate on an overseas tour of duty purchases a property in the United Kingdom in the course of a leave period, and uses that property as an only or main residence for a period of not less than three months before his return to the place of his overseas employment, he will be regarded as satisfying the condition that the property was being used as his only or main residence before he went away, and MIRAS will be applied.

5.6.2 Expatriates who let their property while overseas

From 6 April 1994 new rules were introduced which limit the circumstances under which a loan can remain within MIRAS. Only by making an election in writing to the Inland Revenue when letting commences can the loan remain in MIRAS. But if such an election has been made, interest relief on that loan cannot be claimed against income from property. For a loan in excess of £30,000, therefore, where an election has been made, tax relief is limited in 1995/96 to 15 per cent of the interest paid on £30,000. In many cases it will not be beneficial to make such an election, thereby ensuring that unrestricted relief is given against letting income. In these circumstances it is necessary to advise the mortgage lender to take the loan out of MIRAS, since failure to do so will result in the Inland Revenue clawing back relief when this is discovered. The interaction of MIRAS and relief for interest against income from property is complex and advice on this issue should always be taken in advance of the commencement of the letting. Elections can be made or withdrawn within specific time limits on an annual basis in the light of the individual's circumstances.

5.7   Capital gains tax: principal private residence

The disposal of UK residential property by an expatriate during a tax year throughout which he is not resident and not ordinarily resident for UK tax purposes does not give rise to a charge to CGT.

For the tax year of return to the United Kingdom, Extra-Statutory Concession D2 provides that:

> a person who is treated as resident in the United Kingdom for any year of assessment from the date of his arrival here but who has not been regarded at any time during the period of 36 months immediately preceding the date of his arrival as resident or ordinarily resident here, is charged to CGT only in respect of the chargeable gains accruing to him from disposals made after his arrival in the United Kingdom.

However, extra-statutory concessions will not be given in any case where an attempt is made to use them for tax avoidance, and after the judgment in *R v IRC, ex p Fulford Dobson* (1987), care should be taken in respect of any transaction involving a chargeable gain undertaken in the period 5 April to the date of arrival in the United Kingdom.

Expatriates who retain their home in the United Kingdom during their period of absence overseas should carefully consider the conditions to be satisfied after returning to the United Kingdom for exemption from CGT on a subsequent sale. These conditions are as follows:

(1)   The property must be the individual's only or main residence throughout the period of ownership except for all or any part of the last 36 months of ownership (24 months for disposals before 19 March 1991). If the property has been an only or main residence for part of the period of ownership the gain is apportioned between the exempt and non-exempt periods.

(2)   The exemption applies to dwelling houses and land comprising garden and ground which are for the occupation and enjoyment of the main residence up to the permitted area. The permitted area is

defined as 0.5 of a hectare, being approximately 1.25 acres (inclusive of the site of the dwelling house), although in any particular case the permitted area may be a larger area as the 'Commissioners may determine, if satisfied that, regard being had to the size and the character of the dwelling house, that larger area is required for the reasonable enjoyment of it as a residence'. (TCGA 1992, s 222 (3).)

(3) Certain periods of absence from the dwelling are treated as periods of residence provided the dwelling house was the only property eligible for relief and was occupied as such both before and after the periods of absence. These periods which can be used on a cumulative basis are:

(a) any period or periods of absence which do not in total exceed three years; and

(b) any period of absence throughout which the individual worked in an employment or office all the duties of which were performed outside the United Kingdom; and

(c) any period or periods of absence not exceeding four years in total throughout which the individual was prevented from residing in the dwelling house in consequence of the situation of his place of work or because his employer required him to live elsewhere so that his duties of employment could be effectively carried out.

Expatriates need to pay close attention to condition (b). It is clear that all duties of employment must be performed outside the United Kingdom. This is in contrast to income tax rules where incidental duties performed in the United Kingdom may be disregarded under the provisions of TA 1988, s 335. The performance of such incidental UK duties could inadvertently jeopardise the CGT relief. The condition is also framed in terms of employment or office and does not cover self-employment.

The requirements as to occupation of the property both before and after the period of absence are of considerable significance. If the expatriate returns to the United Kingdom and does not occupy his former main residence because he owns another property, then a chargeable gain may arise on disposal. Extra-Statutory Concession D4 provides assistance to the expatriate where he is unable to resume residence in his previous home because the terms of his employment require him to work elsewhere. The concession deems the condition of reoccupation after the period of absence to be satisfied.

Where an expatriate has sold his UK home during his overseas absence and purchased another property which is to be occupied on his return to the United Kingdom, the gain attributable to the period of time from purchase to actual occupation may be chargeable to CGT on disposal. This arises if the property has not been occupied as the main or only property on purchase, even though it replaces a former main residence occupied as such, before leaving the United Kingdom. Such transactions can present an unfortunate tax pitfall for the expatriate, although the legislation contains specific relief for expatriates who live in job-related accommodation overseas. This is defined as where it is necessary for the proper performance of the duties of the employment that the employee should reside in that accommodation.

Another point to consider carefully is that for the principal private residence exemption to apply, the expatriate must have no other property eligible for CGT exemption as an only or main residence throughout the period of absence. This creates a difficulty, as the expatriate may have an interest in an overseas residence—either by way of ownership or rental—which will be a residence eligible for relief. In these circumstances the expatriate should consider submitting to the Inland Revenue an election under TCGA 1992, s 222(5) that the UK property is the expatriate's only or main residence to satisfy the statutory requirements. There is a two-year time limit from acquisition of the interest in the additional property to make the election.

If part of the gain on a principal private residence is in charge to CGT and the property has been wholly or partly let as residential accommodation during the period of ownership a further relief is available. The relief is the lesser of £40,000 (£20,000 for disposals before 19 March 1991) and the gain otherwise exempt under the general rules referred to at (1)–(3) above.

5.8   Inheritance tax

Non-resident, UK domiciled individuals remain liable to IHT on their worldwide estate. A UK will should specifically cover the disposition of all UK properties. Where a UK domiciled person is married to a non-UK domiciled person, property transactions can be structured to minimise the exposure to inheritance tax. Professional advice should be sought at the time the property is acquired, particularly if an offshore company or trust is being considered. Additionally, the relevant tax and legal issues should be reconsidered on a regular basis in the light of changes in legislation.

6 Capital gains tax

6.1 Residence

The Taxation of Chargeable Gains Act 1992 (TCGA 1992), s 2 provides
that an individual resident or ordinarily resident in the United Kingdom
is subject to CGT on his worldwide capital gains. In order, therefore, to
avoid UK CGT it is essential to cease to be ordinarily resident in the
United Kingdom. This normally requires three complete tax years of non-
residence or, when the individual concerned is in full-time employment
overseas, one complete tax year of non-residence. Exemption from CGT
then normally applies to gains accruing to the individual from disposals
made after the date of his departure (ie he does not have to wait for a new
tax year, or for a full tax year to elapse: Extra-Statutory Concession D2).
The liability to CGT of an expatriate returning to the United Kingdom is
discussed in detail in Chapter 12.

6.2 Husband and wife

The residence statuses of a husband and wife are determined independently. Despite this, the CGT exemption for assets transferred
between spouses married and living together is none the less preserved. In *Gubay v Kington* [1984] STC 499, it was held that the transfer of a chargeable asset by a UK resident spouse to a non-resident
spouse was not a chargeable event. The scope for transferring an asset
from a resident to a non-ordinarily resident spouse before sale to avoid
CGT is limited as was illustrated in *R v IRC, ex p Fulford Dobson*
[1987] STC 344. In this case a wife transferred a farm to her husband
who went to work in Germany and the farm was sold four days after
his departure. The Revenue's refusal to apply Extra-Statutory
Concession D2, because an attempt had been made to use it for tax
avoidance, was upheld.

6.3   Emigration

A person emigrating from the United Kingdom would normally leave the disposal of his assets showing capital gains until after his departure (taking due account of his liability in the new jurisdiction). The disposal should be deferred until after the following 5 April because the Revenue is likely to refuse to apply Extra-Statutory Concession D2. Investments showing losses would normally be sold before the date of departure in order to crystallise a loss which might be of use on any future return to the United Kingdom.

If the assets in question are used in, or in connection with, a business, there are further important considerations. See **6.5**.

6.4   Property

Although non-residents may be exempt from CGT in respect of a disposal of most investments, it is necessary to look rather more carefully in the case of land and buildings. Section 776 of TA 1988, provides that a capital profit from dealing or developing land directly or indirectly is assessed to tax under Schedule D, Case VI as UK income irrespective of the residence of the owner. Section 777(9) of TA 1988 enables the Board to direct that basic rate income tax may be withheld from the sale proceeds, although in practice this has proved ineffective in many cases, as the Revenue has not been aware of the disposal until too late to raise the necessary direction and the non-resident has received the sale proceeds gross. Section 776 does not apply to private residences exempt from CGT as a main residence.

6.5   Business gains

6.5.1   Sale of a business

A not uncommon spur to emigration occurs where a person resident or ordinarily resident in the United Kingdom is intending to dispose of his business, consisting either of shares in a company or the goodwill of an unincorporated business. This gives rise to a number of problems. Although under Extra-Statutory Concession D2 a person emigrating from the United Kingdom is *normally* regarded as neither resident nor ordinarily resident from the day following the day of departure this is a purely concessional treatment as, at law, a person resident for part of the tax year is resident for the entire tax year. The Revenue is likely to refuse to apply the concession so the contract for the disposal of the shares or business should be deferred until after the following 5 April. Even then the problems are not necessarily over as the Revenue or the courts might infer a prior oral contract, or prior agreement sufficient to constitute a contract, where all the terms and conditions of the sale were finalised before final sale. In this connection there is precedent for holding that correspondence between the parties before the final contract can create a binding contract (*J H & S Timber Ltd v Quirk* [1973] STC 111) and that the beneficial ownership can pass before any transfer of legal title (*Ayerst v C & K (Construction) Ltd* [1975] STC 345, *Wood Preservation Ltd v Prior* (1968) 45 TC 112). Gains in the year of departure would also be outside Extra-Statutory Concession D2 if the business was carried on in the United Kingdom through a branch or agency (press release of 6 April 1989, amending ESC D2).

Section 28 of TCGA 1992 states that the date of disposal for CGT is the time the contract was made, and if the contract is conditional it is the time when the condition is satisfied. It would, however, be hazardous to enter into arrangements designed specifically to postpone the date of disposal in order to allow time for emigration, as this might give rise to a series of transactions or a single composite transaction, the effect of which can be considered together and might result in a date of disposal before emigration (*Furniss v Dawson* [1984] STC 153). In particular Lord Bridge's comments in this case are of interest.

> 'When one moves however from a single transaction to a series of interdependent transactions designed to produce a given result it is, in my opinion, perfectly legitimate to draw a distinction between the substance and the form of the composite transaction without in any way suggesting that any of the single transactions which make up the whole are other than genuine. This has been the approach of the United States Federal Courts enabling them to develop a doctrine whereby the tax consequences of the composite transactions are dependent on its substance and not its form. I shall not attempt to review the American authorities nor do I propose a wholesale importation of the American doctrine in all its ramifications into English law. But I do suggest that the distinction between form and substance is one which can usefully be drawn in determining the tax consequences of composite transactions and one which will help to free the Courts from the shackles which have for so long been thought to be imposed on them by the Westminster case.'

The *Westminster* case held that the form of a transaction takes precedence over its substance in taxation matters (*IRC v Duke of Westminster* (1936) 19 TC 490): this applies only in the absence of a pre-ordained series of transactions or one single composite transaction.

This warning having been given, it is obviously possible to enter into negotiations before leaving the United Kingdom which do not amount to a contract to dispose of the shares or business and to conclude these arrangements by a contract for sale after having become neither resident nor ordinarily resident in the United Kingdom. As has been explained earlier, to acquire non-ordinary residence will normally require a period of absence from the United Kingdom of at least three complete tax years. However, the Inland Revenue in a letter dated 10 July 1979, quoted in *Moores Rowland's Yellow Tax Guide*, stated:

'I can confirm that where an employee left the UK on 4 April 1979 and did not return until 6 April 1980 and was on a full-time service contract throughout that period he would be regarded as not resident and not ordinarily resident in the UK throughout the year 1979/80.

However this practice would not be extended to a taxpayer who was only partly in employment and partly self-employed during a similar period. In such circumstances the normal rules for determining an individual's residence status would apply and on the basis that no visits were made during the intervening period the taxpayer would be regarded as not resident but ordinarily resident for the year 1979/80 in these circumstances.'

'These circumstances' would be that there was not a full-time service contract covering the complete tax year.

It is obviously dangerous to rely on a full-time service contract overseas unless this can be substantiated by the facts of the case. The Revenue is unlikely to be easily persuaded that a person who has emigrated on selling his business in the United Kingdom for several million pounds is likely to take full-time employment; and a lot more is required than a mere service contract with some offshore company ostensibly requiring full-time duties, usually of a somewhat indeterminate nature.

If the emigrant disposing of the shares is not granted provisional non-resident and non-ordinarily resident status the CGT would have to be paid and recovered in due course when the non-resident and non-ordinarily resident status was established, retrospectively to include the date of disposal.

In the case of a disposal of an unincorporated business, as opposed to shares, it is important to remember that a business carried on by a non-resident through a branch or agency in the United Kingdom remains subject to UK CGT under TCGA 1992, s 10. It is therefore necessary for the business to cease while the owner is still resident in the United Kingdom and for him then to depart and thereafter conclude the disposal of the business assets, including goodwill of the former business. This is not easy to do without having entered into a binding contract before leaving the United Kingdom despite what the paperwork may purport to provide. In such circumstances it might even be more practical to transfer the business into a company in exchange for shares and claim the rollover under the provisions of TCGA 1992, s 162, then to emigrate, and then to sell the shares in the UK company. The transfer to the company should be done before entering into any negotiations with possible purchasers, otherwise this would be regarded as a series of transactions within the *Furniss v Dawson* principle. Alternatively, it might be possible to show that the purchasers required the protection of limited liability so that this was the business purpose for the transfer of the business to a company.

Rather than try to argue that the contract was actually entered into after leaving the United Kingdom it might well be preferable to give the intended purchaser an option enabling him to acquire the shares after the vendor has become non-resident (TCGA 1992, s 28(2)). 'Conditional contract' refers in particular to a contract conditional on the exercise of an option and makes it clear that the date of the disposal is the date the option is *exercised*. It is tempting to consider entering into a put and call option, but the Revenue has argued strongly in the case of development land tax transactions that a put and call option is the equivalent of a contract for sale and that they are entitled to treat it as a disposal at the date the option was entered into.

If it is not possible to postpone the date of the contract for disposal until the vendor has become non-resident it might be possible to take a large proportion of the proceeds in the form of loan stock. If it can be shown that there is a good commercial reason for the issue of loan stock a claim for roll-over relief on the disposal of the shares should be available under TCGA 1992, s 135, with clearance under s 138. If clearance is obtained it should be possible for the vendor to become non-resident and then dispose of the loan stock, thus crystallising the gain on the shares rolled into the loan stock. It is probably unwise to arrange before departure from the United Kingdom for the loan stock immediately to be redeemed or placed with some financial institution, as the Revenue could then argue that the issue of the loan stock was merely an inserted step in what was in reality a sale for cash, again relying on *Furniss v Dawson*.

It should be noted that capital gains on Lloyd's investments as an underwriting name are basically subject to CGT as arising from a business carried on in the United Kingdom through an agent (TCGA 1992, s 10). However, syndicate investments which form part of the Lloyd's American Trust Fund and Lloyd's Canadian Trust Fund are regarded as not situated in the United Kingdom and non-UK securities in the Lloyd's sterling trust fund are also regarded as situated outside the United

Kingdom. Exempt gilts held as part of a Lloyd's fund would retain their CGT exemption.

Where it is not possible to shelter a gain on going non-resident, retirement relief may be of assistance. This applies to a disposal of the whole or part of a business or shares in a personal trading company by someone reaching the age of 55 or retiring earlier on grounds of ill-health. The relief is exemption on the first £250,000 of chargeable gains and for half the balance up to £1 million, TCGA 1992, ss 163, 164 and Sched 6.

6.6   Reinvestment relief

From 1 December 1993 individuals and some trusts can postpone CGT on any asset (not just shares) to the extent that the gain is re-invested in qualifying unquoted shares, including Enterprise Investment Scheme shares and up to £100,000 pa in Venture Capital Trusts. The provisions are complex and hedged about with many anti-avoidance provisions. Only the gain (and not the whole proceeds) need be reinvested, TCGA 1992, s 164A–N.

The relief applies where the reinvestor makes a disposal and acquires a qualifying investment within the qualifying period, ie a period beginning 12 months before the disposal and ending three years thereafter, subject to Revenue discretion to extend this period.

The qualifying reinvestment must be in ordinary shares, not within the business expansion scheme, in a qualifying unquoted company which carries on one or more qualifying trades or is a holding company of qualifying subsidiaries carrying on qualifying trades. Where the asset disposed of consisted of shares or securities in a company, the qualifying company cannot be the same company or in the same group as that company. There is no requirement that the reinvestor is an officer or employee of the new company nor that the reinvestor holds a minimum number of shares.

The activities of the company follow many of the extensive restrictions of the former business expansion scheme although farming and property development are permitted. The company does not have to be incorporated in the United Kingdom. The roll-over relief is clawed back if a triggering event occurs within the relevant three-year period after the acquisition of the eligible shares in the qualifying reinvestment company unless the shares have already been disposed of, or the disposal is to the reinvestor's spouse who takes over the reinvestor's position. A triggering event is the shares in the reinvestment company ceasing to be eligible or the company ceasing to be a qualifying company, or the reinvestor becoming non-resident other than on taking up a full-time employment lasting for less than three years, or if the shares are exchanged for qualifying corporate bonds under TCGA 1992, s 116. The reinvestment relief therefore cannot be used to roll over a gain with a view to eliminating it by subsequently going non-resident within three years although subsequent emigration would not crystallise a charge. Gifts of business assets also qualify for roll-over relief under TCGA 1992, ss 165–169, but the relief is not available on a gift to a non-resident and the held-over gains would crystallise on the donee becoming non-resident within six years.

6.7 Foreign taxes

It is beyond the scope of this book to consider non-UK tax liabilities, but if a business or shares are sold after having left the United Kingdom the taxpayer may well have become resident in some other country which imposes a CGT charge or assesses capital gains as income. The general advice given with regard to UK CGT may be overruled if the effective rate of overseas tax on the chargeable gain would be greater.

Local advice should be taken before concluding the contract for disposal, as to whether there is a potential tax charge in the country of residence, and if so what, if anything, can be done about it.

6.8 Trusts

The UK resident beneficiary of a non-resident trust is liable to CGT if the settlor was UK domiciled and resident when he made the settlement and if the beneficiary is resident when the gain is distributed to him. If, however, the beneficiary is not domiciled in the United Kingdom, TCGA 1992, s 87(7) exempts him from a CGT charge. See also Chapter 8.

6.9 Offshore funds

Before 1984, it was possible for a UK resident to invest in certain offshore funds known as 'roll-up funds', where income to the funds was not distributed but accumulated tax free—when the investment was realised the accumulated profit, both gain and income, was subject to UK CGT only. Complicated rules were introduced to take effect from 1 January 1984 (FA

1984, ss 92–100, now incorporated into TA 1988, ss 757–764) which mean that a UK resident investor is now liable to tax on his entire gain in an offshore 'roll-up' fund as if it were income, under Schedule D, Case VI. If the investor is domiciled outside the United Kingdom the tax liability will only apply to any gain actually remitted to the United Kingdom.

In the case of a UK expatriate there will be no liability to UK tax on realisations of gain from a 'roll-up' fund, so long as he remains non-resident and non-ordinarily resident in the United Kingdom, but realisations of gain after he returns home will attract the full liability to UK income tax. This future heavy exposure to UK taxation can be avoided by investing in offshore funds that have been granted 'distributor status'. The Finance Act 1984 provided that where a fund meets certain rules—the most important is that the fund must distribute at least 85 per cent of the income received—the investor will be taxed on his income and gain in the normal way, ie Schedule D, Case VI in respect of the income distribution and CGT in respect of realised growth.

The Revenue has attacked offshore roll-up funds which take the form of personal bonds, where the investor appoints the investment advisor, as a transfer of assets subject to tax on the income of the bond as it arises under TA 1988, s 739. In *IRC v Willoughby* [1995] STC 143 the Court of Appeal held that such bonds were not tax-avoidance devices and were protected by TA 1988, s 741. They also held that a transferor (investor) would only fall under TA 1988, s 739 if he were ordinarily resident in the United Kingdom at the time of the transfer. The Special Commissioner in this case held that a tax deferral was a tax advantage and it seems that TA 1988, s 740 could apply to assess benefits from investments to a UK resident even where the investment was made while abroad if the escape route for *bona fide* commercial transactions not designed to avoid tax in TA 1988, s 741 did not apply.

6.10   Gifts from non-residents

If an asset given by a non-resident to a UK resident is subsequently disposed of by the donee, the donee is treated as acquiring the asset at market value at the time of the gift, and is liable to CGT only on any excess over the acquisition value.

6.11   Non-sterling bank accounts

Under TCGA 1992, s 275(l) a non-sterling bank account belonging to a non-UK domiciled individual is treated as located outside the United

Kingdom and therefore exempt from CGT on currency movements unless the account is held at the UK branch of a bank and the individual is resident in the United Kingdom.

6.12 UK investment managers

An investment manager in the United Kingdom whose normal business it is to buy, sell and manage investments on behalf of a non-resident with whom he is not connected is normally protected from a UK tax charge by the provisions of FA 1995, s 127. There are cases where the protection can be lost, such as if the transactions can be taxed as part of a wider trade (insurance, for example) carried on in the United Kingdom through the same agency. The investment manager must be acting as an independent agent or as manager of a quoted collective investment fund such as a unit trust.

7 Inheritance tax

As has already been seen, the non-resident expatriate can, to a very great extent, avoid any liability to UK income tax and CGT. The main determinant of liability for income tax, apart from the location of the income source, is the individual's residence for tax purposes, and CGT is generally only chargeable on persons resident or ordinarily resident in the United Kingdom. This is not the case for IHT.

A charge to IHT may arise whenever there is a transfer of assets, (other than lifetime gifts to an individual (or certain kinds of trust) made more than seven years before the donor's death), no matter where the assets are located, made by a person who is, or was at death, domiciled or deemed to be domiciled (see Chapter 1) in the United Kingdom. In addition, IHT may be charged on a transfer of assets located in the United Kingdom by a person not domiciled in the United Kingdom.

So far as most British expatriates are concerned, although they may be non-resident for many years, their domicile remains the United Kingdom and, in consequence, they remain liable to IHT.

What follows is a necessarily brief outline of IHT with the emphasis placed on those aspects which are likely to be of greatest interest or relevance to expatriates. More detailed information is to be found in this book's companion volume, the *Allied Dunbar Tax Handbook*.

Note:
It is important to remember that expatriates who do manage to change their legal domicile from the United Kingdom remain liable for IHT for three years following that change because of the 'deemed domicile' provisions described in Chapter 1.

It is also important to remember that many other countries also have gifts taxes which apply to lifetime transfers and estate duty, IHT, or acquisitions tax on death. There may be limited relief for double taxation as there are relatively few double taxation agreements covering estate and gifts taxes and unilateral relief, if available, may be difficult to apply, particularly where there is an acquisitions tax in the country of residence which taxes the donee, and a chargeable transfer for UK IHT on the donor or deceased. Gifts and estate taxes often apply lower rates to close relatives (or the United Kingdom exempts most transfers to spouses) but these would not apply to people living together who are not legally married.

7.1   Chargeable transfers

IHT may be payable whenever there is a chargeable transfer of assets. In general terms, a chargeable transfer is one which reduces the value of the transferor's total assets or his estate: in general parlance, a gift or bequest. Tax is chargeable on the cumulative total of chargeable transfers made during the donor's lifetime and on the value of his estate at death. The period of accumulation is restricted to seven years, ie in year 8, the cumulative total of transfers made will be those of years 2 to 8, and transfers made in year 1 will drop out of account. Following death, the IHT due will be calculated on the value of the estate at death plus chargeable transfers made in the preceding seven years.

For transfers on or after 6 April 1995 the first £154,000 is charged at a nil rate and the excess is charged on death at 40 per cent and on lifetime transfers at a reducing percentage of the 40 per cent rate, depending upon the number of years between the transfer and the death of the donor. Up to three years the full rate is payable, four years is reduced to 80 per cent, five years 60 per cent, six years 40 per cent, seven years 20 per cent and thereafter no IHT is due.

Following death, chargeable transfers made within the previous seven years are reassessed and the additional tax then becomes payable, but there is no revaluation of the asset transferred at the date of death.

It is fundamental to an understanding of IHT to appreciate that the amount of tax payable is calculated by reference to the total loss to the donor, ie, the amount by which his estate has been reduced by the transfer. It is not the value of the gift in isolation. In practice, this is of greatest importance in connection with unquoted shares. If a father has 55 per cent of the shares in a family company and transfers 10 per cent to a discretionary trust, those shares might be worth, say, £100 per share as a small minority interest. However, the father's shareholding has fallen from a 55 per cent controlling interest (shares worth £500 each) to a 45 per cent large minority holding (shares worth, say, £300 each). If there were 10,000 shares in issue, the chargeable transfer (loss to the father's estate) would be not £10,000 (1,000 × £100) but £1,400,000 (from 5,500 × £500 to 4,500 × £300).

7.2 Exemptions and reliefs

The IHT legislation contains many provisions exempting certain transfers of value from tax. The most important of these are described below.

7.3 Potentially exempt transfers

A lifetime transfer by an individual to another individual is a potentially exempt transfer (PET). This means that if the transferor survives for seven years it is exempt, but if he dies within seven years it is chargeable. This also applies to transfers to an interest in possession trust, an accumulation and maintenance trust or a trust for a disabled person.

7.4 Transfers between spouses

Where both spouses are domiciled in the United Kingdom any transfer of assets between them is exempt. Where the recipient spouse is not domiciled in the United Kingdom at the time of the transfer, the total exemption is restricted to £55,000 (by IHTA 1984, s 18(2))—(see also later). Additional transfers would fall first into the usual zero rate band. The practical effect of this is that for transfers on or after 6 April 1995, no tax is charged on the first £209,000 of the estate. The spouse exemption applies to both lifetime transfers and transfers at death. There is no similar restriction in other cases where the transferee is non-UK domiciled and the transferor is domiciled in the United Kingdom. This may give rise to opportunities for channelling gifts through a non-UK domiciled individual who subsequently settles a discretionary trust, subject to anti-avoidance provisions in IHTA 1984, s 268 and the extended definition of settlor in IHTA 1984, s 44.

7.5 Annual allowances

A person may make as many small gifts to as many people as he wishes in a year without incurring any IHT. In order to qualify for this exemption, the maximum gift to any individual in the year is £250 (IHTA 1984, s 20(1)). If the gift is greater than £250 it will be taxable unless it can be covered by one of the other exemptions described below. In addition to the small gifts allowance, there is an annual allowance of £3,000 (IHTA 1984, s 19). This allowance, to the extent that it is unused in the year, may be carried forward for one year only. However, where an annual allowance or part of that allowance is carried forward it can only be used once the annual allowance for the second year has, itself, been exhausted.

Example: Inheritance tax—annual allowance

A does not expect to live long and gives £2,000 to her daughter in Year 1; she makes no other transfers in that year and therefore has an annual allowance totalling £4,000 in Year 2 (£1,000 balance of year 1 and £3,000 year 2). If, however, she only gives away £2,000 in that year, her surplus to carry forward to Year 3 is not £2,000, but £1,000 again. She has lost the amount carried forward from Year 1 because she did not fully utilise her Year 2 allowance. Had she given £3,000 in Year 2 she would have nothing to carry foward.

These annual allowances are available separately to husband and wife and the value of the gift is calculated without tax, ie it is not grossed up. These allowances are available only against lifetime transfers.

7.6   Normal expenditure out of income

A gift made during a person's lifetime will be exempt if it is shown:

(1)   to be part of that person's habitual expenditure;
(2)   that, taking one year with another, it is made out of income; and
(3)   that allowing for all such transfers out of income, the transferor is left with sufficient income to maintain his usual standard of living.

On the occasion of the first gift of income it will be considered as exempt if there is clear evidence of further gifts to be made, such as insurance policy premiums on a policy written in trust (IHTA 1984, s 21).

7.7   Gifts in consideration of marriage

Wedding gifts into trust or within seven years of death are exempt so far as they fall within the following limits:

(1)   up to £5,000 from a parent of either party to the marriage;

(2)   up to £2,500 from one party to the marriage to the other or from grandparents or remoter ancestors of either party;

(3)   up to £1,000 in any other case.

As with the two previous exemptions, this one is also only available for gifts made during the donor's lifetime (IHTA 1984, s 22).

7.8   Dispositions for maintenance of family

This exemption applies to dispositions from one spouse to another and includes any made on the dissolution of a marriage (IHTA 1984, s 11). It also covers those made for the children of either spouse (including any illegitimate child of the transferor) until the end of the tax year in which the child attains the age of 18 or, if later, until the child finishes full-time education or training. Where any person makes a disposition to a child who has been in that person's care for a substantial period, the exemption also applies, even though the person is not the child's parent. Finally, the exemption applies for the maintenance of a dependent relative and, by concession, to a disposition from a child to his or her unmarried mother who is financially dependent on the child.

7.9   Other exempt transfers

The previous exemptions have primarily concerned transfers to individuals which are in any case exempt if made more than seven years before death. There are several other exempt transfers of a more impersonal nature. These include transfers to charities, gifts for national purposes, to political parties and for the public benefit (IHTA 1984, ss 23–26).

Finally, no IHT is payable on the estate of anyone who dies from a wound, accident, or disease contracted while on active service (IHTA 1984, s 154). By concession, this exemption is extended to the estates of members of the Royal Ulster Constabulary where death is as a result of terrorist activities in Northern Ireland.

7.10   Business property relief

Relief is given for the transfer of certain property which is 'relevant business property' by way of a reduction in the valuation of the property under IHTA 1984, ss 103–114. Before relief can be given, there are certain conditions to be met. As well as being relevant business property, the transfer must be of property from a qualifying business (basically a business carried on for gain other than a business which is primarily concerned with dealing in land or securities or holding investments), and the property must have been owned for a period of at least two years prior to the transfer.

Relevant business property falls into four classes:

(1)   unincorporated business—property comprising a business or interest in a business attracts relief of 100 per cent;

(2)   shares or securities—if the company was an unquoted company and they gave the transferor control of more than 25 per cent of the voting rights, they attract relief at 100 per cent immediately before the transfer;

(3)   land, buildings, machinery or plant used in a partnership or a controlled company or, by the transferor, which was settled property in which he was entitled to an interest in possession—relief is at 50 per cent;

(4)   unquoted minority shareholdings and quoted shares which gave the transferor control of a company—these attract relief at 50 per cent.

Note:
Shares dealt with on the Alternative Investment Market are treated as unquoted securities for tax purposes.

7.11   Agricultural property relief

Agricultural property in the United Kingdom, the Channel Islands or the Isle of Man attracts relief at 100 per cent under IHTA 1984, ss 115–124 where it has been occupied for the two years before the transfer by the transferor for the purposes of agriculture, or where it was owned for the seven years before the transfer but farmed by persons other than the transferor. A further condition to be satisfied for the 100 per cent relief is that the transferor must enjoy vacant possession or be entitled to it within 24 months or where a tenancy was granted by the transferor after 31 August 1995. In other cases the relief is restricted to 50 per cent.

7.12 Potentially exempt lifetime transfers of agricultural and business property

In circumstances where such transfers become taxable due to the death within seven years of the transferor, the conditions necessary for obtaining the relief must still be met at the date of death. Effectively, therefore, the recipient of such transfers must continue to own the property and continue to use it in the manner which qualifies it for relief for seven years after the transfer, or risk forfeiting the relief.

7.13 Persons not domiciled in the United Kingdom

Overseas assets owned by persons not domiciled in the United Kingdom are generally excluded property for the purposes of IHT (IHTA 1984, s 6(1)). That is, any transfer of such property will not give rise to a liability. However, where such persons own assets in the United Kingdom, then any transfer of such assets may give rise to a charge to tax. There are, as usual, several exemptions and reliefs available to offset this general rule, in addition to the general potential exemption for transfers to indivdiuals.

Under a double taxation agreement, property may be deemed to be located abroad, thus making it excluded property (see Chapter 11). The property of members of visiting forces or of staff of allied headquarters is excluded property. Where a person holds certain UK government securities, then these will be excluded property if the holder is not domiciled and not ordinarily resident in the United Kingdom (IHTA 1984, s 6(2)). For this latter exclusion, it is legal domicile as opposed to the artificial deemed domicile which applies (IHTA 1984, s 267(2)).

Where overseas property is settled property, it will only be excluded property if at the time the settlement was made the settlor was not domiciled in the United Kingdom (IHTA 1984, s 48(3)(*b*)). If that is not the case then the settled property will not be excluded, regardless of any subsequent change of domicile of the settlor and regardless of the domicile of any beneficiaries. A reversionary interest in overseas settled property does not come under these rules but is determined according to the general rule which is that if the person beneficially entitled to the reversionary interest is domiciled in the United Kingdom, there is a liability, and if he is not, then it is excluded property (IHTA 1984, s 48(1)).

7.14   Location of assets

Where an asset is located has to be determined according to the laws of England and Wales, Scotland or Northern Ireland except where these are superseded by special provisions in a double taxation agreement. The commoner types of assets are normally considered to be situated as follows:

(1)   cash—where physically located;
(2)   bank accounts—the location of the bank or branch (note: foreign currency accounts owned by a non-UK domiciled person but held in the United Kingdom are exempt);
(3)   registered securities—the location of the share register;
(4)   bearer securities—the location of the title documents;
(5)   land and buildings—their actual location;
(6)   business assets—the place where the business is conducted;
(7)   debts—the residence of the debtor (or for specialty debts, such as a life assurance policy issued under seal, the place where the document evidencing the debt is located and, for judgment debts, the country where the judgment is recorded).

7.15   The non-UK domiciled spouse

Before 1 January 1974, a wife assumed her husband's domicile on marriage. When the marriage ended, either by death or divorce, the wife retained her husband's domicile unless and until she acquired a new domicile of choice. The current position of women married before 1 January 1974 is that they retain their husbands' domicile (originally a domicile of dependence) as their deemed domicile of choice until, by their own positive actions, they acquire a new domicile of choice. For marriages contracted after 1 January 1974, a wife has had complete independence of domicile and will retain her domicile of origin or any pre-marriage domicile of dependence until she chooses to acquire a new domicile of choice which may or may not be the same as her husband's domicile.

For IHT purposes, a couple of mixed domicile (where one of them is domiciled in the United Kingdom and the other is not) have to take extra care in their tax planning. Their situation does, however, offer some opportunities not available to couples where both are UK domiciled.

Dealing first of all with the restrictions, it has already been mentioned that a transfer from a spouse domiciled in the United Kingdom to one who is not so domiciled, is exempt only up to a total transfer of £55,000. The reason behind this is obviously to prevent the avoidance of tax which would arise by simply using the non-domiciled spouse as a conduit for transfers of non-UK sited assets to other parties such as children. None the less, substantial value can still be transferred because the UK domiciled spouse will have, in addition to the £55,000 exemption, an additional amount of £154,000 which on transfer will be within the nil rate band. Further transfers may be made using the annual allowance and any subsequent increases in the exempt allowance or the width of the nil rate band. After seven years, the £154,000 transferred initially within the nil rate band will fall out of account.

Where the spouse who is not domiciled in the United Kingdom makes any gifts or transfers, there will be no IHT liability so long as the property concerned is excluded property—generally property located outside the United Kingdom. One possible pitfall for the non-UK domiciled spouse arises following the family's assumption or resumption of residence in the United Kingdom. The Inland Revenue may seek to claim that the originally non-domiciled spouse has acquired a new domicile of choice in the United Kingdom. However, they cannot have it both ways. There is a great reluctance in the absence of very strong evidence to accept that a person has shed his or her UK domicile—it should follow, therefore, that there should be equal reluctance to accept that a person has shed a non-UK domicile of origin and acquired UK domicile by choice. But as with most aspects of British taxation, the onus is on the individual to prove the Revenue wrong. The pointers to a change of domicile given earlier should be considered in this light.

In any event, even the person accepted as not being domiciled in the United Kingdom in the legal sense, will be deemed to be so domiciled for IHT purposes after a period of 17 years' residence here. Strictly, the requirement is to have been resident in the United Kingdom in not less than 17 out of the 20 years of assessment ending with that in which the chargeable transfer occurs.

7.16 Settled property

If the IHT rules are generally seen as very complex, this is nowhere more true than when considering the question of settled property. There are several types of trusts or settlements which have a useful application for IHT mitigation and these are discussed in some detail below, in Chapter 8.

For details of the settled property provisions, reference must be made to more specialist textbooks but the following points illuminate, however briefly, some important aspects.

Generally, settlements are themselves subject to IHT at lifetime rates if, when the settlement was made, the settlor was domiciled in the United Kingdom. The settlement of any property after 26 March 1974 is a chargeable transfer by the settlor (assuming he is domiciled in the United Kingdom) unless the trust is for transfers into an interest in possession trust, an accumulation or maintenance trust or a trust for a disabled person: these are potentially exempt transfers. A person having an interest in possession in any property, is deemed to possess that property for IHT purposes so that when that interest ends, there is deemed to be a potentially exempt transfer of the value of the property, under IHTA 1984, ss 49–53. There is no chargeable or potentially exempt transfer if a person becomes absolutely entitled to the property in which he previously had an interest in possession. The special rules relating to discretionary trusts and accumulation and maintenance trusts are discussed later.

A reversionary interest in a settlement of UK property is excluded property under IHTA 1984, s 48(1) unless it had been acquired for value, is one in which the settlor or his spouse has a beneficial interest or is a reversionary interest under a lease for life treated as a settlement.

7.17   Inheritance tax planning

For every tax, there soon springs up a tax-avoidance scheme, or many of them. This continuing game between legislators and tax consultants is as obvious in the area of IHT as anywhere else although the Revenue's success in ignoring purely fiscal moves in a composite transaction in *Furniss v Dawson* [1984] STC 153 should be noted.

As stated at the beginning of this chapter, the recast IHT is in some aspects similar to estate duty (the predecessor to CTT), which was considerably easier to avoid than the tax which replaced it. On the other hand, the ease of avoiding IHT—by simply making gifts to individuals more than seven years before death—depends on the donor's ability to make outright gifts and lose the benefit of the associated income, because it is no longer possible, as with CTT, to make gifts with reservation of interest.

Basic IHT planning is very straightforward, such as simply making use of the various exemptions and reliefs, particularly the exemption for lifetime gifts to individuals. However, rather than merely disposing of cash, some thought might be given to transferring assets which might be expected to grow in value but which have a relatively low value at the time of transfer. Another frequent suggestion is the equalisation of estate between husband and wife with the first to die leaving a substantial part of his or her estate other than to the spouse. In this way maximum use can be made of each spouse's entitlement to allowances and the nil rate band.

Example: Inheritance tax—estate planning

A husband has an estate worth £268,000 and the wife £40,000; in their wills each leaves his or her estate to the other. On the second death, everything goes to the children. Under these provisions there would be no IHT payable on the first death and, assuming no previous chargeable transfers, an IHT charge of £61,600 (£308,000–£154,000 × 40%) on the second death. If, however the husband transferred £114,000 to his wife during his lifetime and they each decided to leave £154,000 to their children with the balance to the spouse, there would still be no IHT to pay on the first death and on the second death, when the estate is £154,000, the IHT payable would be nil, a saving of £61,600.

One reason for equalising the estates rather than simply making enough available for the wife to use the nil rate band is to allow maximum flexibility on the first death following which a written variation of the will (see below) could be used in the light of prevailing circumstances.

The transferor should not so reduce his estate that the surviving spouse cannot sustain a required standard of living. In addition, payment of IHT should be postponed from the date of the first death to the second death by leaving the estate on the excess over the nil rate band to the surviving spouse.

7.18   Insurance policies

To use these policies, the transferor or the intending transferor effects a policy on his life written in trust for his beneficiaries. The sum assured under such a policy should be the amount of the anticipated IHT which will be due on the estate passing at death. Where there is a relatively short period of liability to the tax as, for example, when a person emigrates permanently but remains deemed domiciled in the United Kingdom for three years, a three-year term policy would be the cheapest and simplest form of IHT protection. Similarly, if a major transfer of assets is made to take advantage of the lower lifetime rates of tax, it may be worth insuring for the difference between the tax paid, if any, and the tax which would become payable if death occurred within seven years of that transfer. In most circumstances however, a term policy is unlikely to be the wisest course because as the potential transferor gets older renewing the policy can become very expensive. A better solution is to take out a whole of life policy and write it in trust at a reasonably early stage. Premiums paid by the life assured/settlor in respect of the policy in trust are, of course, transfers of value into the trust and hence can amount to either immediately chargeable transfers or potentially exempt transfers depending on whether the trust is a discretionary trust. However, the exemption for gifts out of income and where necessary, the £3,000 annual exemption can normally be applied to those transfers of premium and, where this is so, the payments will be totally exempt. These exemptions can also be applied to the premiums paid on an investment-oriented policy written in trust and this, too, can be a useful way of transferring a growing asset to others.

7.19   The family home

One asset which can sometimes prove difficult to plan for effectively is the family home, and for many people this is their main asset. Normally a couple will own their house as joint tenants. On the death of one of them the deceased's share is automatically transferred to the survivor. Assuming the couple are married, and are both either UK or non-UK domiciled, there will be no IHT payable on this occasion but on the second death, the whole value of the house will be counted in calculating the tax. The effect of this is illustrated in the following example.

Example: Inheritance tax—the family home

A couple have joint net assets of £390,000, of which £300,000 represents the value of their house, the remaining £90,000 being invested to provide income. The house is owned under a joint tenancy and each holds about £45,000 of investments. Under their wills each leaves his or her estate to the other. The couple have two children who will inherit everything on the second death. Because the survivor after the first death will still require a similar income, it is not practicable to leave anything to the children on that occasion so the eventual IHT bill will be £94,400.

The bill can, however, be reduced by changing the way the house is owned. If the couple own the house as tenants in common, rather than as joint tenants, their individual shares do not automatically go to the other on death but may be dealt with in the same way as any other asset. Thus, in the previous example, although the income-producing assets could not be left to the children, a share of the house could be.

If, on the death of the first spouse his or her half-share in the house was left to the children, this would be a chargeable transfer of £150,000 with no IHT payable. The estate on the second death would be £240,000 on which the IHT would be £34,400, a saving of £60,000.

But tenancies in common are not without their drawbacks. There must be a high degree of trust among all the parties so that the widow or widower can continue to live in the property only half of which she or he will own. There can also be a problem if the co-owner is declared bankrupt. It is very important for anyone contemplating such an arrangement to discuss it fully with his lawyer who will also give an indication of the cost of changing an existing joint tenancy to a tenancy in common, which usually requires only a simple notice of severance served on the co-owner.

8 Wills, settlements and trusts

8.1 Wills and assets in more than one jurisdiction

Anyone whose assets are other than negligible should make a properly drawn-up and witnessed will, unless he has no concern about the disposition of those assets after his death. Anyone who dies without leaving a valid will dies intestate, and his property will be disposed of according to the laws of intestacy. This procedure will seldom coincide with the deceased's wishes. This is especially true if the deceased held assets in more than one jurisdiction. Not only that, but intestacy may also give rise to prolonged legal arguments and transactions, which in some countries have been known to go on for half a century or more.

This brings out an important point for the expatriate, particularly. If he has UK domicile, he should not only have a valid UK will which allocates all his worldwide property according to his wishes, but he should also have a will covering any assets held outside the United Kingdom which is valid in the jurisdiction where those assets are held.

Under private international law, where there is a will, the passing of assets from the deceased's estate to his heirs is governed by the law of the deceased's domicile in the case of movable property (such as bank deposits or securities) and by the local law in the case of immovable property. It will often be the case, therefore, that any decision of, say, an English court relating to immovable property overseas will not be effective in the overseas jurisdiction until it has been approved by a court there. The overseas court may also insist on a local grant of probate or Letters of Administration, which can be a relatively expensive procedure.

A further point to bear in mind about assets held overseas is that not all countries allow the testator complete freedom to dispose as he pleases. In many countries the children of the deceased are legally entitled to inherit a minimum portion of the estate, or of part of the estate. In other countries, the incidence of estate duties or IHT varies according to the kinship or other relationship of the heirs to the deceased. Even in the United Kingdom, with very liberal laws in this respect, a will may be challenged and the dispositions altered by the court if, for instance, no provision has been made for a person who was financially dependent on the deceased. A will may be challenged in the United Kingdom on several other grounds also, but this matter lies beyond the scope of the present Handbook.

It will be clear even from the above simple generalisations that the administration of an overseas estate can be an extremely complex business. But one thing is certain: the trouble and expense (in the way of legal fees payable both in the United Kingdom and elsewhere) incurred in sorting matters out properly in advance amount to a mere fraction of the trouble and expense that will be incurred by the executors or administrators if proper arrangements have not been made. Indeed, an individual with assets in more than one country owes it morally to his executors as well as his heirs to make proper arrangements, even if this means writing several wills and consulting with several lawyers in several jurisdictions.

Apart from the simple efficiency in dealing with a local estate under local law that only a locally acceptable document makes possible, there are two further important practical points. First, proper testamentary arrangements regularly reviewed are essential to IHT or estate duty planning. They are the only way to protect the heirs from the full ravages of taxation. Secondly, from the UK viewpoint, a grant of probate or Letters of Administration will not be given until any IHT has been paid. Since assets will not normally be released until the grant is made, the only way to pay the tax bill is to borrow the money. If overseas assets can be speedily released through a local probate, these can be used to pay the UK tax and thereby hasten the release of assets held in the United Kingdom.

8.2   Will trusts

A UK will may grant an absolute interest to a beneficiary or may create a will trust under which the assets are left to trustees for the benefit of various beneficiaries. The types of possible trust are discussed below. The commonest will trust is to leave the majority of the estate to the surviving spouse for her life with the remainder to the children or grandchildren. The advantage of this arrangement is that the life interest to the surviving spouse is treated for IHT purposes as her absolute interest and therefore the IHT exemption on leaving assets to a surviving spouse still applies. However, the ultimate destination of the assets is assured so that should, for example, the wife remarry and have further children by the second marriage, the deceased former husband's estate passes through to his own children and cannot be diverted to the children of the second marriage. It is possible to leave the reversionary interest to the grandchildren rather than to the children and so avoid an IHT charge on the death of the children. Whether this is desirable of course depends on the children's assets and the respective ages of the parties.

8.3   Incidence of inheritance tax

It is also important to bear in mind when drafting the will the incidence of IHT. Section 211 of IHTA 1984 following *Re Dougal* [1981] STC 514 makes it clear that IHT on death in respect of personal property and of real property in the United Kingdom is a general testamentary expense payable out of residue in the absence of contrary provisions in the will. If, therefore, the intention is that any legacy should bear its own share of IHT, it is important that the will makes this clear. There are complicated provisions in IHTA 1984, ss 38–42 to deal with the case where part of the residue is left on an exempt legacy such as to the surviving spouse, and part on a chargeable legacy such as to the children.

Overseas assets subject to IHT will normally be subject to their proportionate share of the IHT applicable thereto. For the avoidance of doubt, it is preferable to draft the will so that it is made perfectly clear which, if any, legacies are to bear their share of IHT.

As already noted, the provisions of a will can largely determine the amount of IHT which will fall due. A will can, in fact, be looked upon as an IHT planning tool. However, if family circumstances at the date of death are significantly different from what was envisaged when the will was prepared, or if the will is highly inefficient in a tax-planning sense, the will provisions may be altered by a written variation. If this is done within two years of death, no IHT will be charged on the variations or rearrangements if the parties concerned so elect, and the tax payable will be computed on the basis that the varied provisions were effective at death. Stamp duty is no longer payable on the value transferred under a written variation (FA 1985, s 85).

8.4   Written variations

The problem with the written variation is that it requires any beneficiary whose share is being reduced to be legally competent (ie adult and of

sound mind), as any attempts so to modify the interest of a child beneficiary would require the consent of the court. In practice, it may be preferable to leave that part of the estate which, for example, may or may not
be required by the surviving spouse to trustees of a discretionary settlement with the intention that the trustees would, within two years of the
date of death, redistribute the assets among the various beneficiaries in
accordance with their needs.

Written variations are treated for IHT purposes as a disposition on death
under IHTA 1984, ss 17 and 142 and for CGT purposes by TCGA 1992,
s 62(6). However, for income tax purposes, the income in the period from
the date of death to the date of the variation (or distribution from any discretionary trust) remains that of the original beneficiaries. It is also likely
that a variation in favour of children would be argued by the Revenue to
be an indirect settlement by the original beneficiary so that, for income
tax purposes, any income distributed to the child during his minority
would be treated as the income of the parent under TA 1988, s 660B. A
variation or two-year discretionary trust should therefore be regarded as
a useful opportunity to fine tune the dispositions given by will rather than
a substitute for a carefully planned will reviewed at frequent intervals.

Example: Inheritance tax—written variation

Mr Bird died in July 1995. His net estate was valued at £400,000 including a house worth
£100,000. Apart from £25,000 to his son, the estate was left to Mr Bird's widow. When Mr
Bird's will was drawn up many years previously the value of his estate was only about
£150,000 with the house worth £50,000. He felt at the time that his widow would require
£75,000 to provide her income and that was his rationale for the structuring of his will.

As it happens, in 1995, there will be no IHT to pay following Mr Bird's death (he has made
no previous transfers) but there is a potential tax charge on Mrs Bird's death, assuming she
leaves her estate to the son (she has personal assets worth £50,000) of £108,400. She and
her son therefore effect a written variation whereby the son receives £144,000 instead of
£25,000 and his children receive £10,000 in total. There is still no IHT payable on the estate.
The potential charge on the death of Mrs Bird is reduced from £108,400 (on £425,000) to
£56,800 (on £296,000). The written variation has therefore saved IHT of £51,600.

8.5   Trusts

A trust or settlement is a legal relationship which is established when a
person transfers assets into the care of others for the benefit of a third
party. The three parties concerned in this relationship, the settlor, trustees,
and beneficiaries respectively, may all incur tax liabilities stemming from

the trust in different ways. A detailed explanation of trust law is beyond the scope of this book and readers are referred to the *Allied Dunbar Tax Handbook* for further information. Trusts constitute an extremely complex area of the law and good professional advice is essential.

This chapter can only provide an outline of the major tax-planning aspects of trusts as they affect, or might affect, the expatriate. It must be stressed that to establish a trust is not a job for a layman. Perhaps more than in any other field of tax planning, trust work requires the assistance of expert professional advice.

8.5.1 The residence of trusts

For most income tax purposes, a trust with a UK resident, ordinarily resident or domiciled settlor at the time of creation is resident outside the United Kingdom only if all the trustees are themselves so resident and the administration and management of the trust are carried out overseas, TA 1989, s 110 (*Kelly v Rogers* (1935) 19 TC 692, *Reid's Trustees v IRC* (1929) 14 TC 512). If there is a UK resident trustee of a trust settled by a non-UK resident and domiciled settlor which also has a foreign trustee, the UK resident trustee is deemed to be non-resident for income tax purposes (FA 1989, s 110(1)(*b*)). Similar provisions apply to personal representatives under FA 1989, s 111. For CGT purposes, TCGA 1992, s 69(1) only requires a majority of trustees to be non-UK resident. A trust which is not resident in the United Kingdom may enjoy substantial tax advantages over the domestic settlement but there are numerous provisions in the UK legislation which seek to prevent tax avoidance by the use of such vehicles by or for the benefit of persons ordinarily resident in the United Kingdom. The three main UK taxes, income tax, CGT and IHT can each have an impact on trusts and on each of the parties involved. Tax liabilities are determined not only by the residence of the trust and the individuals concerned but also by the type of trust which is involved. The following section on the taxation of trusts outlines the tax consequences which attach to each of the main types of trust with which the expatriate may be concerned.

8.5.2 Resident trusts

It may be useful to make the first distinction between types of trusts as between those where the settlor is alive and those where he is deceased. The main thrust of the anti-avoidance legislation is concerned with preventing a settlor using a trust mechanism to provide himself with a tax-sheltered 'piggy bank' for his own or his wife's benefit. To that end there are numerous provisions which seek to tax trust income as that of the settlor and these are described below. Where the settlor has died, whether the trust was set up during his lifetime or under his will, the taxation rules are somewhat less complex.

In general terms, a UK trust is liable for basic rate income tax on all its income, wherever arising. Where trust income has already suffered tax at source or is accompanied by a tax credit, this will be accounted for in the trust assessment. Where the trust has overseas income which has been taxed abroad then relief for double taxation may be available either to the trustees or the beneficiaries. The income of discretionary trusts and accumulation trusts, after deducting expenses, is also liable at the 'rate applicable to trusts' (the excess of 35 per cent over the basic rate, or lower rate for dividends, as appropriate)—TA 1988, s 686. The income tax assessment of trusts is generally made in the name of the trustees and the tax due is payable out of the trust funds. Where trust income is distributed to beneficiaries it is treated as received net of tax at 35 per cent under TA 1988, s 687 (or 25 per cent in the case of a beneficiary absolutely entitled to the income, that is where the trust is not a discretionary trust).

A non-resident trust is liable to UK tax on its UK income at the basic rate and, on accumulations, at the 'rate applicable to trusts' as well. See *IRC v Regent Trust Co Ltd* [1980] STC 140.

In the case of dividends from UK companies, from 1993/94, the liability is at the lower rate (TA 1988, s 207A), usually equivalent to the tax with-held under the advance corporation tax rules which is allowed as a credit. The 'rate applicable to trusts' is charged on the dividend plus related tax credit. An overseas trust is taxed only on the dividend at 35 per cent with no available credit (subject to double tax relief) unless there are no current or potential UK beneficiaries, in which case there is no additional tax charged from 1995/96. There is no tax credit on a foreign income div-idend, but a UK resident recipient is only charged at the 'rate applicable to trusts' on the dividend grossed up at the lower rate, in the same way as for stock dividends.

Trusts are also liable for CGT in much the same way as individuals but the annual exemption is restricted to 50 per cent of that available to indi-viduals. For 1995/96, the trust exemption is therefore £3,000. For trusts formed after 6 June 1978, this exemption is split among all trusts with the same settlor, ie, if he made four trusts, each would be entitled to exemp-tion on the first £750. For trusts formed before that date, the full £3,000 is allowed. Certain trusts for the mentally disabled and those in receipt of attendance allowances are entitled to the same exemption as an individ-ual; TCGA 1992, Sched 1.

Some of the aspects of IHT and trusts were mentioned in the preceding chapter. *What is perhaps of the greatest importance is to note that, for IHT purposes, the residence of the trust is largely immaterial.* A trust may incur a liability to IHT on its worldwide assets if, at the time it was set up, the settlor was domiciled in the United Kingdom (IHTA 1984, s 48(3)(*a*)). If the settlor was domiciled elsewhere, the IHT liability will be restricted to transfers of trust assets located in the United Kingdom.

8.5.3 Trusts created *inter vivos*

Where a settlement is made during the lifetime of the settlor, the taxation rules are particularly rigorous to prevent the avoidance of tax. An outline of these anti-avoidance provisions is given below.

8.5.4 Income tax

The basic rule a settlor must obey in order to avoid having the trust income assessed on him, is fully to divest himself of the assets he is transferring into the trust. If he retains an interest in either the income or the assets of the trust then any income not distributed to beneficiaries will be treated as the settlor's income (TA 1988, s 660A–J, 677 and 678). A retained interest is widely defined but generally means that the settlor or his or her spouse is able to obtain some benefit from the income or assets of the trust at any time. Even where the income is distributed to others any excess of higher rate tax over the basic or lower rate on the distribution will be charged to the settlor.

Included in retaining an interest is a power to revoke the trust. If the trust can be revoked in whole or in part, and on revocation the trust property reverts to the settlor or his spouse, then the income of the trust (or a part thereof corresponding to the partial revocation) will be treated as the income of the settlor (TA 1988, s 660A). The power of revocation may be immediate or postponed, but in the latter case, if the power cannot be used for at least six years, the income will not be treated as that of the settlor until the power becomes exercisable. Power to revoke includes a power to advance the whole of the capital, or to diminish the assets of the trust or the income receivable by beneficiaries other than the settlor or his spouse. Whether it is the settlor or another person who has the power to revoke is immaterial.

Where there is a settlement of income such as a covenant, it is essential that the payments should be capable of being made for a period of at least six years (TA 1988, s 660). The six-year rule applies to settlements generally but is normally of particular relevance to income settlements. Where a covenant fails on this rule, it will be treated as income of the settlor and not the payee. Nevertheless, the payment will still be deemed to have been made to the covenantee and then returned to the settlor: the settlor is then treated as receiving investment income, even if the payment was made out of earned income or capital. As a result, the settlor may find that he has more tax to pay because of a failed covenant than he would had he not instituted it in the first place (*Ang v Parish* [1980] STC 341). However, since 15 March 1988 there have been no tax advantages in covenanting money to an individual.

Where a capital sum (which includes a loan or loan repayment) is paid by trustees to the settlor, his spouse, or a third party directly or indirectly at the settlor's direction, that sum is treated as the income of the settlor and is assessed on him under TA 1988, s 677. The assessment, however, is restricted to the amount of undistributed income in the trust but includes income previously accumulated. The tax charge is based on the amount of undistributed income grossed up at the basic rate plus the additional rate and credit is given for tax already charged on the trust. Where the undistributed income is less than the capital sum, there is provision to carry forward the excess of the capital sum to subsequent years. The settlor will then be charged to the extent of undistributed income in those years until the capital sum is fully extinguished. For capital payments made after 5 April 1981, the period for carry forward is restricted to 11 years (capital payments made before that date are to be treated as made on that date so as to fall within the new rules, so far as they have not been charged).

Under a discretionary trust, that is, one where the trustees may apply the trust property and/or income at their discretion, the settlor and his spouse must be specifically excluded from benefit, otherwise the income will be charged on the settlor whether or not he receives it. This does not apply where the benefit may accrue to the widow or widower of the settlor.

Settlements for the benefit of the settlor's infant children do not generally provide an income tax advantage, in view of the effects of TA 1988, s 660B. The exception to this rule is an accumulation settlement. Any income belonging to a child which is derived from a parental source is deemed to be the income of the parent for tax purposes. This applies not only to settlements made by parents but to any transfer of assets from the parent to his or her child. For example, if a parent gave his child shares in a company, any dividends paid to the child until he reached the age of majority would be treated as the parent's income. Similarly taxed too would be the interest in a child's bank account where the capital came from a parent, subject to the *de minimis* exemption where the child's income does not exceed £100, TA 1988, s 660B(5). Where there is a court order directing a father to make payments directly to his child, the Inland Revenue does not regard these payments as creating a settlement. Under these circumstances, the child's income would not be aggregated with that of either parent.

The use of accumulation trusts is one way to create a settlement for the benefit of minor children. Where there is an irrevocable settlement of capital and the trustees are empowered or directed to accumulate the income arising from it for the ultimate benefit of the settlor's children, the settlor will not incur any income tax liability so long as the income is actually accumulated. The trust income is taxed at 35 per cent in the name of the trustees. If any sums are paid to or for the benefit of the child before his or her eighteenth birthday or earlier marriage, such sums will be treated as the settlor's income. When the accumulated income is paid to adult beneficiaries, it is normally treated as capital in their hands. See also Chapter 7 and below, regarding the favourable treatment of these trusts for IHT purposes.

All of the above provisions apply generally but where the settlor is either not domiciled, not resident, or not ordinarily resident in the United Kingdom, certain other considerations come into play. Under TA 1988, s 660I(1), income arising under a settlement includes any income chargeable to income tax and any income which would have been so chargeable if it had been received in the United Kingdom by a person domiciled, resident and ordinarily resident in the United Kingdom. But where, in any year of assessment, the settlor is not resident, etc, in the United Kingdom then the settlement income in that year will not include any income which would not have been chargeable on the settlor, had he been entitled to it, by reason of his non-residence, etc.

The other consideration concerns settlements for the settlor's children. Where the settlor is not taxable as a UK resident then there is no aggregation. Any income from such a settlement paid to the child will not be treated as the parent's income for any year in which the parent is not resident in the United Kingdom. Under these circumstances, the child beneficiary will be able to reclaim the tax deducted on his income from the trust up to the amount of the single person's allowance. Where tax has been deducted at 35 per cent he will also be able to reclaim the tax at the 'rate applicable to trusts' on the income beyond his personal allowance.

8.5.5 Capital gains tax

Capital gains tax (CGT) may become payable on the creation of a trust, on gains made in the trust, and on certain deemed disposals of trust assets. On the first of these the liability is likely to fall on the settlor, while on the second and third, the tax will be payable by the trustees out of the trust funds.

Whether a settlement is revocable or otherwise, a transfer into a settlement is considered to be a disposal of the entire property which becomes settled (TCGA 1992, s 70). This implies a deemed disposal by the transferor and the disposal will be treated as being made at market value. If this results in a capital gain then the transferor may elect to have the gain held over, if the asset consists of business assets (TCGA 1992, s 165) agricultural property (TCGA 1992, Sched 7) or where the transfer is chargeable to IHT (TCGA 1992, s 260) or reinvestment relief applies (TCGA 1992, s 164A–N). If the deemed disposal shows a loss then this loss may normally only be utilised by the transferor against subsequent gains arising in his transactions with the trust (TCGA 1992, s 18(3)). Gains may only be held over where the trustees are resident in the United Kingdom (TCGA 1992, ss 166, 261).

During the administration of a trust, gains and losses will accrue to the trustees as they would to an individual managing his portfolio. Net gains are chargeable at 25 per cent (or 35 per cent for a discretionary or accumulation settlement) subject to the restricted exemption mentioned earlier. In the case of trusts where the settlor or settlor's spouse could receive any benefit, the gains are aggregated with the settlor's to determine the rate of tax.

When property ceases to be settled property, if, for example, it is distributed or a person becomes absolutely entitled to it, that is a deemed disposal and an occasion of charge on any gain (TCGA 1992, s 71(1)). Where property ceases to be settled on the death of a life tenant, there is also a deemed disposal but there will be no chargeable gain (TCGA 1992, s 72). If the trustees and recipient of the disposed property agree and so elect, the gain accruing on property eligible for roll-over relief may be held over provided that the recipient is resident in the United Kingdom (TCGA 1992, Sched 7). Where a life interest in settled property comes to an end, there is no charge if the property remains within the settlement; there is no deemed disposal.

8.5.6 Inheritance tax

When a person creates a settlement there will be a diminution of the settlor's estate unless he settles the property on himself for life (IHTA 1984, s 3). This transfer of value may give rise to a liability for IHT. The IHT legislation treats differently settlements where there is or are interest(s) in possession, and those where there is no interest in possession.

Where a person is beneficially entitled to the interest in possession of settled property, he is treated as being beneficially entitled to the property in which the interest subsists (IHTA 1984, s 49(1)). Thus if two people had equal interests in possession of a trust worth £200,000, each would be treated as being entitled to £100,000. On the death of one of these persons IHT would be payable on the deemed transfer of £100,000 in addition to any other estate the deceased might have. Other events will also be treated as dispositions of the property by the person beneficially entitled to the interest in possession; if, for example, the interest is terminated during the life of the person or if it is disposed of by way of assignment or surrender. Where the disposal is for a consideration in money or money's worth, IHT will be charged on the value transferred less the consideration received.

There are, however, exceptions to this rule. If a person becomes absolutely entitled to the property or to another interest in possession, that will not be treated as a chargeable transfer (IHTA 1984, s 53(2)). Other exceptions include where the property reverts to the settlor or his spouse (if she, or he, is domiciled in the United Kingdom) or to the widow or widower of the settlor within two years of the death of the settlor (IHTA 1984, s 53(3)–(5)).

A reversionary interest is a future interest under a settlement, eg that of a remainderman who will inherit on the death of the life tenant. For IHT purposes, a reversionary interest is normally excluded property unless it was acquired at any time for money or money's worth (IHTA 1984, s 48(1)).

With one major exception, trusts where there is no interest in possession are treated harshly for IHT purposes. The major problem with the normal discretionary trust is the liability for the periodic charge under IHTA 1984, s 64. This charge is levied every tenth anniversary of the settlement date (falling after 31 March 1983) and is charged at 30 per cent of the rate which would be payable on a notional transfer of the value of the property in the trust at the end of the ten-year period. The rate is the lifetime rate of the settlor and is calculated on the settlor's previous chargeable transfers in the ten years preceding the creation of the settlement: IHTA 1984, ss 65 and 67. For further details, see the *Allied Dunbar Tax Handbook*.

Inheritance tax is also payable on other occasions when property is distributed from the trust to beneficiaries (including the settlor and his or her spouse) in anticipation of the ten-year charge (IHTA 1984, s 65).

The exception to this highly taxed regime is the accumulation and maintenance settlement. Such settlements are greatly favoured and narrowly defined by IHTA 1984, s 71. They are settlements where one or more beneficiaries will, upon attaining a specified age not exceeding 25, become entitled to an interest in possession in the settled property; no interest in possession subsists in the settled property and the income from the property is to be accumulated in so far as it is not applied for the maintenance, education, or benefit of a beneficiary; and either not more than 25 years have elapsed since the trust was created or became an accumulation and maintenance trust, or all the persons who are or have been beneficiaries are or were grandchildren of a common grandparent.

The commonest use of such trusts is along the following lines: S creates a settlement under which his children obtain an interest in possession at age 21 and at age 35, say, or upon earlier marriage, they receive the capital. Income up to age 21 is to be accumulated apart from any payments made for the beneficiaries' maintenance. No lifetime IHT is payable on transfers into accumulation trusts, on any maintenance payment made, on the beneficiaries' acquisition of the interest in possession, or on the release of capital and accumulated income (IHTA 1984, s 71(3)). Neither is there a periodic charge on these settlements (IHTA 1984, s 58(1)(*b*)). But one point to bear in mind if a payment is made for the benefit of the child under age 18 and unmarried, is that it will be treated as the income of the settlor if the settlor is the parent, under TA 1988, s 660B.

Accumulation and maintenance settlements offer one of the most tax-efficient ways of transferring capital to children or grandchildren.

8.5.7   Non-resident trusts

Non-resident trusts may have a particular appeal to the expatriate who is used to having his investments sheltered from the Inland Revenue and who wishes to retain a similar advantage on his return either for himself or for the benefit of his children. There can certainly be advantages in setting up non-resident trusts but the anti-avoidance legislation is a real minefield for the unwary. It is essential to consider this legislation most carefully before opting to place substantial sums in what can be an expensive attempt to establish shelter and then finding that it does not achieve its main aim.

As mentioned earlier in this chapter, a trust settled by a UK resident, ordinarily resident or domiciled settlor, will be treated as resident in the United Kingdom unless the general administration of the trust is carried on outside the United Kingdom and the trustees, or, for CGT purposes, a majority of them, are not resident or not ordinarily resident in the United Kingdom.

The UK income of a non-resident trust is liable to UK income tax at the basic rate and, so far as it is to be accumulated or is payable under a discretion, at the 'rate applicable to trusts' (see **8.5.4** and *IRC v Regent Trust Co Ltd* [1980] STC 140). It should be noted, however, that where the income has tax deducted at source or has an accompanying tax credit, the rate applicable to trusts is charged only on the net income. For example, a non-UK resident trust receiving dividends of £800 (with tax credit of £200) would be liable for additional tax of £800 × 15 per cent=£120 leaving a net income of £680. A UK resident trust would have suffered total tax of £350 (tax credit of £200 plus £1,000 × 15 per cent) leaving a net £650.

From an income tax point of view, general principles can be applied which indicate that income paid to a beneficiary, where he is entitled to that income, will form part of his income for tax purposes. Where the trust is an accumulation trust, then accumulated income will not be taxable on the beneficiary and this may be paid to the beneficiary as capital in due course. General principles apart, there are several anti-avoidance provisions which also come into play.

The most important of these income tax provisions are contained in TA 1988, ss 739–746. Section 739 is seen as one of the most widely drawn anti-avoidance provisions. Where an individual ordinarily resident in the United Kingdom transfers assets so that someone not resident or domiciled in the United Kingdom receives any income from these assets, and that income can be used currently or at some future time by the individual who transferred the assets, then that income will be treated as income of the transferor.

What this means in the context of trusts is that if an individual, at the time ordinarily resident in the United Kingdom, has established a non-resident trust under which he may benefit, then the income of the trust will be treated as his income whether or not it is distributed. It will be similarly taxed if the settlor's spouse may benefit. Section 739 will not apply while the settlor is not ordinarily resident, but a non-resident trust established during a period of non-residence will be caught when the expatriate returns to the United Kingdom. This section relates only to income and does not, therefore, operate to tax capital gains (see later). If income from or accruing to a non-resident trust is to escape UK income tax then the settlor and his or her spouse must be totally precluded from any possible benefit, and the words 'power to enjoy' are widely construed under TA 1988, s 742(2). Alternatively, if it can be shown that the trust was established for *bona fide* commercial reasons, such as the establishment of a pension scheme, and that the avoidance of tax was no part of this reasoning, the section will not operate (TA 1988, s 741). This will be very difficult to prove especially since exchange controls (once a useful commercial reason) no longer operate in the United Kingdom.

It should be noted that non-UK life assurance policies held in a non-resident trust are subject to UK tax on maturity under TA 1988, s 553(5).

On a more positive note, non-resident trusts can be established for the benefit of, for example, the settlor's children without any UK tax liability on the income as it arises overseas (see earlier for income arising in the United Kingdom). This is all well and good so long as the trust funds are accumulated. Unless the settlor and his spouse are excluded from benefit, TA 1988, s 660B can deem the trust income to be that of the settlor. Where there is a distribution of income that income becomes chargeable on the beneficiary under TA 1988, s 740 if he or she is ordinarily resident in the United Kingdom. Where a benefit is received under the trust, then that benefit will be taxed to the extent that the trust has relevant income. Where the benefit exceeds the relevant income then the excess will be taxed in later years as the trust accrues further relevant income. Relevant income is income of the trust which can be used to provide a benefit but is restricted to income which arose on or after 10 March 1981. If, for example, a non-resident trust established in 1975 accrued income at the rate of £2,000 a year, then in May 1995, the total income is £40,000, of which, say £28,000 is relevant income. During that year, £36,000 is paid to a beneficiary. The beneficiary's income tax liability in 1995/96 would be on £28,000 and, if income continues to accrue to the trust at the same rate, a further liability on £2,000 a year for the next four years. If, however, the trust also had realised capital gains accrued since 10 March 1981, then to the extent that there is insufficient relevant income in the year of distribution, the surplus or a part of it will be allocated to the accrued capital gains and taxed accordingly.

In general terms, a non-resident trust established prior to 19 March 1991 by a UK domiciliary is not liable to UK CGT (except where it is carrying on a trade in the United Kingdom). However, where the settlor was domiciled and either resident or ordinarily resident in the United Kingdom when the trust was established, or in a relevant subsequent year when trust gains, or gains of companies owned by such trusts, TCGA 1992, s 97, are distributed to a UK domiciled beneficiary (FA 1981, s 80), those gains will be treated as accruing to the beneficiary and taxable on him. Gains of the trust are computed each year and the cumulative total of gains is treated as trust gains for the year. When a capital payment is made to beneficiaries, the trust gains will be attributed to them in proportion to the capital payment received by them up to the amount of that payment. Unattributed gains, ie where total gains are in excess of the capital payment, will be carried forward as trust gains for subsequent years. Gains are not apportioned to non-UK domiciled or non-UK resident beneficiaries. Tax on gains apportioned to a UK resident and domiciled beneficiary after 6 April 1992 may be increased by 10 per cent per annum as if it were interest for a maximum of six years (TCGA 1992, ss 91–97).

Trusts which emigrate from the United Kingdom on or after 19 March 1991 as a result of the appointment of non-resident trustees are deemed to have sold and reacquired their assets at market value immediately before emigration, which could crystallise a CGT charge on exit (TCGA 1992, s 80) unless the emigration is caused by the death of a trustee and the trust is reimported within six months (TCGA 1992, s 84). Past trustees may be made liable for the tax (TCGA 1992, s 82). Anti-avoidance provisions cover trusts benefiting from double taxation treaties, dual resident trusts and disposals of settled interests (TCGA 1992, ss 83–85). A UK domiciled settlor setting up a non-resident trust after 19 March 1991, or adding to an existing trust after that date, is taxed on the trust's capital gains as they arise if he or his spouse, child or child's spouse, or a company controlled by them, is a beneficiary (TCGA 1992, s 86 and Sched 5). This is under the provisions of TCGA 1992, ss 77–79, which assess the settlor of a UK trust who retains an interest.

As far as IHT is concerned, non-resident trusts are treated in very much the same way as resident trusts. The important point for the tax liability of these trusts is the domicile of the settlor at the time the trust is first established. If the settlor is not UK domiciled, then trust assets located outside the United Kingdom will be excluded from any IHT liability. The professional adviser has a duty to return details of any non-resident trusts established for a UK domiciled individual under IHTA 1984, s 218. Reference must be made, however, to any double taxation agreement in force. Where a non-resident trust has an IHT liability, this normally falls on the trustees but if, for whatever reason, the liability is not met by them, the Inland Revenue may obtain the tax from any of the following under IHTA 1984, s 201:

(1)   any person entitled to an interest in possession in the settled property;

(2)   any person for whose benefit the property or income therefrom may be applied at or after the time of the transfer; or

(3)   the settlor, if the transfer is made within his lifetime.

In summary, non-resident trusts can be very useful in tax planning. Where the settlor and his or her spouse are precluded from income, the income payable to beneficiaries is effectively taxed on a remittance basis. The rules for capital gains are now rather complex, as summarised above, but do not affect non-domiciled settlors. Before embarking on any trust scheme, the expatriate must be totally clear on what he hopes to achieve and must be professionally advised in order to achieve it.

9 Other UK taxes

9.1 Value added tax

United Kingdom VAT is payable at the standard rate of 17.5 per cent in respect of goods or services supplied in the United Kingdom by a registered business. Registration is compulsory where the taxable turnover exceeds £46,000 a year. Certain items are exempt from VAT, while others are zero-rated, for example, most food; gas, electricity and fuel oil are charged at 8 per cent. So far as the expatriate is concerned, the most important VAT relief is that relating to exports of goods or services. If goods are exported from the United Kingdom the sale is zero-rated, and therefore VAT should not be charged. Certain supplies of international services are also zero-rated; for example, an expatriate obtaining advice from a UK business, on his personal tax affairs, will receive a zero-rated bill if he is resident outside the EC. However, if he is resident inside the EC the charge will be standard-rated. A supply to the expatriate of taxation advice for business purposes is zero-rated whenever he is resident outside the United Kingdom.

Value added tax due on imports of goods is paid at the time and place of entry or, if the importer has approval for deferment, by direct debit covered by banker's guarantee on the fifteenth of the month following the month in which the goods enter the United Kingdom. However, from 1 January 1993, businesses which import goods from EC member states only account for VAT on their next VAT return.

9.1.1 VAT exemptions and zero-rating

The main VAT exemptions are set out in the Value Added Tax Act 1994 (VATA 1994), Sched 9: the main headings are land (but see **9.1.2**), insurance, finance, education, health, burial and cremation.

Zero-rating for VAT purposes is given by VATA 1994, Sched 8, the main headings of which are food, books, news services, construction of dwellings, international services (see below), transport, caravans and houseboats designed for permanent habitation, gold, medicines, certain supplies to or by charities and children's clothing.

International services include services relating to land outside the United Kingdom, letting goods for hire outside the United Kingdom, the supply of cultural, artistic, sporting, scientific, educational or entertainment services performed outside the United Kingdom, valuation of goods outside the United Kingdom, the supply to a person in his business capacity of services listed in VATA 1994, Sched 5 to a member of the EC and in any capacity to a person belonging elsewhere, and the supply of insurance and allied services and export and transhipment services. Goods sent to the United Kingdom for repair and subsequently re-exported are also included in this heading. Schedule 5 refers to services treated as supplied where received, such as transfers and assignments of intellectual property, advertising services, professional services of consultants, engineers, lawyers, accountants, etc, banking, financial and insurance services, the supply of staff, hiring of goods and certain restrictive covenants.

If these services are supplied by a person who belongs outside the United Kingdom to a UK business registered for VAT, then the same consequences apply as if the recipient had himself supplied the services in the United Kingdom and that supply was a taxable supply, ie he would have to account for VAT on the value of that supply by the overseas person. Therefore if the UK business was partially exempt for UK VAT purposes, and these services received related to exempt supplies, it will suffer a disallowance of VAT input tax on these expenses. A UK business will therefore not obtain an advantage by using services supplied from abroad, which do not have a VAT charge on them, as opposed to services supplied in the United Kingdom which will bear VAT.

9.1.2   Property

Expatriates with property in the United Kingdom should appreciate that although the purchase price of domestic property is free of VAT, alterations as well as repairs and maintenance are subject to VAT. The construction of buildings for industrial and commercial use and in the community and civil engineering sector is standard-rated for VAT: the landlord has the option to charge VAT on rents and capital sums received on the supply of non-domestic buildings and developed land used for non-domestic purposes. By electing for this, the landlord is able to recover input tax on repairs and maintenance expenses. Therefore expatriate owners of commercially let property in the United Kingdom should consider whether or not to register for UK VAT and appointing an agent in the United Kingdom to deal with their UK VAT affairs.

9.2 Cars

Cars supplied in the United Kingdom other than for export are subject to VAT. The separate car tax has been abolished.

An expatriate returning to the United Kingdom and importing a car could be liable to VAT on the value of the car at the time of importation, plus import duty if the car is not of EC origin unless it qualifies under the personal belongings heading (see below). The exemption for a car on which VAT was originally paid in the United Kingdom has now been abolished.

9.3 Excise duties

Many items imported into the United Kingdom suffer excise duties in addition to VAT. Examples include the obvious ones of alcohol and tobacco, perfume and gold and other less likely items such as cigarette lighters. Items acquired in the United Kingdom for personal export may be acquired in duty-free shops or those operating a personal export scheme under which the VAT, but not excise duty, may be recovered.

9.4 Personal belongings

The importation of personal belongings is normally subject to import duty and VAT (if relevant). The value for import duty is basically the secondhand value (exclusive of VAT) in the United Kingdom of identical or similar objects. The value for VAT is the same but inclusive of import duty.

There are relieving provisions and these relate to three categories of belongings:

(1) cars, aircraft and caravans;
(2) boats; and
(3) other effects.

The appropriate customs formalities including the claiming of the reliefs must be complied with:

(1)   Motor cars, motor bikes, aircraft and mobile homes can be admitted entirely tax and duty free if belonging to a person coming into the United Kingdom for a stay of at least six months which are already his personal property and have been owned and used abroad by him or his spouse for six months excluding time he has spent in the United Kingdom. Furthermore, the vehicle must be for personal use and not sold, hired, etc for one year from importation under penalty of forfeiture. Release may be granted, if all duties and tax are paid. There is also a temporary importation relief for a visitor intending to stay less than six months in the United Kingdom, but the vehicle must be exported at the end of this period (see Customs and Excise Notice 3, and the Private Vehicle Memo).

(2)   Boats are not in any case subject to import duty if more than 12 metres long. All boats designed or adapted for recreation or pleasure are subject to VAT as are other boats of less than 15 tons gross. The relieving provisions are virtually identical to those for motor cars (see Customs and Excise Notice 8A and later Customs and Excise Notice 8).

(3)   Other baggage, personal and household effects (including pets) are relieved in the same way as cars, etc, except that these goods need only have been owned and used in the expatriate's normal home for three months if he is returning from the EC: the six-month rule applies if he is returning from outside the EC and the goods are not disposed of for 12 months. These rules also apply to someone setting up a secondary home in the United Kingdom. Certain prohibited or restricted goods are not within this relief, eg, goods bought under a tax-free scheme. The normal duty-free allowances apply in addition to this relief (see Customs and Excise Notice 3).

(4)   In addition to the above reliefs, a person who is resident outside the EC and who intends to become normally resident in the United Kingdom on the occasion of his marriage can bring in, duty and VAT free, wedding gifts up to a value of £800 each provided that they are from non-residents. Personal and household effects need not have been used abroad, but the goods should be imported within two months before, or four months after, the wedding.

9.5   Stamp duty

Stamp duty on the conveyance of UK stocks and shares is chargeable at ½ per cent. In the case of property the charge is 1 per cent or nil if the value transferred is £60,000 or less. There is no longer any stamp duty on gifts.

Of particular interest to expatriates is the stamp duty provision under which a stampable document signed outside the United Kingdom and kept outside the United Kingdom is only stampable within 30 days of being brought into the United Kingdom (Stamp Act 1891, s 15(2)(*a*)).

10 The taxpayer's rights and obligations in his country of residence*

Whatever the expatriate's position in his present country of residence, whether, that is to say, he is living in retirement, in full-time employment, or self-employed, he will be well advised to have a clear idea of his basic rights and obligations *vis-à-vis* the local tax administration. Although in many countries these rights and obligations will be similar to those in force in the United Kingdom, the expatriate is likelier to find himself in a situation calling for some knowledge of them than he would have been if he had never left his native shores. It can be dangerous, in other words, for the expatriate to take anything for granted as far as his host country's tax system is concerned. To give a specific example of the kind of thing the expatriate needs to be aware of, many countries require a person leaving after a stay of several months or more to have a clearance certificate from their tax authorities before he is allowed to go. Again, some countries levy local taxes without sending any notification directly to the taxpayer concerned: it is up to the taxpayer to find out from some official publication or other that a tax payment is due from him.

10.1 Taxpayers' rights

Insistence on the political rights of taxpayers first appears in history in the 18th century. 'Taxation without representation is tyranny' was a watchword of the American Revolution, and Art 14 of the 1789 French Declaration of Human Rights laid it down that citizens have the right to decide themselves, or through their representatives, on the necessity for public contributions and the use to which they should be put, and to determine the amount, base and duration of such levies. Article 14 also states that citizens should have an obligation to pay these taxes.

*This chapter is based on the OECD publication *Taxpayers' Rights and Obligations: A survey of the legal situation in OECD countries*, Paris, 1990

In the modern world, democratic governments at least take the political rights of taxpayers for granted. In this chapter we are concerned rather with what might be termed administrative rights, the rights, in other words, that govern the individual taxpayer's actual dealings with the tax authorities. We are also concerned primarily with income tax. There is no international convention on such rights, but in many countries there is a growing awareness on the part of government that taxpayers need more explicit and comprehensive provisions to protect their rights at a time when tax levels are high, tax legislation grows more complex from year to year, and new technology is both making it easier in principle for information from different sources to be exchanged and checked, and allowing more co-operation between tax authorities in different jurisdictions.

The 25 member states of the Organisation for Economic Cooperation and Development all recognise, whether implicitly or explicitly, the following basic principles of taxpayer protection.

10.1.1   Right to be informed, assisted and heard

Taxpayers are entitled to have up-to-date information on the operation of the tax system, with its complexity duly reflected, and the way in which their tax is assessed. They are also entitled to be informed of their rights, including their rights of appeal.

10.1.2   Right of appeal

The right to appeal against any decision of the tax authorities applies to all taxpayers, and to almost all decisions taken by the tax authorities, whether as regards the application and interpretation of the law or of administrative rulings, provided the taxpayer is directly concerned.

10.1.3   Right to pay no more than the correct amount of tax

Taxpayers should pay no more tax than is required by the tax legislation, taking into account their personal circumstances and income. The tax authorities, however, and whatever tribunals or courts may be concerned try to make a distinction between legitimate tax planning and forms of tax avoidance or minimisation that can be proved to go against the intention of the legislators. Taxpayers are also entitled to a reasonable measure of assistance from the tax authorities so that they receive all the reliefs and deductions to which they are entitled; but in many countries tax reliefs are not automatically given even if all the information is available to the authorities.

10.1.4   Right to certainty

Taxpayers have the right to a high degree of certainty as to the tax consequences of their actions. A related point is that legislation and changes in the administrative interpretation of tax laws should not normally be retroactive.

10.1.5   Privacy

All taxpayers have the right to expect that the tax authorities will not intrude unnecessarily upon their privacy. In practice, this is interpreted as avoiding unreasonable searches of their homes and requests for information which is not relevant for determining the correct amount of tax due.

10.1.6   Confidentiality and secrecy

The information available to the tax authorities on the affairs of the taxpayer is confidential and will be used only for the purposes specified in the tax legislation.

With regard to exchanges of information between tax administrations in different countries, requests may be refused if the requested authority believes there is a risk of disclosure. Some countries require the tax authorities to inform the taxpayer before any information is passed to another government department or foreign tax authority.

In the majority of OECD member countries the tax administration has the statutory power to override bank secrecy and to obtain specific information from the bank for tax purposes, although this power is normally used with reserve and not unless there is some serious matter at issue. The rules and practice on this score, however, vary considerably from one country to another.

10.2   Taxpayers' obligations

Taxpayers also have certain **obligations** enforceable by law, the chief of which, administratively speaking, is to file an annual return. This often has to be done within a specified deadline, with a penalty for failure to comply. In many countries taxpayers must supply additional information or specified documentation on the request of the authorities. In some countries there is a specific legal obligation to report on a change in the taxpayer's situation, such as the formation of a partnership, initiation of some professional activity, or acquisition of a new source of income.

Further details about taxpayers' obligations in OECD member countries and the consequences if the requirements of the tax authorities are not met are set out in the following table.

Table 10.1 **Taxpayers' obligations**

Country	Obligations to make annual return	Population receiving tax returns	Other obligations	Consequences if requirements are not met
Australia	All taxpayers are legally obliged to file a return following a notice requiring filing signed by the Commissioner.	All taxable persons and companies (except taxpayers with income mainly from employment) who filed a form in the preceding year.	Upon notice from the Commissioner taxpayers must furnish necessary information, attend and give evidence, produce books and documentation, furnish special returns, keep business records if certain deductions are claimed and records of acquisitions and disposal of assets owned since 19 September 1985.	Assessment by Commissioner, penalty of double the amount of tax assessed can be imposed, prosecution and penalties of up to $2,000 (1st offence), $4,000 (2nd offence), $5,000 or up to 12 months' imprisonment (3rd offence) plus additional measures.
Austria	Follows from the respective tax laws or from a specific request issued by the tax office.	Taxpayers with income subject to assessment with certain limitations (does not cover employment which is subject to withholding tax).	Taxpayers obliged to notify to the tax office all relevant facts or circumstances relevant for existence or scope of tax liability.	Administrative fines (max Sch 20,000) and/or penal proceedings. Delays can be punished by surcharge up to 10% of assessed tax.

(continues)

Country	Obligations to make annual return	Population receiving tax returns	Other obligations	Consequences if requirements are not met
Belgium	All taxpayers (except individuals with low income) must file an annual return.	Persons and corporations receiving taxable income.	The tax administration has at its disposal rights to obtain certain supplementary information from taxpayers.	Assessment by tax office, increase of assessed tax between 10 and 200%, administrative penalties (BF200–10,000) or legal prosecutions.
Canada	All corporations (except charity) and all individuals with tax payable must file a return.	All corporations and individuals who filed a return in the previous year.	To take advantage of certain special provisions in the Income Tax Act a special form must be filed.	Failure to file returns in time results in penalty equal to 5% of unpaid tax plus up to 1% of unpaid tax per month (maximum 12 months).
Denmark	All taxpayers are legally obliged to file an annual return.	All taxable persons and corporations.	On request taxpayers must supply information, eg, documentation for deducted expenses.	Assessment made by tax authorities.
Finland	All taxpayers (except non-residents paying final withholding tax at source) must file a return.	Residents who received income in the previous year.	Specific rules for non-resident taxpayers.	Increased tax depending on degree of negligence.

France	All taxpayers are legally obliged to file a return.	All taxable persons and corporations.	Taxpayers must supply supplementary information on certain tax allowances.	After the order of tax authority is given, assessment interest of 0.75% per month, tax increase of 10, 40 or 80%, allowance may not be accepted if no documentation is supplied.
Germany	All persons subject to taxation with the exception of certain employed persons subject to withholding tax on wages.	All known taxpayers with the exception of employed persons with final tax payments by withholding tax on wages.	Authorities must be notified of the setting up of corporations and partnerships, agricultural and forestry undertakings, business enterprises and self-employment as well as of certain direct investments abroad and the manufacture of excisable goods.	Estimation of income and supplementary charges.

(continues)

Country	Obligations to make annual return	Population receiving tax returns	Other obligations	Consequences if requirements are not met
Greece	All natural persons with taxable income earned. All legal entities.	All individuals having filed a tax return in previous years.	Individuals and companies must notify the tax office of changes in their situation, eg, commencement, interruption of business, legal modifications of the company, the value of own stocks, various contracts of construction of buildings, etc.	Failure to file returns in time or accurately results in a fine. Fine differs in kinds of cases, but without considering intention to evade taxes.
Ireland	All persons liable to tax by Direct Assessment and all other persons who are required to do so by a notice from the tax inspector.	Employed taxpayers liable to income tax and pay related social insurance by deduction at source through the PAYE system (with allowances other than basic) plus full issue of returns to taxpayers liable to tax by direct assessment.	Persons and corporations must on request supply additional information on accounts, books and documents and assets. Chargeable persons who have not been required to do so must file a return and new companies must furnish basic data on the company.	Administrative assessment of taxable income, penalties and — if failure is wilful — additional penalties.

Italy	All persons with income (varies by source of income) above a certain level are required to file a return.	All taxable persons and corporations.	Taxpayer must supply supplementary information on request.	Prosecution, imprisonment (up to 5 years) and fine (amount varies).
Japan	Each taxpayer must assess his own income tax and file a return.	All persons estimated to be liable to file a final return.	Persons receiving gross income of more than Y30 million from business shall submit special report unless final return submitted.	No penalty.
Netherlands	All taxpayers are legally obliged to file a return.	Persons who are suspected to be liable to tax or required to withhold tax.	Taxpayers must supply relevant documents. Legal entities must submit a list of directors.	Assessment on an estimated basis by tax inspector, in some instances with a surcharge of 5% or a criminal fine up to GLD 10,000. In criminal cases up to 4 years' imprisonment and/or fines up to GLD 25,000. In cases of reassessment or additional assessment a surcharge of 100% may be imposed on tax levied.

(*continues*)

Country	Obligations to make annual return	Population receiving tax returns	Other obligations	Consequences if requirements are not met
New Zealand	All persons with assessable income except employees subject to withholding tax with earnings less than certified amount.	Every person with an IRD identification number and for whom a current address is held.	Details of payments made to non-residents (eg dividends, interest) subject to non-resident withholding tax, information on all interest paid or credited in the course of business and information from employers on payments or benefits made or given to employees.	Prosecution and fines up to $6,000.
Norway	All persons and companies with income or capital taxable in Norway must file a return, except certain categories of pension recipients.	All persons and companies with assessed income in the previous year plus those who inform authorities that they will have taxable income.	Taxpayers operating business enterprises must supply additional information (annual balance of accounts).	Taxpayer can lose right of administrative appeal, authorities can make discretionary assessment, or an additional penalty can be imposed.
Portugal	All persons with an income above certain limits and all companies.	No tax return is sent to taxpayers.	Taxpayers subject to corporate tax are required to provide some	Fines of varying size, assessment by inspector and interest on tax due.

Spain	All taxpayers, and individuals who have taxable income greater than Ptas 840,000.	Tax returns are not sent to taxpayers.	additional information (eg depreciation, expenses, royalties, etc). Taxpayers are required to report to the authority on initiation and termination of their business or professional activities, as well as on change in their fiscal domicile.	Fines are imposed. After a tax audit, taxpayers are punished with withdrawal of tax reliefs, in certain cases by legal prosecution.
Sweden	All persons with an income of at least SKr 10,000 (with certain exceptions), except certain categories of pension recipients plus nearly all corporations.	All filers for previous year plus – according to information held – persons obliged to file a return for year in question.	All taxpayers are obliged to furnish any piece of information necessary for a correct assessment (normally submitted together with tax return).	Administrative fines, administrative assessment, combined with increase in tax, legal prosecution.
Switzerland	All taxpayers must file a tax return.	All taxpayers.	Obligation to furnish information on the request of tax administration.	Administrative assessment, administrative fines or legal prosecution.

(continues)

Country	Obligations to make annual return	Population receiving tax returns	Other obligations	Consequences if requirements are not met
Turkey	All persons and corporations with income subject to tax (with certain exceptions).	Tax returns are not sent to taxpayers.	Taxpayers or other related persons and public institutions must furnish all necessary information to tax authorities.	Special penalties (up to TL 240,000).
United Kingdom	Only taxpayers receiving a return from the inspector.	All taxpayers with income subject to assessment, but only approx. one-sixth of taxpayers with income mainly from employment.	Any new source of income must be notified.	Penalties of up to 100% of the tax due.
United States	All taxpayers are in principle obliged to file a return (exceptions being some persons with gross income below a certain limit).	Persons who filed a form the preceding year.	Taxpayers are required to pay estimated tax in instalments during the taxable year. Reporting is required in special cases (eg. US residents having interests in a foreign corporation or in a foreign financial	Fines of 5% of tax for a late return and 5% for each month late up to 25%. Fines of 20% of underpayment for certain failures to file an accurate return. Fines equal to the amount of interest on

account). Payments of certain income to non-resident alien individuals, foreign corporations, and foreign partners are subject to reporting and withholding tax.

underpayments of estimated tax instalments. Special fines concerning information on foreign corporations. (Persons required to deduct and withhold tax on income to a foreign person are liable for the tax.)

Source: *Taxpayers' Rights and Obligations: A survey of the legal situation in OECD countries*, Paris, 1990

11 Double taxation agreements

11.1 Fiscal residence

The United Kingdom taxes the worldwide income of a UK resident and domiciled individual and it also taxes the income arising in the United Kingdom of a non-resident. It will be appreciated that as many other countries do likewise, it is possible to be subject to tax on overseas income both in the country of residence and in the country in which the income arises. In many cases this problem is alleviated by a bilateral double taxation agreement between the two countries involved.

The United Kingdom currently has more than 90 double taxation agreements, some of which relate only to particular types of income (see Inland Revenue booklets IR146 and IR6). This book is aimed at the British expatriate, and it is therefore necessary to consider in the case of income arising in the United Kingdom whether there is a double tax treaty between the United Kingdom and the taxpayer's country of residence or not. If there is such a treaty, it is then necessary to consider the taxpayer's fiscal residence under the treaty.

Consider for example the case of the expatriate who has retired to Spain, where he spends the majority of the winter, but who has retained his house in the United Kingdom where he spends the summer months. Article 4 of the Anglo-Spanish Double Tax Treaty provides that it is necessary first of all to consider residence according to the rules of the country concerned. Under UK law, if he spends an average 91 days a year or more in the United Kingdom, he is resident in the United Kingdom. As he spends some eight months of the year in Spain, he is resident in Spain for Spanish tax purposes.

It is then necessary to consider in which country he has a permanent home available to him. As he has a home in both countries, it is then necessary to consider his centre of vital interests—ie the state with which his personal and economic relations are closer. This is debatable. He spends two-thirds of his time in Spain but has by no means severed his ties with the United Kingdom. If the country in which he has his centre of vital interests cannot be determined, it is necessary to look to the country in which he has a habitual abode. But as he has such an abode in both countries it is then necessary to look to his nationality. If he is a UK national, he will be regarded as resident in the United Kingdom and non-resident in Spain and taxed accordingly. If he is a Spanish national, however, on the same facts he would be regarded as resident in Spain and not resident in the United Kingdom. If he is a national in neither the United Kingdom nor Spain, the tax authorities in each country will agree his place of residence. In the circumstances envisaged this would probably be Spain and he would therefore be regarded as not resident in the United Kingdom, notwithstanding the fact that he has a home here which would normally make him resident under the UK residence rules.

A number of the older treaties do not have this tie-breaker clause with regard to residence and it is therefore possible to be resident in both countries. This also applies where there is no double tax treaty. In this case, the tax liability must be calculated in accordance with the rules of each country and advantage taken of any remaining relief under the treaties and unilateral relief where available.

Exceptionally, the second protocol to the Anglo-US treaty (SI 1980 No 568) provides that for income tax purposes a woman with US citizenship who married a UK domiciled man before 1 January 1974 and therefore acquired a UK domicile of dependence is deemed to have married on that date and may therefore retain her US domicile of origin unless she acquires a UK domicile by choice.

11.2   Dividends

A non-resident in receipt of dividends from the United Kingdom is not entitled to the tax credit that is available to a UK resident unless the appropriate treaty so provides. The treaty with Spain for example provides in Art 10, para 3 that a Spanish resident entitled to dividends from a UK company is entitled to the same tax credit as a UK resident and is subject to Spanish tax on the gross equivalent of the dividends. However, the UK authorities subject the dividend to a withholding tax of 15 per cent on the gross equivalent and this tax is allowed as a credit against the Spanish tax payable. If therefore a British company paid a dividend of £80, the resident in Spain would receive £80 from the company and the UK Inland Revenue would repay the difference between the tax credit available to a UK resident of £20 and 15 per cent on the gross equivalent: that is £5. He would therefore receive £85 from the United Kingdom and would be regarded in Spain as having received dividends of £100 on which tax of £15 had already been paid.

If he were a resident of a non-treaty country, he would be treated as receiving income of £80 and would pay such local tax on that income as would be levied by the country of residence.

To avoid having to apply to the UK Inland Revenue for the repayment of part of the tax credit, it is possible to arrange for the company paying the dividend to repay the appropriate part of the tax credit at the same time. This requires the consent of the company and of the Inland Revenue under the Double Taxation Relief (Taxes on Income) (General) (Dividend) Regulations, SI 1973 No 317. (Usually known as the G arrangement.)

11.3   Interest

Interest arising in the United Kingdom to a non-resident is normally taxable in the United Kingdom under Schedule D, Case III, under TA 1988, s 18(3), but the charge is limited to the tax deducted at source, if any, FA 1995, s 128. Annual interest, that is, on a loan exceeding 12 months, paid to a person whose usual place of abode is outside the United Kingdom, is subject to deduction of tax at the basic rate at source under TA 1988, s 349(2)(*c*) unless it is bank or building society interest. A non-resident can arrange that such interest is paid gross, see **4.3**.

Interest paid to a non-resident may suffer a reduced rate of withholding tax or be liable in the United Kingdom for a reduced rate of tax under the treaty. Article 11 of the Anglo-Spanish Treaty, for example, reduces the tax in the country where the interest arises to 12 per cent which would be credited against the liability in the country of residence. It is possible to arrange with the Financial Intermediaries and Claims Office (FICO) to deduct tax at the reduced treaty rate, if any, on payment of interest to a non-resident under the Double Taxation Relief (Taxes on Income) (General) Regulations, SI 1970 No 488. This applies to both interest and royalties.

11.4   Royalties

Royalties paid from the United Kingdom to a non-resident are subject to a withholding tax at the basic rate of 25 per cent if they are royalties in respect of a UK patent under TA 1988, s 348(2)(*a*) or 394(1)(*b*) or in respect of copyright, and are paid to the owner of copyright whose usual place of abode is not within the United Kingdom under TA 1988, s 536. This section refers to a usual place of abode outside the United Kingdom, not residence outside the United Kingdom, although for practical purposes this will normally be the same. It should also be noted that copyright royalties paid to an author whose normal place of abode is outside the United Kingdom are not subject to withholding tax under TA 1988, s 536 in view of a Parliamentary Answer of 10 November 1969 (*Hansard* Vol 791, col 31).

Other royalties arising in the United Kingdom are not subject to withholding tax unless they are pure income profit where the non-resident provides no services whatsoever for the royalty received. If it is pure income profit, the tax would be withheld at source at the basic rate in the same way as for any other annual payment. Under the appropriate double tax treaty, it may be possible to reduce the rate of withholding tax and in the treaty with Spain, for example, the rate of withholding tax on royalties is reduced to 10 per cent by Art 12 of the treaty. As for interest, permission may be obtained from the FICO to pay the interest subject to this reduced rate of withholding tax.

11.5   Income from real property

Income from immovable property is normally taxed in the country in which it is situated, as under Art 6 of the Anglo-Spanish Double Tax Treaty. Income from property in the United Kingdom is subject to withholding tax under TA 1988, s 43 or 42A at the basic rate of tax where payment is made to a non-resident, although by concession it is normally possible to arrange with the Inland Revenue for payment to be made subject to a reduced or nil level of withholding tax if it can be shown that the income arising will be reduced for UK tax purposes by, for example, mortgage interest paid, and from 6 April 1996 where the non-resident agrees to comply with his UK tax responsibilities under self-assessment the tenant or rent-collecting agent will be authorised to pay rents gross under TA 1988, s 42A regulations.

11.6   Businesses

Business profits are normally only taxed in the country of residence unless there is a permanent establishment in the other country, see, for example, Art 7 of the Anglo-Spanish Double Tax Treaty. Permanent establishment is very often defined by the treaty, for example, in Art

5 of the double tax treaty with Spain, and includes a place of management, branch, office, factory, workshop, mine, oil well, etc, and in the case of Spain, a building site which exists for more than 12 months.

If there is a permanent establishment of a non-resident in the United Kingdom, it will be subject to UK tax on the profits. The assessment may be made in the name of a UK representative, ie a branch or agent who is made responsible for the tax under FA 1995, s 126/127, and who may withhold UK tax when accounting to the non-resident. A non-resident trading with the United Kingdom is not, under general law, subject to UK tax and it is specifically provided that a non-resident trading in the United Kingdom through a broker who is a general agent is not liable to UK tax in view of FA 1995, s 126/127. If he is otherwise trading in the United Kingdom but not through a permanent establishment the treaty will normally protect him from UK tax. In the case of a business being carried on by a non-resident it is common for the treaty to reinforce the transfer pricing provisions of TA 1988, s 770 to ensure arm's length pricing between the United Kingdom and overseas business and in the case of Spain this is contained in Art 9 of the treaty.

11.7 Capital gains

A non-resident is not normally liable to UK CGT except in the case of assets used for a branch or business in the United Kingdom under TCGA 1992, s 10. Article 13 of the Anglo-Spanish Double Tax Treaty would allow the United Kingdom to tax immovable property in the United Kingdom, although in fact it does not do so, except for land development profits under TA 1988, s 776.

11.8 Independent personal services

The self-employed activities of a non-resident will not normally be subject to tax in the United Kingdom unless there is a fixed base in the United Kingdom, as under Art 14 of the Anglo-Spanish treaty.

11.9 Dependent personal services

Employment income of a non-resident from activities in the United Kingdom would normally be taxable under Schedule E, Case II although this liability may be reduced by treaty relief. For example, under Art 15 of the Anglo-Spanish treaty, if the employer is not resident in the United Kingdom and the non-resident employee is present for a period not exceeding 183 days in the fiscal year, he would not be liable to UK tax under Schedule E, Case II for his work in the United Kingdom. On the other hand, directors' fees from a UK company would be subject to tax in the United Kingdom, in the case of Spain under Art 16 of the treaty.

11.10   Entertainers and sportsmen

There are often special provisions relating to the remuneration of non-resident entertainers and sportsmen whose remuneration may be very large. The treaty will usually provide that they are taxable in the country in which the performance is given even though they would otherwise be protected by the treaty, see, for example, Art 17 of the Anglo-Spanish treaty, withholding tax at the basic rate from the UK earnings of non-UK resident entertainers and sportsmen.

11.11   Students and teachers

There are often special provisions in double tax treaties relating to students and teachers. For example in the treaty with Spain, Art 20 provides that a previous resident of Spain who comes to the United Kingdom for training and who receives money for his maintenance, education or benefit is not taxable in the United Kingdom. This is obviously useful where the children of expatriates come back to the United Kingdom for the purposes of their education. Teachers, as in Art 21 of the Anglo-Spanish treaty, are often allowed a two-year period, in total, *IRC v Vas* [1990] STC 137, in another country without becoming liable to tax therein.

11.12   Pensions

Under most of the double taxation agreements that the United Kingdom has with other countries, pensions are normally only taxable in the country of residence. The exception is pensions which result from Government Service; these are normally taxable only in the country from which the pension originates unless paid to a national of the country of residence. For example, under the Anglo-Spanish treaty, a UK pension paid to a resident of Spain would be liable for tax only in Spain, by virtue of Art 18. However, if the pension resulted from service with HM

Government or a local authority, it would be taxable only in the United Kingdom under Art 19(3), unless the recipient was a Spanish national in which case it would be taxable only in Spain.

Clearly the operation of the agreement is straightforward where the pension is paid gross—the return is simply made to the appropriate authority. Where the pension is normally subject to deduction of tax at source, obtaining treaty relief is a little more involved. (Those pensions subject to tax deduction at source were outlined in Chapter 4 but briefly, they are likely to be any pension other than state pensions—Old Age Pension and State Earnings Related Pension—which are paid gross.) Authority for pension or retirement annuity payments to be made gross is granted by the FICO (see **4.4**).

The Inspector will grant permission on receipt of confirmation that the individual in question is resident for tax purposes in the other jurisdiction. There is an official confirmation form for each country with which the United Kingdom has a double taxation agreement—the form may be obtained from either tax authority and is printed in both languages. For instance, in the case of a resident of Spain Form SPA may be obtained from FICO or from the local office of the *Delegación de Hacienda del domicilio fiscal del residente de España.*

11.12.1   UK State Retirement (Old Age) Pension

This is always paid gross to the recipient wherever resident and would normally be taxable in the country of residence.

11.12.2   Occupational pensions in respect of government or local authority service

These pensions, for example of civil servants, members of the armed services, state system school teachers etc would be paid subject to deduction of tax under PAYE at the appropriate code number. If the recipient is living in a treaty country it is unlikely that there would be a local tax liability in the country of residence on this income.

11.12.3   Occupational pensions (not government)

Occupational pensions would normally be subject to deduction of tax under PAYE. A non-resident should be able to arrange for a no tax notice of coding from his local district, if he still submits UK income tax returns, or from FICO. Such pensions will normally be taxable in the country of residence.

11.12.4   Retirement annuities and personal pensions

These are normally subject to deduction of tax at the basic rate although a non-resident should be able to obtain the appropriate authority from FICO for the annuity to be paid gross. Such income would normally be taxable in the country of residence.

11.13   Other income

In some treaties there is an article which provides that any other income arising in the treaty country will only be taxed in the country of residence. This article could, for example, apply to maintenance payments from the United Kingdom to a non-resident who would therefore receive the income gross or be able to recover the tax from the Inland Revenue. In the treaty with Spain 'other income' is in Art 22.

11.14   Non-discrimination

Treaties often contain what is known as a non-discrimination article which says generally that a non-resident shall not be treated worse than a resident for tax purposes. In the Anglo-Spanish treaty this is contained in Art 25. Non-discrimination clauses are very often more useful as a negotiating tool than for actual invocation.

11.15   Mutual agreement procedure

Most treaties also contain a mutual agreement procedure whereby a resident may ask his own tax authority to negotiate with the overseas tax authority if he considers that he is being unfairly treated, or the double taxation treaty is being ignored or misinterpreted. The mutual agreement procedure is, for example, often invoked or threatened to be invoked in negotiating with the Internal Revenue Service in the United States, who tend to have a somewhat cavalier view of the application of double tax treaties with other countries.

11.16   Exchange of information

One of the points to watch in living in a country where there is a double tax treaty with the United Kingdom, is that the treaty will usually contain a clause overriding the normal secrecy provisions and allow the appropriate tax authorities to exchange information relating to the taxpayer's financial affairs. Inland Revenue information gathering powers may now be used on behalf of other tax authorities within the European Community (FA 1990, s 125).

Although most treaties are similar in many respects, it is extremely important to refer to the actual treaty currently in force when considering the likely taxation charge as there are significant differences.

11.17 Inheritance tax

The United Kingdom has only ten double taxation treaties covering IHT and consequently they are generally of not so much importance as the income tax treaties. The countries with which agreements have been concluded are:

France	Republic of Ireland
India	Republic of South Africa
Italy	Sweden
Netherlands	Switzerland
Pakistan	United States

In some circumstances the treaties can change the fiscal domicile of an individual for IHT purposes which would obviously be of extreme importance in determining his UK IHT liability. For instance, under Art 4 of the IHT Double Taxation Treaty with South Africa, a South African national with a UK domicile who had not been ordinarily resident in the United Kingdom for seven years would be regarded as domiciled in South Africa and not in the United Kingdom. This seemingly arcane illustration is mirrored in other ways in other treaties and must serve as an example of the need to seek professional advice in situations where an individual is living in one jurisdiction and has assets in another.

Where two countries both have a claim to the same assets (for IHT purposes) the potential exists, despite the treaty, for double taxation to occur. For this reason most treaties contain a double taxation relief clause which will remove or, at the least, mitigate the double liability. Where there is no double taxation treaty between countries, unilateral relief against double taxation may be available whereby a credit for the overseas tax paid will be set against the UK IHT liability. The provisions are somewhat complex and are contained in IHTA 1984, s 159.

11.18   Unilateral relief

Double taxation relief is often given unilaterally where there is no treaty or the treaty does not cover the income in question. A UK resident is given unilateral relief under TA 1988, s 790. Unilateral relief will normally give credit for direct overseas taxes suffered but, for example, would not normally give an individual relief for the underlying taxes on a company's profits out of which a dividend is subsequently declared. As far as possible relief is given as if there had been a double taxation treaty in force, see SP 7/91.

11.19   Treaty shopping

In certain cases, it is possible to use a third country's double taxation agreement to reduce a withholding tax. For example, UK patent royalties paid from the United Kingdom to a resident of Hong Kong would normally suffer UK tax at 25 per cent. If, however, a Netherlands company were interposed, the UK royalties should be paid gross to The Netherlands under the UK-Netherlands Double Tax Treaty and 7 per cent or so of the royalties would remain in The Netherlands subject to Netherlands tax. The remaining 93 per cent would, however, be paid on to Hong Kong free of withholding tax as The Netherlands does not levy a withholding tax on royalties.

This could not however be done for dividends from the United Kingdom as there is a specific anti-avoidance provision in the UK-Netherlands treaty to prevent the use of the treaty by a third country resident.

Care is required, however, because, as in all tax matters, if there is first, a pre-ordained series of transactions and second, steps inserted which have no business *purpose* apart from avoidance of tax, the inserted steps will be ignored for tax purposes: see *Craven v White* [1988] STC 476.

12   The returning expatriate

The successful handling of an expatriate's financial affairs requires careful planning before he leaves the United Kingdom, continuous awareness of the taxation consequences of his actions while overseas, and, perhaps most important of all, careful planning and sound advice before his return home. It would, after all, be rather unfortunate to have spent many years building up a substantial amount of capital only to have a large slice of it taken by the Inland Revenue through a lack of foresight on return. Fortunately, much can be done to mitigate potential tax charges, but it is essential for these mitigating devices to be put in train before the expatriate comes back to the United Kingdom. Effective tax planning the day after return will, more often than not, prove to be impossible or, at least, illegal or ineffective.

This chapter, in common with the rest of the book, is concerned primarily with taxation and investment, but the returning expatriate has more to consider than this, and an indication of some of the other areas of concern is also provided.

12.1   Tax liabilities on return

As already mentioned, the main determinant of a person's liability to UK income tax or CGT, apart, that is, from having an income or a capital gain, is his tax residence position. The mere ending of an overseas employment or a visit to the United Kingdom need not result in a change of residence. The change from non-resident to resident will only come about if any of the following circumstances apply:

(1)   the person returns to the United Kingdom intending to remain permanently or for a number of years; or
(2)   he spends 183 days or more in the United Kingdom in any particular tax year;

(3)   he visits the United Kingdom regularly for periods which average 91 or more days each year over a period of four consecutive tax years.

For the majority of returning expatriates, the first condition above will apply. But before going on to review the consequences of this, it is worth considering the not uncommon situation of the expatriate who returns home for a period, perhaps at the end of a contract, but with the intention of finding another overseas job at the earliest opportunity. A person in these circumstances need not become resident in the United Kingdom, but many do under the second condition above. Unlike the majority, this temporary resident will not become resident and ordinarily resident from the date of arrival: rather, he will become resident but not ordinarily resident for that year. The tax consequences here are quite different from those pertaining to the new permanent resident.

12.1.1   Taxation on remittance basis

An individual who is resident but not ordinarily resident will be taxed on the remittance basis, that is, on the income he actually brings into the United Kingdom. In some respects this can be a more onerous burden than that of the permanent resident. Income which arises in the United Kingdom will be wholly taxable; overseas investment income will be assessed on the remittances made during the preceding tax year (or the current year if the income source arose after 6 April 1994 or from 1997/98). Any remittances from an overseas trade or profession will be charged on a current year basis.

The remittance of earnings in the year of return from an overseas employment will also be taxable in the year of return. Earnings arising in the year of return or previous years from a trade within Schedule D will also be assessed on amounts remitted in the year of return. This latter liability is one of the major differences between the treatment of those who become ordinarily resident, who are assessed on an arising basis unless domiciled outside the United Kingdom; and those who do not. Taxable remittances can be in cash or kind, or they can be constructive remittances arising through various debt arrangements and similar devices. An expatriate who is likely to find himself in this position would be well advised to seek professional assistance at an early date, before his return, because the degree of tax liability will be determined by many individual factors which are beyond the scope of a general treatment here.

From 6 April 1995, if the business was started on or after 6 April 1994 or 6 April 1997 in other cases there will be a deemed cessation of a business on a change of residence, at the date of arrival if concessionary treatment applies or previous 6 April if not. Remittance of past profits in the years following the year of return are not taxable because the source has ceased. On the change to self-assessment in 1996/97, if the current year basis does not apply in that year, the assessment is based on half of the total remittances in 1995/96 and 1996/97. In 1997/98 and future years, where the remittance basis applies the amount assessable is the total of the remittances in the fiscal year.

So far as CGT is concerned, an individual resident but not ordinarily resident will be fully liable on any gains made worldwide unless he is not domiciled in the United Kingdom. In the case of the non-domiciled individual he will be liable in full for gains made in the United Kingdom and on any gain remitted to the United Kingdom which arose abroad.

12.1.2 Tax on worldwide income

Returning to the majority case, the erstwhile expatriate will become resident and ordinarily resident from the day of his return. From then on, he will be fully liable to UK taxes on his worldwide income and capital gains. There are, however, one or two important exceptions and adjustments to this general rule. The first of these concerns any earnings from the overseas employment. Because, by concession, the tax year is split in the year of return into a resident and non-resident part, the overseas earnings before return escape tax. Subsequent payments including terminal leave pay, bonuses, gratuities, or lump sums from provident funds or in commutation of pension rights, used to be allowed tax free where they related to the overseas employment, but ceased to be from 6 April 1992, under SP 18/91. Any pension which arises overseas and which is payable by reason of overseas employment is taxable in the United Kingdom (whether remitted or not) but 10 per cent of the amount received is exempted from tax under TA 1988, s 196.

Where the returned expatriate has a continuing source of overseas investment income this, too, will become taxable on his return. This type of income is taxed under Schedule D, Case IV or V, and the basis of assessment is the income arising in the previous year, up to and including 1995/96, and from 1997/98 the current year basis applies, 1996/97 being a transitional year—see below. Because of this previous year basis, the new arrival could find himself with an immediate tax bill on income which arose while he thought he was safely beyond the reach of the Inland Revenue. By a further concession the Revenue do not seek to obtain the full amount of tax chargeable. The assessment for the year of return is restricted to that part of the overseas investment income which corresponds to the fraction of the year during which the taxpayer is actually resident. For example, if an expatriate returns to the United Kingdom on 5 August 1995 he will be resident in the United Kingdom for eight months of tax year 1995/96. If his overseas investment income for 1994/95 was £9,000, the amount assessed for 1995/96 on his return would be:

$$£9,000 \times 8 \div 12 = £6,000$$

If he were to delay his return until 5 March 1996, the assessment then would be on one-twelfth of £9,000, ie £750.

Much as the reduction in these assessments may be welcome, the net result is still a tax liability on income which arose during the non-resident period. In certain circumstances the whole liability can be avoided.

12.1.3   Current year basis

The preceding year basis of assessment, as stated above, is based on the income arising in the previous year. But where there was a new source of income before 6 April 1994, the assessment for the year in which the income first arose was based on the actual income for that year. This is known as the current year basis which also applies generally from 1997/98. One way, therefore, that the returning expatriate can avoid taxation on the previous year basis, is to ensure that when he returns his investments are all recently purchased. This does not mean that the expatriate should make no investments until just before his return. He should, however, sell his securities and repurchase them the next day for a new account or preferably purchase other securities. Similarly, bank deposit accounts should be closed, the money transferred to a current account for a short period and a new deposit account should then be opened.

One point to bear in mind when contemplating the return home and what to do with bank deposits is the period of notice required for withdrawals or closure of the account. Many investors use fixed-term deposits for three, six, or 12 months and if the interest rate remains attractive at the end of the term, they simply roll the money over for a subsequent term. Breaking a fixed-term account, if it is permitted at all, will always involve a stiff penalty in interest forfeited. It is essential, therefore, to ensure that all accounts can be terminated before the return date.

The taxation advantage of using this capitalisation or closure procedure can be best illustrated by an example:

Example: Capitalisation of investments

Mr Swan has been abroad for ten years; he opened a deposit account in a Channel Islands bank five years ago and for the last two years the deposit has been standing at £100,000. Interest has been, and for the purpose of illustration, will continue to be, paid at the rate of 10 per cent a year. The interest earned and paid in June and December has always been withdrawn by Mr Swan and invested elsewhere. Mr Swan's contract ended on 31 December 1994 and he intends to return to the UK on 5 January 1995. If Mr Swan did nothing about his account before coming home he would be assessed for 1994/95 on his interest as follows: interest arising in 1993/94 × ¼ (the portion of the tax year during which he is resident), ie £10,000 × ¼=£2,500.

If he is taxable only at the basic rate this will mean a bill of £625 payable within 30 days of the issue of the notice of assessment.

If, on the other hand, Mr Swan had closed his account on 31 December 1994 he would have no liability for interest in 1994/95 at all because the first interest payment due from the new source would not be made until June 1995. His first liability would be in 1995/96 and would be calculated on the interest arising in that same year.

The advantage is magnified if, as is often the case, the returned expatriate withdraws a substantial amount of his accrued capital to purchase a house or a business, perhaps.

Although this is one of the simplest pieces of tax planning for the returning expatriate, it is often missed. But it works only for overseas bank accounts. If the expatriate has held his money on deposit in the United Kingdom he would have had no liability during his period of non-residence but in the year of return this concessionary exemption is lost completely. If nothing is done about a UK account, the full amount of interest paid will be assessed on the previous year basis. There is no apportionment related to the part of the year during which the investor is resident.

If the account is closed before return this will make little, if any, difference. The assessment would then be on the current year basis from the beginning of the tax year to the date of closure and on the same basis from the date of reopening until the following 5 April, ie a full year's interest. The only way around this is to close the UK account in the tax year preceding the tax year of return, transfer the money offshore then use the capitalisation procedure on that offshore account. Because of the hassle involved in this, as well as the need to know the expected return date well in advance, it is better if the expatriate stays clear of UK deposits altogether. The same interest rates, with the same banks, can be obtained outside the United Kingdom.

From 1997/98 the current year basis will apply generally under the new self-assessment regime. Investment income will be taxed on the amount arising in the fiscal year, including income from abroad unless the remittance basis applies. Income from an overseas trade managed and controlled overseas is taxable under Schedule D, Case V on the income of the accounting year ending in the fiscal year, as is the income from a UK trade or profession under Schedule D, Cases I and II. The current year basis applies to new sources of income and new businesses from 1994/95. For existing sources 1996/97, the first year of self-assessment, is assessed on the average income of the transitional period, usually the two years ending in 1996/97 or on 5 April 1997. The deemed cessation on a change of residence applies to all trades and professions and investments but losses may be carried forward through the change. There are anti-avoidance provisions, with penalties to discourage attempted exploitation of the transitional provisions. Foreign partnership income remains taxable under Schedule D, Case V and UK partnership income, including partnership investment income, is taxed on the current year basis on the income of the accounting period ending in the fiscal year.

12.2   Capital gains tax

Turning to the question of CGT, there is now less scope than there used to be for some tax planning tactics. The basic rule is that where a person is not resident and not ordinarily resident throughout the tax year, he will have no liability to UK CGT. By concession, where the tax year is split into a non-resident and resident part in the year of return, no CGT will be charged on gains made during the period of non-residence (ESC D12). But to qualify for this treatment, the person must have been non-resident for a continuous period of 36 months. If this condition is not met, then any gains made in the tax year in which the return falls will be taxable whether made before or after the return. For short-term expatriates, therefore, any imminent or potential gains should be realised in the tax year before the year of return. For the longer-term expatriate, gains may be taken without penalty up to the day before returning to the United Kingdom.

The returning expatriate's aim should be to realise his gains before he returns and hold his losses until he rejoins the UK tax system. The converse, of course, will apply if there is a local CGT regime which is more burdensome than that in the United Kingdom. In most cases, however, the investor will not necessarily want to dispose of his holdings. In the case of a married couple where one spouse was resident and the other (the investor) was not resident, the non-resident spouse could transfer the gainful assets to the resident spouse. TCGA 1992, s 58, which normally exempts transfers between husband and wife, does not apply if one of them is non-resident; TCGA 1992, s 288(3) and TA 1988, s 282 *Gubay v Kington* [1984] STC 99. This transfer would be deemed to be carried out at market value and the recipient spouse would have this market value as the acquisition cost. When both spouses were resident in the United Kingdom once more, the asset could be transferred back exempt from tax. Assuming both spouses to be UK domiciled, there would be no IHT complications. On eventual sale, the base cost would be that market value crystallised on the first transfer, the overall effect being to wipe out gains which arose during the period of non-residence.

Another simple step is the 'bed and breakfast' operation under which investments are sold and repurchased the following day. The repurchase following the previous day's sale (theoretically, and usually in practice too, at the same price or thereabouts) crystallises any underlying gain and gives an enhanced acquisition cost against which to compute the gain on the eventual disposal. It appears from the exchange of correspondence between the Institute of Chartered Accountants and the Revenue, published on 25 September 1985 as TR 588, in para 16, that the *Furniss v Dawson* doctrine would not normally be applied to a properly executed bed and breakfast transaction.

Where the intention is to dispose of certain assets in the near future, perhaps to purchase a house or business, the simplest course might be to sell before return and hold the proceeds on deposit until required. If the assets are showing losses, they should be retained until after return.

So far, this chapter has illustrated ways of reducing the returning expatriate's immediate tax bills. That may be sufficient planning for some expatriates who intend to spend their capital soon after return but for many others it does not go far enough. In particular, where the returning expatriate intends to use his capital to provide an income either to supplement a lower UK salary or to provide a pension in retirement, what is required is longer-term planning and the use of a 'tax shelter' and, in this context, good advice is essential.

12.3 Dangers of evasion

Many expatriates believe when they return home that so long as their money is left outside the United Kingdom they will have no UK tax liability on any income arising from that money or any capital gains made. Others believe that they will only have a liability when they remit the income to the United Kingdom. For the British expatriate returning home this is, of course, untrue. Then there are those expatriates who know this to be the case but still take the view that if they leave their money off-shore and 'forget' to declare it, the Inland Revenue will never find out. That view, to say the least, is extremely inadvisable. Just one or two points might help to dissuade some expatriates from this course of action.

Assuming that the unlawful evasion goes undetected for a year or two, our evasively minded individual may decide to spend some of his cash on a new house: the Inland Revenue will receive details of the transaction and any half-awake tax inspector will ask where the balance of the purchase price came from. The claim that it was a legacy from Aunt Freda will not be accepted without sight of the probate documents.

Another myth which should be exploded concerns bank secrecy. More and more countries are co-operating with each other in the transfer of information about taxpayers of mutual interest, and there is often provision for this in double taxation agreements. Even the Swiss banks, those bastions of security where it is a criminal offence to divulge any information about a bank customer, have not proved impregnable to attacks by both the French and American tax authorities. Finally, an incautious word in the golf club may find its way back to the taxman and the subsequent investigation will not be a pleasant experience, quite apart from the substantial costs which will inevitably be incurred.

12.4   Miscellaneous investments

The steps to be taken and the points to be considered with a portfolio of conventional investments have largely been covered, but many expatriates also acquire a range of other investments, whether Persian carpets, Chinese ceramics, precious metals such as bullion, coin or jewellery, and so on. Where these are wanted at home for reasons of aesthetic enjoyment as well as as an investment, the investor should be prepared to pay any necessary duty, including VAT, incurred on importing them. If it is only their investment potential that is of interest, these charges can be avoided by importing them to the Channel Islands and depositing them there. The cost of safe storage and the high cost of insurance, however, must be taken into account.

Income from and expenditure on woodlands in the United Kingdom were taken out of the tax system with effect from 15 March 1988, subject to transitional provisions, but woodlands remain a tax efficient investment. They still attract IHT privileges.

12.5 Unremittable overseas income

Where a person has overseas investment income which cannot be remitted to the United Kingdom or otherwise released from the overseas country, any tax chargeable in the United Kingdom on the income will be held over until such time as the income is released. The unremittability of the income must be by reason of the laws of the overseas country, or executive action of that country's government, or the impossibility of obtaining foreign currency there. In addition the investor must not have realised the income outside that territory for a consideration in sterling or any other freely remittable currency. Where this relief is due it must be claimed before any assessment on the income becomes final. When the income is finally released it will become taxable at that time, and relief will be given for any overseas taxes paid. If the investor dies before the income is released, then any later release will be charged to his personal representatives.

12.6 National Insurance

Some of the benefits available under the British social security system will be accessible to the returning expatriate immediately, regardless of his National Insurance record while overseas, but the major benefits such as unemployment benefit, sickness and invalidity benefit and maternity grants and allowances will only be given where there is an acceptable level of contributions.

Where the returning expatriate has been receiving a National Insurance Retirement Pension at a lower level than that currently prevailing in the United Kingdom he will be entitled to have it uprated to the full rate on his resumption of UK residence.

12.7 Other matters

The returning expatriate must also consider various legal matters. First, he must make sure to give his tenants sufficient notice if he has let his house and wishes to resume living there. It might be considered wise to seek to terminate the tenancy a month or so before the expected date of return to give time for eviction proceedings to be pursued, should the tenants resist moving. The lost rent is unlikely to be as much as the cost of staying in hotels while the law takes its course.

Another point worth watching is the expatriate's will. It may be that he has made a will under his local legal framework while abroad—this is generally no bad thing. The will should be reviewed on return. It may be worth retaining the overseas will, suitably amended, in so far as it relates to property in the overseas country and to have a new will in the United Kingdom. This may assist in releasing overseas assets to the executors in order to pay any IHT required before a grant of probate on the UK will (see also Chapter 8).

Finally, in some countries a tax clearance certificate is required before an exit visa is granted. Where such a certificate is necessary, it is usually essential to apply in good time. There is not a lot of point in turning up at the airport only to be told that you first have to satisfy the local taxman that you have paid all his taxes.

13 Constructing an investment portfolio

Peter Ashton, Operations Manager, Allied Dunbar International Assurance Ltd

13.1 Introduction

For the internationally orientated investor, the sheer range of investment vehicles and the diversity of criteria for their appraisal are bewildering enough. But in constructing a portfolio there are also many personal factors peculiar to the individual investor that have to be taken into account.

The whole subject is so wide-ranging and important that it merits a book on its own, and for a comprehensive treatment the reader may well like to refer to the *Allied Dunbar Investment and Savings Handbook*, which is revised annually to update such key information as stock market performance and changes in UK tax rules.

This chapter and the following chapters aim to bring out the main points for appraising the major investment media likely to be considered by an expatriate investor. In the following pages we also refer to some of the important tax considerations, but these have been treated in more detail in Chapters 4–11. In choosing an investment, however, the expatriate should bear in mind that the investment itself is generally the primary consideration, and the taxation treatment secondary.

13.2 Establishing objectives

When designing an investment strategy, the expatriate should begin with the basic precept that any investment proposal must address specific financial circumstances. It is not possible to make a considered choice of an investment medium until the objective or purpose of the investment has been established. In essence the investor must ask three broad questions:

(1)   What do I want my investments to achieve?
(2)   In what time-scale?
(3)   Within what constraints?

Obviously, the more general the question, the more difficult it is to give an accurate, satisfactory and qualified answer. The individual factors that need to be taken into account to arrive at a considered investment strategy are many and varied. The following list is not necessarily exhaustive but it does include the major questions that should be asked:

(1)   What amount is available for investment, and when?
(2)   What proportion of the total investment portfolio does this represent?
(3)   What other investments are held?
(4)   What part should this investment play in the overall spread and balance of the total portfolio?
(5)   What is the investor's base currency?
(6)   What is the currency of the country to which the investor intends to retire?
(7)   What known liabilities are to be met?
(8)   Is there any expectation of adding to the investment, and when?
(9)   What is the age of the investor and, where relevant, the age of any of his dependants?
(10)   What is the investor's attitude to risk?
(11)   What are the access requirements and the likely time-scales involved?
(12)   What are the personal motivations of the investor?
(13)   What is the rate of inflation in the country in which the investor is, and will be, resident?
(14)   Is immediate income required from the investment and if so at what level?
(15)   Where relevant, what is the required balance between high immediate income and future growth in income?
(16)   Is capital appreciation alone the principal present aim?
(17)   What are the personal tax liabilities of the investor, both current and expected, and will different rates of tax be applied to income and realised gains?
(18)   Are there IHT considerations which may affect the choice of investment?
(19)   Are there any other relevant constraints which may limit or influ-

ence the choice of investment; for example, exchange controls, protective securities legislation, investment subject to trust, double tax treaties etc?

13.3   Risks and rewards

There is an element of risk in all investment. 'As safe as houses' is a proverbial comment, but in Britain many people bought a flat or a house at the top of the property boom, only to find that they were paying much higher interest on their building society loan than they had planned, while the market price of their property fell or the property proved unsaleable. Similarly, bank deposits are usually thought of as the most risk-free investment you can make, but the purchasing power of the money on deposit can be eroded by inflation which sometimes outstrips interest payments. There have been painful reminders, too, in the last few years that even banks can default. Expatriates are likely to be more exposed than other people to currency risks, and this is such an important consideration that we have devoted an entire chapter of this Handbook to it. In this section of the Handbook we are primarily concerned purely with the 'financial risk' that investors face.

The dictionary defines risk in general as 'the possibility of incurring misfortune or loss', and applied to financial investments this can be further defined as 'the possibility that expected security returns will not materialise and, in particular, that the securities held will fall in value'.

For the mathematically minded, 'financial risk' is defined as the variance or standard deviation of returns over time. In other words, a security is risky if its return from year to year is likely to depart appreciably from its average annual return. This means that a security that yields exceptionally good returns as well as exceptionally bad returns is risky in mathematical terms, although in everyday usage only the possibility of the bad or disappointing returns is seen as constituting a risk.

In theory, higher rates of return on an investment incorporate a premium for bearing additional risk. The market with its infinite knowledge (though not its infinite wisdom) is supposed to correlate risk and return in this fashion. Some well-documented studies have shown that it is indeed historically true that investors have received higher rates of return for bearing greater risks. Two American researchers, for example, were able to show that between 1926 and 1983, ordinary shares yielded an annual average rate of return more than three times that of US Treasury Bills, while their risk, calculated in terms of standard deviations, was nearly seven times as great. (In one year in three, shares showed a negative return, which was true of Treasury Bills in only one year out of the 58 surveyed.)

An important practical consequence of this relationship between risk and reward is that the investor should always look very hard indeed at any investment which claims to yield a well-above-average return. For one reason or another, such an investment or investment proposal is bound, in risk terms, to be even more-than-well-above-average. After all, the American research just quoted showed that investors had to take on seven times as much volatility to get three times as much return, and as this research covered the entire stock market, it took care only of average or market risk, and not the particular risk inevitably associated with an individual stock or investment scheme.

A particular word that should put all investors on their guard is 'guaranteed'. This word has no legal force unless it really does mean a bankable guarantee—implying some form of collateral backing the claimed return. If an intermediary claims to guarantee a specific return, ask who or what guarantees it, and whether the guarantee has any legal status.

The best way of reducing financial risk is through diversification. Here the proverbial wisdom about not putting all your eggs in one basket really does apply (and its truth has in fact been demonstrated by rigorous mathematical argument). In spite of this, it is surprising how many investors pay little heed to this truth. But in diversifying or spreading their investments, the investor should bear in mind that there is a general market (sometimes called 'systematic') risk besides the risk inherent in the shares of a particular company ('unsystematic risk'). In other words, it is possible to see widely spread equity investments all go down together (as they may all rise together in a bull market).

13.3.1   Some rules of thumb

Below is a list of points to consider:

(1)   The degree of future risk in any investment is always a matter of judgment. Mathematical measures of performance, volatility or risk hold water only when applied to the past.

(2)   The longer investors are prepared to tie up their money, the greater the return they will be entitled to expect.

(3)   The riskier an investment appears to be, the greater the return should be.

(4)   In general, the various investment media can be put on a scale of financial risk as follows:

(a)   Commodities: extremely risky.

(b)   Equities (shares in public companies): here the risk varies greatly from company to company, but there is also the general market risk referred to above.

(c)   Corporate bonds: less risky than equity, because the capital itself is not normally at risk.

(d)   Collective investments (unit trusts, mutual funds, investment trusts): less risky still, because the investment is spread among many different shares, bonds, or other media.

(e)   Life assurance: the only risk arises if the investor is unable to keep paying the premiums, as there may be a heavy penalty for early cancellation.

(f)   Bank and building society deposits: normally no risk at all.

(g)   Government stocks: such as gilts—the fixed-interest stocks issued or guaranteed by the British government. Financially the safest investment of all (but depending on the issuing government and on the investor's base currency, still subject to the risk of erosion by inflation and to currency risk).

13.3.2   Investor protection

After some notorious cases of fraud and malpractice (some of them on a vast scale) in recent years, jurisdictions all over the world are reviewing and tightening their authorisation and regulation of financial intermediaries of all kinds.

In the United Kingdom, the Securities and Investments Board (SIB) acts as an umbrella organisation for a number of Self-Regulatory Organisations (SROs) set up to provide proper regulation of the investment business carried on in different financial sectors. The SIB is a private limited company whose costs of operation are met by the UK financial services sector (embracing the stock market, unit trusts, life assurance, pension fund management and private portfolio management), but it reports directly to ministers of the Crown. Its board members are appointed jointly by the Economic Secretary at the Treasury and by the Governor of the Bank of England. The SIB's powers derive from the FSA 1986 (see **1.2.2**), and this Act also makes provision for recognised professional bodies such as the three Institutes of Chartered Accountants and the Law Society to authorise their members to carry on investment business (mainly in the form of advice) as part of their professional services to their clients.

Expatriates investing in the United Kingdom, or taking advice from or in some way availing themselves of the services of a UK intermediary should make sure that the company or intermediary concerned is a member of an SRO or recognised professional body. A list of relevant addresses is given in Appendix III.

The self-regulatory system seems to be peculiar to the United Kingdom, most other jurisdictions regulating the financial services sector directly from the Central Bank or equivalent body, or a government department or agency, or from a combination of these two entities. When planning to invest offshore, investors should find out which is the local authority responsible for authorisation and regulation, and then make sure that the particular investment or company they are contemplating is properly subject to this authority. Further details about particular offshore centres are also given in Appendix II.

13.4 Constructing a portfolio

Choosing the individual components of an investment portfolio can be confusing. Performance statistics often serve to mislead rather than inform. There is a disturbing tendency these days, among some sectors of the financial press, to measure investment performance over unrealistically short time-scales. Apart from causing confusion when attempting to compare the performance of different shares, sectors or investment funds, it makes comparisons between different investment media meaningless. Perhaps the most important difference between the mainstream investment areas is the time-frame within which they can be expected to provide effective performance. The prudent investor should use published investment statistics with caution, taking care to obtain sufficient information to indicate clearly the track record of the proposed investment.

So armed with all this information, what kind of investment do expatriates need to satisfy their aims? Where should they start looking?

Leaving aside the esoteric sorts of 'investment' opportunities—emeralds, rare stamps, coffee futures and the like—most private investors will find their needs catered for by the mainstream investment areas—bank deposits, government bonds and equities. These three areas account for well over 90 per cent of privately invested monies. Before we go on to examine specific investment vehicles, we will look at the main characteristics of these media.

Monies placed on deposit have a secure capital value in money terms, but the income produced will vary depending on the prevailing interest rate.

This means, contrary to popular belief, that the overall return from a deposit is far from guaranteed. If we go further and consider the overall return in real-value terms (as opposed to the meaningless 'money' return), it is clear that in an inflationary climate the longer the investment is held the more vulnerable it becomes.

An investment in government bonds is almost the reverse of this situation in that the income is generally guaranteed (in money terms) but now the capital value will fluctuate, depending again on the prevailing interest rate climate. The bond will usually have a guaranteed capital value at redemption, of course, but once again only in money terms, not in real value.

It will be seen that in the case of the two main investment areas where genuine guarantees are common, the main effect of the guarantee is to provide a secure and dependable return in the short term, but to restrict the overall return over the longer term. If one is looking for realistic growth rates over longer time-scales, experience has shown that they have only been achieved by investments in real assets such as shares, which produce both income and a capital return.

There can be no guarantees or predictions, but in a capitalist society, which is expected to remain so, security will more likely be achieved in the long term by investing in a well-balanced, carefully managed portfolio of equities—providing the investor's time-scales are long enough to iron out the fluctuations caused by the ebbs and flows in world market conditions and the changes in market sentiment generated by political climates. Historically, five years upwards has been the right sort of time-scale to consider equity investment to have sufficient security. If equity investment is contemplated over shorter periods than this, it stands the risk of being speculation rather than an investment.

Most investment advisers would, for the majority of their clients, recommend a balance between short-term bank/money market deposits, and the longer-term equity-linked investment, offering capital appreciation, with characteristic fluctuations in value and a lower but secure percentage income yield. The actual income will rise as the capital value appreciates and this element of the portfolio is therefore the key to providing the growth in income that is necessary to offset the erosive effects of inflation. The middle ground will be held by government bonds (such as gilt-edged stock or Eurobonds).

Quite how the proportion between deposits, government bonds and equity-linked investment will be determined, depends on the list of points to consider at **13.3.1**, and hence the particular needs of the individual investor. As a rule of thumb (and a potentially hazardous one, since any such rule must make assumptions about average needs) a classically constructed portfolio might have something in the region of 10 per cent on deposit. Of the balance, somewhere between 25 per cent and 35 per cent in government bonds, with the rest in equity-linked investments (frequently mutual funds such as unit trusts or offshore funds).

To summarise:

(1)   There must be a spread of investment sufficient to contain the volatility and depreciation risks that are incurred with an overly weighted exposure to one investment medium, one market sector, one country or one currency.

(2)   Within individual stock-market holdings there should be a balanced mix of investment sectors, eg manufacturing, engineering, property, finance, leisure etc.

(3)   The resulting portfolio must be under active daily management to ensure that the results obtained continue to meet the investor's needs.

Clearly, this is an ideal situation which average investors may find difficult or impossible to achieve by direct investment. They may not have the expertise to guide their choice or the time to manage a balanced portfolio actively. Even where the time and expertise are to hand, the required spread may be impossible to achieve in all but the largest private portfolios without striking 'minimum bargains' where the dealing costs are disproportionately high.

For many investors, the answer is to construct their portfolio from large building blocks such as the wide range of collective investment media that are available. The main areas from which the choice may be made are described in the following chapters.

14 Bank and building society deposits

14.1 Banking services for expatriates

Whether an individual's financial affairs are very simple or extremely complex, successful financial planning begins with establishing proper and effective banking arrangements. Apart from providing a home for money in its own right, a bank provides the mechanisms which link and give access to whatever other financial arrangements need to be made.

Specific individual requirements will depend on personal circumstances, but most expatriates are likely to need some or all of the following services from their bank:

(1) sterling current account: expatriates tend to keep higher balances than their onshore counterparts so this should, preferably, be interest bearing;
(2) sterling deposit account: as mentioned earlier this forms an important part in constructing a secure investment portfolio;
(3) currency deposit account: many expatriates are paid in foreign currency and, according to their domestic arrangements, may well have this currency as their base currency giving rise to a need for appropriate deposit facilities;
(4) currency conversion facilities;
(5) loan facilities: expatriates may need both short- and longer-term borrowing, perhaps in the latter instance to buy a home in the United Kingdom;
(6) standing orders;
(7) direct debit facilities;
(8) international money transfers;
(9) Eurocheque facilities;
(10) credit card payment facilities;
(11) international money orders and drafts.

Most banks, whether in the United Kingdom or offshore, can provide these services. But apart from considerations of tax (discussed immediately below), there are other good reasons for expatriates to conduct as much of their banking business as possible offshore. In the first place, they have many particular requirements and problems that UK residents do not have, and these are more likely to be understood and catered for by an offshore bank or branch that specialises in the banking needs of expatriates.

There are two further important advantages to expatriates if their bank or branch operates from either the Channel Islands or the Isle of Man:

(1)   These offshore centres are outside the UK tax jurisdiction, but have access to the UK banking network. This means that the full facilities of a UK clearing bank, such as cheque books and credit and other plastic cards for use in the United Kingdom, can be made available.

(2)   Jersey, Guernsey, and the Isle of Man have comprehensive financial services legislation enacted which assures investors of substantially the same safeguards and protection as if they had made their financial arrangements with an institution in the United Kingdom. The Isle of Man, moreover, is the first offshore centre to operate a deposit protection scheme, which covers 75 per cent of the first £20,000 of a deposit, whether in sterling or in a foreign currency.

14.2   Bank and building society deposits

At the beginning of Chapter 13, we said that taxation was generally a secondary consideration to the actual nature of a particular investment medium. But in the matter of bank or building society deposits taxation can often be the first question to consider. This is because interest arising on an account or deposit in a bank or building society in the United Kingdom is a UK source of income for a non-UK resident. In certain circumstances, under an extra-statutory concession, this interest is not taxable for non-residents, but the rules are complex, especially as they apply to the non-resident's year of departure from and year of return to the United Kingdom. These rules are explained in full detail in Chapter 4.

There is the further point that for an investor not domiciled in the United Kingdom, a deposit in the United Kingdom is treated as a UK sited asset for purposes of IHT, unless the deposit is in a currency other than sterling. This point is explained in greater detail in Chapter 7.

Many, though not all, of these UK tax problems can be avoided by non-residents if they put their bank deposits offshore. This is an area in which banks and building societies compete, and there is a very wide range of savings or deposit accounts on offer. But broadly speaking, the accounts fall into three main categories:

(1)   deposit or savings accounts with variable interest rates (the rates changing from time to time in line with base rates or money market rates);
(2)   interest bearing cheque accounts (often money market accounts);
(3)   fixed-term deposits, where interest rates are usually based on prevailing money market rates for the duration of the term, and the interest is paid at the end of the term of the deposit.

The differences between the terms offered by rival institutions relate to such matters as the minimum deposit required and the minimum notice of withdrawal (which also tend to affect the rate of interest offered), the variation between the rates of interest paid on deposits of different amounts, and the timing of crediting the account with interest. Surveys of the terms and conditions offered by offshore institutions are published from time to time in the *Financial Times* magazine for British expatriates, *Resident Abroad*.

As far as deposits are concerned, there is no difference in principle between an offshore bank or branch of a bank and an offshore branch of a UK building society. In recent years, moreover, the major UK building societies have extended their range of services to include many that previously only banks supplied, such as cheque books and plastic cards, standing order/direct debit facilities, and so on. But they may be unlikely to provide the full range of services required by the expatriate investor.

Finally, one general caveat applies to deposits, whether in a bank or a building society: this part of an investor's portfolio should not be allowed to grow out of proportion to the rest of the portfolio, because there is no possibility of growth of the original capital in the case of a deposit (as distinct from any accruals of interest that may be allowed to accumulate).

15 Fixed-interest securities

15.1 British government stocks

British government stocks (also known as British funds, gilts, or gilt-edged securities) are instruments used by the government to raise capital. The stocks are guaranteed by the government and consequently are totally secure. Investors can be sure that the stated rate of interest will be paid and the nominal principal returned, in accordance with the provisions of the loan.

Gilt-edged securities normally have a fixed rate of interest, known as the 'coupon', which is expressed as a percentage of the nominal value; so, for example, the holder of £100 nominal of Treasury Loan 8¾ per cent 1997 will receive £8.75 a year until that date (normally subject to deduction of income tax at the basic rate—but see below) regardless of the price at which the stock was purchased or its market value from time to time. In addition to paying interest during the life of the stock, the government also has a requirement to repay the loan at the nominal or par value of £100, on the date stated—this is known as the redemption date.

The market value at any given time will depend upon the coupon, the amount of time to run to redemption and prevailing interest rate conditions. The closer a stock is to redemption the nearer the market price will be to the nominal value. Stocks are usually classified according to the length of time to run to redemption, as follows:

(1) 'shorts': five years or less to redemption;
(2) 'mediums': between five and 15 years to redemption;
(3) 'longs': over 15 years to redemption.

In addition there are also undated or irredeemable stocks with no final date specified for redemption.

For the mediums and longs, at least, the key factor in determining their capital value from time to time is the prevailing structure of interest rates compared with the coupon on the stock. If the prevailing interest rate falls, the value of the stock will rise. This is because a larger investment is required at the new rate to give an equivalent yield. Conversely, if interest rates rise, then the capital value of the stock will fall. British government stocks are exempt from CGT, no matter how long they are held, and irrespective of the fiscal residence status of the holder.

The expatriate buying gilts directly (as distinct from via a collective investment vehicle) should generally choose from the range of so-called 'exempt' or 'approved' stocks, where the income can be paid gross (ie without the normal deduction of basic rate income tax at source) to an individual not ordinarily resident in the United Kingdom. Details of the stocks currently exempt and advice on the procedure needed to get the interest paid gross are given in Chapter 4 at **4.4**.

Because the investment is guaranteed by the government and the coupon and redemption value are both fixed, gilt-edged securities are ideal for the investor who places a high premium on security. If, however, a gilt-edged security is not held to maturity, the value of the stock will depend directly on prevailing interest rates and will fluctuate accordingly. The wide range of stocks on the market and the complex calculations sometimes needed to compare redemption yields make it advisable to have some expert advice before investing even in these safe securities, and for this reason many investors prefer a collective medium to direct investment.

15.2   Bulldog bonds

'Bulldog bonds' is an informal term used to designate sterling-denominated fixed-interest bonds issued by foreign governments and international agencies in the British domestic market. The structure of such bonds is fundamentally similar to that of the gilts issued by the British government, but they are usually priced to yield ½–1 per cent more than the nearest equivalent gilt. The interest is paid gross on some issues.

15.3   Eurobonds

Eurobonds developed from the market in Eurodollars, which originated in the 1950s as claims for US dollars in the hands of banks and their clients outside the United States who did not want to transfer their money to the United States. The market gradually extended to other major currencies held by persons not living in the country of the currency concerned.

Eurobonds are now issued in most of the world's major currencies, with the Japanese yen and the deutschemark sectors the most active. The bonds are issued by consortia of banks (the primary market) on behalf of the borrowers (mostly large corporations or governments and their agencies), and the banks may then sell them to investors (the secondary market), most of whom are institutions.

Some private individuals find Eurobonds attractive, partly because they are usually issued in bearer form, which means there is no register of holders, and ownership of them can be transferred as easily as ownership of a bank note; and partly because the interest on a Eurobond is always paid (on presentation of the coupon) without any deduction of tax.

There are three main types of Eurobond:

(1) straights: which carry a fixed-interest coupon and a fixed maturity date;
(2) floating rate notes (FRNs): which have an interest rate tied to an agreed (but fluctuating) international rate, usually the London interbank offered rate (LIBOR);
(3) convertibles: which are convertible to ordinary shares on the terms stated.

The *Financial Times* gives extensive coverage to this market on its International Capital Markets page. Its table of Eurobond prices is headed 'FT/ISMA International Bond Service'.

You can buy Eurobonds either through your stockbroker or your bank, but there will not be much enthusiasm on your intermediary's part unless you are investing at least £25,000 in this medium. Another point to consider is that you cannot always sell your Eurobonds when you want to, owing to illiquidity in the market resulting from the attitude of the main players in the market to such factors as currency fluctuations or even political uncertainty. On the positive side, however, for the private investor wishing to have a share of the action in Eurobonds, there are a number of offshore funds (see Chapter 17) specialising in collective Eurobond investment.

15.4   Corporate bonds

The relatively high rate of inflation in the United Kingdom throughout most of the post-war period has caused most private individuals to prefer company shares to bonds, whereas the opposite has been true in countries with historically low rates of inflation, such as Germany and Switzerland. This historical comparison of inflation rates is not so wide in recent years.

Companies issue two types of fixed-interest vehicles: debentures, which are backed by specific assets of the issuer; and loan stocks, some of which are secured while others are not. Corporate bonds offer a higher yield than gilts, because even a blue-chip company is considered riskier than the British government, but against this advantage it is not always as easy to sell corporate bonds back to the market as it is to dispose of gilts. The most convenient way to deal in corporate bonds is through a stockbroker, who will also be able to explain the pros and cons of certain special types of bond such as convertibles and deep discount bonds.

16   Direct investment in equities

16.1   Useful publications

The subject of direct investment in ordinary shares of quoted companies calls not so much for a separate chapter, but for an entire book, if not an encyclopaedia. And not surprisingly, several publishers have already answered that call. The *Investors Chronicle*, the FT's weekly magazine for stock-market enthusiasts, has issued a *Beginner's Guide to Investment* which is both very useful and goes well beyond the mere beginnings of the subject.

The *Allied Dunbar Investment and Savings Handbook*, already referred to in Chapter 13, contains a chapter on listed investments which not only reviews the highlights of the previous year's activity on the UK stock market, with brief references to other important markets round the world, but bravely previews some of the major probable trends in the year ahead. In the same chapter you will also find a detailed explanation of the actual mechanics of dealing on The Stock Exchange.

For investors interested in the strategy and tactics of stock market investment, it is difficult to think of a better book than Burton G Malkiel's modern classic *A Random Walk down Wall Street*, published also in London by W W Norton & Company. Although written primarily for US readers, this book contains a great deal of material of both theoretical and practical interest to investors in equities, wherever they may be. Mr Malkiel tends to take a sceptical view of technical systems and theories, and he stresses the overriding importance of the time element in stock-market investment. Indeed, he defines true investment, as distinct from speculation, as 'a method of purchasing assets in order to gain profit in the form of reasonably predictable income and/or (capital) appreciation over the long term'.

16.2   Individual investors: risks and potential advantages

In spite of the domination of nearly all the stock markets in the world, and certainly the major ones, by professional investors managing institutional funds, all the authors just mentioned express the view that there is still scope for the private individual investor. The editor's post-bag at *Resident Abroad* shows, too, that a great many expatriates are still interested in DIY equity investment, even though they may at the same time hold units in one or other type of investment fund. The well-known investment consultant Peter Doye has a regular column in the magazine intended for such expatriate investors.

It is true that the comparatively small individual investor has high costs in the way of brokerage charges and perhaps fees for ancillary services such as advice, and that the spread between the buying and selling prices of ordinary shares is such that their market price has to rise by 6 or 7 per cent (even more in the case of some of the smaller companies) before the investor can see a profit. But similar considerations apply to investment funds, which also charge annual management fees.

Some individual investors persist down the direct route into equities for the personal satisfaction or even excitement that cannot be experienced when your only stake is in a large pool of assets being managed not only on your behalf but on behalf of perhaps hundreds of other investors. A more important consideration with some individual investors, however, is this: a collective investment by definition spreads the risk, and thereby to some extent limits the possible reward, even if at the same time it limits the possible loss. Spread as a collective investment is across a number of securities, its performance will tend to be related more closely to the market or sector average than will the performance of a particular share. In other words, it is possible if you pick the shares of the right companies to make spectacular profits (and equally astonishing losses if you pick the wrong shares), which is hardly the case even with the highest performing collective funds.

Bernard Gray, in the *Beginner's Guide to Investment*, referred to at the beginning of the chapter, suggests other ways in which the private investor may have the edge over the professional: 'he does not have to produce quarterly figures showing his relative performance, as fund managers do. Nor does he have to remain in the market when he would sooner be out. He can buy shares because he genuinely likes their investment prospects, not because he fears being left behind by the market. And he can buy into all but the smallest companies without moving the market price to his disadvantage'. In spite of the professional's easy access to far more information about companies and markets than is normally available to the private individual, the private individual is sometimes able, by a mixture of common sense, lateral thinking, and a modicum of luck, to pick winners that the professionals miss. One expatriate investor of our acquaintance made a considerable fortune in this way. For example, when one national motorway building programme was getting under way he reasoned, ahead of the professionals, that road sign manufacturers would have a bonanza, and he was able to buy a fair stake in such a company before his and eventually other investors' shrewdness caused it to become a favourite. But here we must put in a word of warning. Playing the stock market in this way can easily be addictive, and grow from something akin to a hobby to a full-time occupation, if not an obsession.

There are between 40 and 50 national stock markets throughout the world, and new ones are established every year. Expatriates will probably have to be very well established in their host country before they deal on the local exchange. They are much more likely to deal through a London stockbroker or bank, through whom they will be able to buy most major stocks in the world. For less adventurous trading than this they will usually be better advised to consider a unit trust or offshore fund specialising in a particular national market, rather than dealing directly.

17 Collective investment vehicles

Pauline Skypala, Deputy Editor, Money Management

17.1 Introduction

Direct investment in the share, fixed-interest and currency markets is often not an option for expatriates, who do not always have the time or the information to run their own investment portfolios, even if they have the expertise and the inclination. And there are few investment managers who are prepared to undertake direct investment on behalf of anyone with less than around £250,000 to invest.

Instead, they advocate the use of collective investment vehicles such as investment trusts, unit trusts and offshore funds, all of which work on the same basic principle: a pooling of resources which enables small investors to participate in a professionally managed portfolio of shares, benefiting from a spread of risk that they could not achieve on their own. However, it is important to realise that you can still lose money—pooled funds do not protect you from a falling stock market.

The main differences between the various types of collective investment vehicle are related to structure, location and taxation. Offshore funds are generally recommended as the most appropriate vehicles for the expatriate investor, but there are also arguments in favour of using UK-based funds in some circumstances. But before reviewing the pros and cons of offshore and onshore funds, it is useful to examine their workings.

17.2 UK investment and unit trusts

17.2.1 UK investment trusts

These were the first pooled funds to be established, although they are probably the least familiar to the investing public. They are public companies, listed on The Stock Exchange, which invest in the shares of other companies in the United Kingdom and overseas. They are described as 'closed end', which means that there is a fixed number of shares in existence and the fund does not expand or contract. Unlike unit trusts, however, investment trusts are permitted to gear up their investments by borrowing.

Investment trusts offer a wide range of investment opportunities: there are general trusts with an international portfolio; specific geographic trusts covering the United Kingdom, North America, Japan, Europe, etc; trusts investing in specific industrial sectors, such as smaller companies, financial and property; trusts that invest for capital growth, and trusts that aim for a high income; plus specialist vehicles such as venture capital and split capital trusts which give the investor a choice between income shares, providing income throughout the life of the trust (usually eight to ten years), and capital shares, which pay out from the accumulated capital when the assets of the trust are eventually sold.

You can buy shares in an investment trust through a stockbroker, bank, building society or other share dealing service. Because of the minimum commission often charged on stock-market dealings, however, this method is mainly suitable for large share purchases. Smaller investors can use an investment trust savings and investment scheme. These allow the occasional investment of lump sums of just £250 plus, or a regular monthly investment of as little as £25. Charges vary, but are in most cases low, and in some cases nil. Most schemes also offer special selling arrangements which are often cheaper than the normal rate of broker's commission.

Annual management charges on investment trusts are also relatively low compared with those on other pooled investment schemes, averaging 0.5 per cent of assets under management.

The prices of investment trust shares are set by the stock market and are governed by the same laws of supply and demand which affect all share prices. The stockbroker's commission payable on purchase and sale of shares is usually 1 per cent, but there is also a 0.5 per cent stamp duty on the purchase of shares. But if shares are bought through an independent financial adviser, the commission is generally 3 per cent. Note that the share price may be at a premium or a discount to the net asset value (NAV) per share, which expresses the actual value of a trust's assets after the deduction of the value of its preference shares and all its liabilities.

If the share price is at a discount to the net asset value you are buying assets at a lower cost than you would pay if you bought them directly on

the stock market; if it is at a premium, you are paying more. Most investment trust shares trade at a discount.

17.2.2 UK unit trusts

These differ from investment trusts in being structured as trust funds
rather than investment companies, in which you buy units rather than
shares. They are 'open-ended', which means the managers can create or
redeem units to match demand, and must increase or reduce their shareholdings depending on whether money is coming in or going out of the
fund. Unit trusts are not usually quoted on the stock market.

You can buy units directly from the management companies, or through
an independent financial adviser. Prices are fixed by the managers in
accordance with rules specified by the Securities and Investments Board
(SIB) and reflect the value of the assets held. Two prices are given, an
offer price which includes the 'initial charge' you pay to buy units, which
is usually between 5 and 6 per cent; and the lower *bid price* for selling.
Annual management charges average 1.25 per cent. You can invest a
lump sum or use a savings plan to invest smaller amounts on a regular
basis. There is usually no extra charge involved in these plans.

Like investment trusts, unit trusts give you access to stock markets
around the world and to specialist investment sectors, including fixed-
interest and money market instruments.

Investments in unit trusts and investment trusts receive the same tax treatment. The funds themselves do not pay CGT on any profits they make,
but UK resident investors may be liable for the tax on any gains realised
when they sell if they are in excess of the annual allowance. Income distributions are paid effectively net of basic rate tax, ie with a tax credit.
Non-taxpayers may reclaim the amount credited.

17.3 Offshore funds

A fund is described as 'offshore' if it is incorporated in a low-tax financial
centre such as the Isle of Man, the Channel Islands, or Luxembourg, and
intended for use by non-residents of that jurisdiction. Such funds generally
pay little or nothing in the way of local taxes, although they may receive
dividends or interest net of withholding tax, depending on where and in
which instruments they invest. They are usually structured as open-ended
investment companies or unit trusts, able to issue and redeem their own
shares or units. Offshore fund prices reflect the value of the underlying

assets, but some funds work on a dual pricing system, quoting both an offer and a bid price, while others work on a single pricing system.

The charging structure of offshore funds is similar to that of UK unit trusts, with an initial charge of nil to 5 or 6 per cent, depending on the type of underlying investment, and an annual charge of 0.5 to 2 per cent, again varying with the type and location of a fund's holdings.

Offshore funds offer a wide choice of investment opportunities and management groups. They provide an investment route into virtually every stock market in the world, most freely exchangeable currencies, Eurobonds, government bonds, commodities, financial derivatives (futures, options and warrants), and even property. If you know which areas you want to invest in you can choose specific funds, or you can opt for an international fund where the investment decisions about which markets to go into are made by the managers.

Many offshore funds are set up as umbrella funds, which simply means that instead of running separate funds the managers run one inclusive fund split into a number of sub-funds. This offers advantages for the managers, mainly in the shape of more cost-efficient administration, and generally makes it easier and cheaper for investors to switch between different investment areas.

Some offshore funds distribute the income they earn on their investments, while others accumulate it within the fund. The latter type are often more convenient for expatriate investors, but may not be suitable if you are intending to return to the United Kingdom in the near future. This is because the tax treatment of offshore funds in the United Kingdom depends on whether the fund has distributor status or not. An investment in a fund with distributor status is taxed in the same way as a UK unit trust. But if you hold a fund without distributor status, you are liable for income tax on both the income from the fund and any capital gain you make on disposal.

Thus, investments in a non-distributor fund need to be sold during a period of non-residence, and unless you can be sure that you will be overseas for some years or that you will have the opportunity to sell your holding in a subsequent period of non-residence, it is sensible to opt for a distributor fund. Most such funds have a reinvestment facility for investors who do not want to receive dividends.

Do not assume that a fund which distributes its income automatically has distributor status. The majority do, but to be granted the status, they have to satisfy certain rules, the most important of which is that they distribute at least 85 per cent of the income earned on their investments.

The major centres for offshore funds are the Channel Islands, Luxembourg, Hong Kong, the Isle of Man, and to a growing extent, Ireland. Also notable are Bermuda and the Cayman Islands, and Gibraltar, too, is competing for offshore fund business. You will find that some funds are incorporated in one jurisdiction but administered and managed from another, usually for tax reasons. For example, a fund based in Bermuda may be run from Jersey, with investment advice coming from London. This is of little concern to investors as far as investment performance or taxation is concerned, but could affect whether or not they are covered by a compensation scheme.

Regulation in these centres is relatively good, having been tightened considerably in recent years in response to changes in the marketplace, such as the advent of the single European market for financial services, the introduction of the Financial Services Act in the United Kingdom, and various scandals—notably the collapse of the Savings & Investment Bank in the Isle of Man and the Barlow Clowes affair.

17.3.1 Ucits funds

The first two factors in particular have occasioned the introduction of different categories of funds, and although this has limited practical significance for the investor, the terminology can be confusing. One of the main distinctions to be aware of is that between so-called Ucits funds and other offshore funds. Ucits is shorthand for Undertaking for Collective Investment in Transferable Securities, and denotes an open-ended fund that has complied with certain requirements, laid down in a European Community Directive, which allow it to be marketed freely in all European Community countries, subject to local marketing regulations. But at present only funds that invest in equities and bonds are covered by the Directive, a proposed second Directive that would have embraced money market funds having been withdrawn by the EU Commission in March 1995.

Ucits funds have to be based in an EU member country, and most of the funds that have been set up specifically to take advantage of the single European market for financial services are based in Luxembourg, although Dublin is also becoming an important centre. However, it makes little difference to the investor whether or not a fund is a Ucits; the significance of a fund's status in this respect is mainly of interest to fund managers and financial advisers.

Other categories of funds you may come across also relate mainly to where the funds can be marketed. Jersey, Guernsey and the Isle of Man, for example, have two or three classifications which funds can slot into, depending on whether or not the managers want to market them in the United Kingdom. There are no Ucits funds in these three centres, as they are all outside the EU for most purposes (with the exception of the free movement of industrial and agricultural goods). But to enable fund managers to promote their products to UK investors, the Channel Islands and the Isle of Man (and Bermuda) applied to become designated territories under the UK Financial Services Act. This entailed providing investor protection at least equivalent to the cover given to investors in UK unit trusts, and to comply with this all the islands set up compensation schemes.

All recognised or authorised class funds in the islands are covered by the schemes. But this by no means includes all the funds based in the islands, so it is wise to check if you want to know for certain whether you are covered by a compensation scheme.

17.3.2   Advantages of offshore funds

The main attractions of offshore funds are their freedom from tax, the confidentiality factor, and the wide range of investments they offer, including currency funds which are not available at all onshore.

Where offshore funds really score on the tax front is on the income side, as they are able to pay the investor an income from investments in instruments such as Eurobonds, deposits, and exempt gilts without the deduction of any tax. In contrast, investors in UK gilt, fixed-interest and money market funds receive income payments net of 25 per cent tax. As a result, fixed-interest and money market funds comprise a significant proportion of the offshore funds available and are widely used by expatriates.

When it comes to investment for capital growth, however, there is little difference between offshore funds and UK unit or investment trusts in terms of tax: they all accumulate investment profits free of CGT. Whether the income and capital gains earned on offshore fund investments remain tax free in the hands of the investor obviously depends on where he is resident when he receives them.

If tax is not the deciding factor in using offshore funds, the scales may be tipped in their favour by other considerations, in particular the currency factor, which plays an important role in the financial affairs of expatriate investors. All UK pooled funds are denominated in sterling regardless of where they invest, whereas offshore funds are frequently denominated in the currency of their main investment area. Thus, North American funds are quoted in dollars, Far East funds in Hong Kong dollars or Japanese yen, and European funds in deutschemarks or Swiss francs.

In addition to providing currency exposure in this way, offshore funds also offer a means of investing in foreign currency deposits and bonds. These funds are available either on a managed basis, where the managers make the investment decisions about which currencies to hold, or on an individual currency basis where the individual decides on the currency mix. The advantage such funds offer over using bank deposits to hold foreign currency is that they give smaller investors access to money market rates of interest.

17.3.3   Disadvantages of offshore funds

There are few real disadvantages to using offshore funds, although some commentators maintain that if you are planning to return to the United Kingdom, it makes life simpler if you stick to UK funds. There is no question then of having to sell your investment at an inopportune moment to avoid unwelcome tax consequences on your return to the United Kingdom, as you might have to if you have any non-distributor funds in your portfolio. Many expatriates prefer to keep their investments outside the United Kingdom while they are non-resident, however, and the simplest way to avoid any tax complications with offshore funds is to make sure you invest only in funds with distributor status.

Another worry with offshore funds is regulation. A widely held view is that offshore fund groups are not as tightly regulated as UK fund groups. There is some substance in this, but as noted above, Ucits, recognised and authorised funds are all allowed to be sold to UK residents, and should therefore be subject to the same degree of regulation by the appropriate authorities. If you are concerned about this aspect of using offshore funds, it is as well to restrict your choice to funds of this type. The other safeguard is to use only funds run by big international groups or by fund managers that are well known in the United Kingdom.

It is sometimes suggested that offshore funds tend to perform less well than UK funds, owing to a combination of higher charges and lower quality investment management. But while it is the case that offshore funds do carry slightly higher charges on average than unit trusts, this is unlikely to have a significant effect on performance. Moreover, the charge that offshore funds do not receive the same attention as a group's UK funds is difficult to prove, and one that many groups keen to earn a good reputation for investment performance on an international stage would doubtless contend.

There is no consistent statistical evidence to support the contention that UK funds are the better performers, and comparisons are in any case questionable because of the currency factor. Much depends on which currency you use to measure performance: a fund denominated in US dollars investing in the United States may look lacklustre compared with a similar vehicle valued in sterling if the pound has fallen against the dollar over the investment period.

17.3.4 How to invest in offshore funds

You can invest in an offshore fund either by contacting the managers directly or via your financial adviser. Many investment managers will run a portfolio of offshore funds for you, or you can put together your own. Some fund managers will accept only lump sum investments, but quite a few also offer a non-contractual regular savings scheme.

You can check the prices of offshore funds in the *Financial Times*, which carries listings every day. The paper lists funds by area and according to whether they are SIB recognised, regulated or other. SIB recognised funds are those which are allowed to be marketed to the general public in the United Kingdom, such as Ucits funds. Regulated funds are those which are not SIB recognised but are regulated by the authorities of the jurisdiction in which they are based. Funds categorised as 'other' are mostly based in jurisdictions such as Hong Kong, the Cayman Islands, the Bahamas, etc, which are neither EU member states nor designated territories under the Financial Services Act. Note that addresses are given only for the managers of SIB recognised funds.

Performance figures for offshore funds are carried in specialist magazines such as *Resident Abroad*, the *International* and *Investment International*. When choosing an offshore fund or fund group, look for consistent performers rather than chart toppers. Ideally, you should select funds run by management groups that can produce above-average performance across the whole range of their funds. This is particularly important if you opt to use an umbrella fund, as you are then relying solely on the investment expertise of one group, and there are only a few that are equally good in all investment sectors.

18 Life assurance

Peter Ashton, Operations Manager, Allied Dunbar International Assurance Ltd

18.1 Introduction

A life assurance policy is a contract between individual policyholders and a life assurance company. The life company maintains the underlying investment funds in its own right but, depending on the nature of the policy, it undertakes to pay the policyholder either a specified sum, or a sum which is increased periodically out of the profits of the company, or one which varies from time to time with the value of that part of the underlying fund 'earmarked' for that particular investor. One of the most important characteristics of the life assurance policy as an investment vehicle, is that it does not produce an income (which would, of course, be exposed to taxation) but is essentially a medium- to long-term accumulator.

Naturally, all life assurance policies provide life cover—a sum assured payable upon death. Most policies, other than temporary assurances, usually also provide investment benefits—sums payable on surrender or maturity of the policy. Life assurance policies may be divided into three categories depending upon the emphasis that is placed on savings or on protection (life cover):

(1)   An endowment policy: has a high savings element and is one under which the benefits are payable at the end of the predetermined period (the endowment term) or on death, if earlier.

(2)   A whole of life policy: one under which the benefits are in general payable on death, whenever it occurs.

(3)   A term policy: a temporary assurance, the sum assured being paid only if death occurs within a specified period.

Term assurances are used entirely for protection against financial hardship on death and will not be considered further here.

18.2   Three types of contract

Within the endowment and whole of life categories the life policies can be one of three different types, depending on the way in which the sums payable by the company are determined:

(1)   With profit contracts are policies under which a minimum sum is guaranteed to be paid by the life company on certain specified events, augmented from time to time by bonuses declared by the company according to its profits. These bonuses may be reversionary (bonuses added to the sum assured, either yearly or triennially) or terminal (bonuses declared at the end of the policy as an increment to the final payment).

(2)   Without profit contracts are policies under which the life company guarantees, on certain specified events, to pay an absolute sum and invests the premiums in such a way as to produce that sum, bearing any shortfall in the return or retaining any profit in excess of the guaranteed return.

(3)   Under unit-linked contracts the life company maintains an underlying fund, which is divided, for accounting purposes, into 'units' and undertakes to pay to the policyholder an amount equal to the greater of any guaranteed sum and the value of the units allocated to the policy. The underlying fund might consist of specific types of investment media (such as property, equities, unit trusts, investment trusts, government securities, local authority and bank loans or deposits, or building society deposits) or the fund may consist of a combination of some or all of these ('managed' or 'mixed' funds).

A life company generally has full investment freedom as to the type of investments it chooses, subject only to the investment being a suitable 'match' for its liabilities. In the case of unit-linked policies, the Insurance Company Regulations permit linkage only to certain types of assets, such as those listed above. If the contract is one which incorporates a guaranteed maturity value, the investor knows that he will get at least that sum. At the same time, in the case of with profit policies, he has the advantage of having the guaranteed sum augmented from time to time by reversionary and terminal bonuses. With unit-linked contracts, the value is augmented by the movement of the value of the underlying fund (capital appreciation plus reinvested income).

Life policies can be subdivided into two main types depending upon how the premiums are payable:

(1)   Regular premium policies are those under which premiums are payable annually, half-yearly, quarterly or monthly, either through-

out the duration of the policy or for a limited premium-paying period. This type of policy is suitable for the regular saver, probably investing out of income, who is looking to amass a capital sum for the future.

(2) Single premium policies, generally known as single premium bonds. For many years these have been, in the main, unit-linked policies often marketed as property bonds, managed bonds, equity bonds, etc by reference to the initial underlying fund to which the policy was linked.

The main investment characteristic of single premium unit-linked bonds is the high allocation of the premium to investment in the underlying fund, with relatively low life cover. Virtually the entire premium is allocated to 'units', save only for the initial management charges, resulting, in effect, in the investment of most of the premium in the chosen fund. Most companies offer a wide choice of unit funds for the bond linkage.

Subsequently, at no cost or for a small administrative charge, the policyholder may switch his investment to one or more of the other funds and is thereby entitled to select a fund which reflects his own view of market conditions. Switching does not amount to a realisation for tax purposes, which is an important investment advantage.

Most unit-linked single premium bonds allow the investor the right to make regular or irregular withdrawals by way of partial surrender to serve as an income. The same result can be achieved by splitting the investment into a number of smaller policies and encashing individual policies in full from time to time.

18.3 Offshore single premium bonds

These follow the basic concept of the UK single premium bond and are normally issued by offshore-based insurance companies with UK parentage. The attraction of these bonds, especially for the expatriate, is the tax treatment of the underlying fund, which (with the exception of some withholding taxes deducted at source by certain countries) grow free of tax.

18.4 Portfolio bonds

These are developments of the offshore single premium bond, which gives the investor the choice of including a wide range of assets within the bond. They were designed for the substantial investor who wants to benefit from the favourable tax treatment of an offshore bond while being able to exercise choice in the management of the underlying assets.

18.5   The UK taxation of offshore single premium bonds

Offshore single premium bonds are subject to their own particular income tax rules which can, in certain circumstances, produce a liability to income tax for the UK resident bondholder, both at basic rate and higher rate. Age allowance too may be affected if a gain or excess occurs.

If the bondholder has cashed in the bond at a profit or makes a partial withdrawal which is in excess of 5 per cent of the original contribution there may be a liability to tax. A potential liability to income tax arises whenever a chargeable event occurs. Chargeable events are:

- the surrender of a bond (where surrender is the total encashment of the bond) or the encashment of any of the individual contracts within the bond;
- amounts withdrawn in a policy year in excess of the cumulative 5 per cent allowance;
- death of the life assured, or the last survivor, in the case of joint life bonds;
- the sale of a bond (ie an assignment for money or money's worth).

In each case there may be a liability to basic rate tax. Higher rate tax will also be payable if the bondholder is already paying higher rate tax or if their taxable income including the gain or excess brings them into the higher rate tax bracket (although they may benefit from 'top-slicing' relief).

18.5.1   Calculation of tax (for gains excesses)

A special tax relief (called 'top-slicing') exists for UK taxpayers if the receipt of a gain or excess from a bond would cause them to move from the basic rate tax band (currently 25 per cent) into a higher rate tax band. Top-slicing has the effect of reducing the amount of gain or excess which is taxed at the higher rate. Where individuals are higher rate taxpayers before the gain or excess is included in their taxable income, the relief does not apply.

18.5.2   Non-residence

If the bondholder has been non-UK resident while owning the bond but subsequently becomes UK resident then the chargeable gain realised while UK resident will be reduced by a fraction relating to the number of years the bondholder has been UK resident and the number of years the bond has been held.

18.5.3 Portfolio bonds

The description of the UK taxation of offshore single premium bonds applies to portfolio bonds which invest in the pooled life funds offered by offshore-based insurance companies.

Portfolio bonds invested in assets chosen and managed specifically by the investor may, under some circumstances, be treated as a 'highly personalised investment vehicle' for income tax purposes by the Inland Revenue under the Taxes Act 1988, s 739. UK residents contemplating investing in such bonds are strongly advised to seek expert tax advice.

19 Pensions

Debbie Harrison, Pension Provision in Europe (a Financial Times Management Report)

Pension planning is one of the more complex areas of personal finance for the British expatriate, and it is a topic that should form part of a comprehensive financial review, rather than be treated in isolation. A point of particular importance is the impact of pension arrangements on the expatriate's position regarding taxation.

In this chapter we aim to provide a basic guide to successful pension planning to two broad categories of expatriate: the employee going overseas on a long-term assignment, and the pensioner planning to spend his or her retirement abroad. We conclude the chapter with a list of useful addresses for those readers who wish to find out more about their current pension options.

19.1 Employees

Pension planning for employees should always start with a detailed analysis of existing provision. This rule applies to everyone, and not just to expatriates, because it is only when the basic building blocks are identified and evaluated that it is possible to fill gaps in provision and plan for the future.

There are three main sources of pension in the United Kingdom and throughout most of the western world:

(1)   state schemes;
(2)   occupational schemes; and
(3)   private plans.

While the same three pillars of pension provision can be recognised in other countries outside the United Kingdom, the emphasis between them varies considerably. For example: in the United Kingdom, employees and the self-employed derive the largest proportion of their total pension from occupational schemes and private plans, whereas in Italy and France and many other countries state schemes provide virtually all of an individual's pension in retirement. In most EU member states, for instance, private individual plans are rare.

19.2 State pensions

Many expatriates ignore their state pension on the misguided assumption that it does not apply to persons with a peripatetic life-style who are also often highly paid. It is true that the UK state pension is not particularly generous—certainly not in comparison with other EU countries—but it forms, nevertheless, a reliable inflation-linked element in an individual's total retirement income.

Few financial advisers fully understand the vagaries of the UK state pension system, and where the eventual pension will be drawn from several sources in different countries, it is vital for the individual to keep a good record of contributions paid and benefits due.

In the United Kingdom the state pension consists of two elements—a basic or 'old age' pension and an earnings-related pension. The full rate of the basic pension for the 1995/96 tax year is £58.85 per week for a single person. Eligibility to the basic pension depends on an individual's National Insurance Contribution (NIC) record.

National Insurance is a form of taxation, and for most employees it is levied at 2 per cent on earnings up to the so-called 'lower earnings limit' and 10 per cent on earnings between the lower and upper earnings limits. These earnings limits are, respectively, £58 and £440 per week for the 1995/96 tax year.

To qualify for the top rate of pension it is necessary to have paid NICs for a full working career of between 35 and 40 years. Where an individual has less than a full contribution record a proportion of the pension is paid. Women who have not paid enough NICs to entitle them to a pension in their own right can claim a Category B pension under their husband's contributions.

The Category B pension is paid only when the husband reaches state pension age of 65, and not when the wife reaches the state pension age which currently is 60 but will rise to 65 during the phased period from 2010 to 2020.

(This will not affect women currently over age 45/46. Those currently aged between 40 and 45 will have a retirement date fixed between 60 and 65 depending on their date of birth. Women currently under 40 will retire at 65.) The Category B pension, which is worth £35.25 per week for the 1995/96 tax year, is added to the husband's single person's pension of £58.85 to give what is known as the married couple's pension, currently worth £94.10.

If a woman is entitled to a small proportion of the basic pension in her own right she can claim this from age 60. Where the Category B pension is worth more, this will be paid when her husband reaches age 65. It is important to remember that the Category B pension replaces and is not paid in addition to the earlier pension.

Women currently under 40 with a full NIC record should note that they will have to work and pay NICs for an extra five years to age 65 in order to qualify for the full state pension. Women between age 40 and 45 should check with the DSS the exact date they will be able to claim their state pension.

The second element of the state pension is known as the Additional Pension or Serps—the State Earnings Related Pension Scheme. Employees automatically belong to Serps if they are not contracted out via an occupational scheme or an 'appropriate' personal pension.

The Social Security Act 1986 reduced the Serps pension for those who retire after the end of the century. Under the original terms of Serps, which was introduced in 1978, the maximum pension was 25 per cent of band earnings assessed over the individual's best 20 years of earnings. However, after 6 April 2000, the 25 per cent maximum will be reduced over a period of ten years to 20 per cent. Also the 'best 20 years' basis of assessment will be replaced by average band earnings over a lifetime. This means that all periods of employment, including periods of low earnings, will be taken into consideration. The overall effect will be to reduce the value of the pension—an important factor for those who expect to rely heavily on their Serps pension.

Few people have a clear idea of what their state pension may be worth. However, the Department of Social Security (DSS) operates a useful pensions forecast service. For details see the contacts list at the end of this chapter.

Fortunately, in most cases, it is possible to continue to build up state retirement benefits when you work abroad. But the rules vary according to the country of employment and the nature of the social security agreement between the foreign country and the United Kingdom.

19.3   EU Multilateral Agreement

The EU, for example, operates the Multilateral Agreement on Social Security. This came into effect following the Treaty of Rome in 1958 which established what used to be called the European Community. Under the agreement, a UK national can work in different EU countries and continue to build up a right to a state pension from each country through the payment of local national insurance contributions. On retirement the individual can retire anywhere in the Union and draw a pension based on the total number of years worked within the EU.

Under normal circumstances an individual who works abroad would pay local national insurance automatically. There are exceptions to this rule, however: for example, where the period of employment is expected to last less than one year. In this case the individual is retained in the UK social security scheme. Occasionally this period can be extended, but this is rare.

The important feature about the Multilateral Agreement is that it allows employees to aggregate the number of contribution years built up throughout the Union in order to claim a proportion of the state pension in each country of employment. The reason for this feature is that different countries have different qualifying periods for the state pension. For example, in the United Kingdom you have to pay NICs for about ten years before you qualify for a proportion of the basic state pension, although under Serps a benefit is earned from day one. In Italy and Spain, the qualifying period is 15 years, so without the agreement an individual could work for ten years in each of these two countries and not have a right to a state pension.

Under the Multilateral Agreement a pension will be paid from each country of employment provided the *total number* of years worked in the Union exceeds the *minimum qualifying period* in each member state.

On retirement, the pensions are claimed from the relevant country and usually they are paid in the local currency. This means that the pension can be subject to currency fluctuations. Each element of the pension is subject to the annual increases applied by the relevant country. Normally the separate pensions are claimed from each member state but they can be claimed through one source, for example through the equivalent of the DSS in the country of retirement.

The Multilateral Agreement makes no allowance for the fact that different pension ages operate in different member states. This means that a woman currently can draw her UK state pension from age 60, but will not be able to draw a state pension from Germany until she is 65 and from Denmark until she is 67. Most EU countries have equalised the state pension or, like the United Kingdom, have announced the date when this will come into force.

19.4 Occupational pensions

In the United Kingdom approved occupational schemes and private plans are the most tax-efficient method of saving for retirement. Employees and the self-employed get full tax relief on contributions (within Inland Revenue limits), while the funds themselves grow free of income tax and CGT. Moreover, part of the eventual fund can be taken as tax-free cash, although the rest must be taken as pension and is taxed as income.

It is important to bear in mind these tax advantages when considering alternative options. But it is equally important to remember that under an approved UK pension the benefits cannot be taken before age 50 at the very earliest, and for most occupational schemes the normal retirment age is 65.

19.5 Retention in home scheme

Many people who work abroad are seconded by a UK employer and can be retained in the UK company's pension scheme. While the employee may not be able to pay into the scheme if there are no UK earnings, it may be possible for the employer to continue contributions. Because of the tax advantages noted above retention in the home scheme is usually the best option. The normal limit on home country scheme membership for overseas secondment is ten years. The arrangement must be approved by the Pension Schemes Office (PSO), a department of the Inland Revenue.

Where it is not practical or possible to stay in the UK company scheme, the employer should make some provision for pension within the salary package. This should at least match the benefits of the main company scheme.

19.6 Final salary

Most company schemes in the United Kingdom operate on what is known as a final salary or defined benefit basis. This means that for every year of service the employee earns a proportion of his or her final salary up to a maximum pension of two-thirds final salary. The most common pattern is to build up a pension at the rate of $\frac{1}{60}$ of final salary for each year of service up to a maximum after 40 years of two-thirds (ie $\frac{40}{60}$ths) of final salary.

This type of pension offers a valuable hedge against inflation since the pension is linked to the employee's final salary which, under normal circumstances, can be expected to outstrip the Retail Price Index (RPI).

19.7   Money purchase

Some schemes offer what are known as money purchase pensions. Under a money purchase pension, contributions are invested to provide a fund at retirement which is used to buy an annuity from an insurance company which, in return for the lump sum investment, guarantees to pay the investor an income for life. This means that the retirement income is dependent on the investment performance of the fund, the charges deducted by the provider, and the annuity rate—that is the income the investor can secure with the fund—at the time of retirement.

Investment performance varies considerably from company to company and annuity rates fluctuate in line with the yields on long-dated gilts— the investments insurance companies buy to back the annuity guarantees. This does not necessarily mean that money purchase is a poor alternative to final salary, but it does place more emphasis on the careful choice of pension provider and the level of contributions. Both employers and employees should seek expert help before choosing a money purchase pension. This should be done with the help of a pensions adviser.

Where an employee is retained in his or her UK company scheme it is important to examine the tax consequences. Many foreign tax authorities will regard the contributions paid by the UK employer as additional salary and will tax these contributions as income.

19.8   Personal pensions

Personal pensions were introduced in the United Kingdom in 1988, and allow employees to contract out of Serps on an individual basis, in addition to making contributions within certain Inland Revenue limits. Unfortunately, it is not possible to continue to pay into a personal pension plan from abroad unless there is a source of UK earned income on which contributions can be based.

If you are planning to go abroad in the near future and would like to take out a personal pension in the meantime then choose the plan carefully. Many people fall into the trap of setting up a monthly premium personal pension plan only to find that there is a hefty financial penalty when it is no longer possible to keep up the payments.

Any planned future changes of employment status should be discussed with a qualified adviser at the outset, so that a suitably flexible plan is selected. If in doubt, it is always sensible to make pension contributions on a single premium basis rather than on a regular basis such as a monthly or annual plan. This avoids any lock-in situation where early termination penalties might apply.

19.9 Pension options abroad

19.9.1 Foreign employer's scheme

If it is necessary to leave the UK company pension scheme when you go abroad it is important to investigate the pensions options available overseas. The most attractive option is likely to be to join the foreign company's pension scheme, as this will probably include the advantage of employer contributions in addition to the employee's own contributions. As in the United Kingdom, most countries award tax relief on contributions to approved pension schemes—an important consideration if you are paying local taxes.

However, there are circumstances when it might not be advisable to join the foreign company's scheme. For example, rather as with state pension schemes, in many countries it is necessary to work for several years before you have what is known as a 'vested right'. The vesting period refers to the number of years you need to be in a company pension scheme before you become entitled to a preserved pension or transfer value when you leave.

A preserved pension is the pension benefit you leave behind in a former employer's scheme. The benefit, which cannot be drawn until retirement, builds up at a modest rate within the scheme. This pension benefit in most cases can be transferred to another scheme (see **19.11**). However, if you leave before the vesting period is completed, you can end up with nothing to show for your contributions.

In the United Kingdom, employees are entitled to a preserved pension after two years. If an employee leaves a company scheme before then all he or she is entitled to is a return of employee contributions (but not the employer's). Moreover, a deduction is made for back payments into Serps for that period of employment, and on top of this a deduction is made for tax.

The United Kingdom is quite lenient, however, in its vesting rules. In Belgium, for example, the vesting period is five years, while in other countries it is necessary to work for 15 years or more before earning the right to a preserved pension.

19.9.2   Individual plans

Where the foreign employer does not offer a company pension scheme or it is inappropriate to join—perhaps because the job is expected to last for just a few years—the next best choice would be a local private individual plan. The foreign equivalent to personal pensions can be a good choice particularly if contributions attract tax relief at the individual's highest marginal rate. But it is worth noting that the United Kingdom is more advanced in its private pensions market than many other countries.

In the United States and Australia similar plans to UK personal pensions are available, but in the EU the personal pensions market is underdeveloped. This is mainly because the combination of state and occupational schemes provides a very high level of benefit and there is no need for other types of pension.

Some countries are beginning to develop an individual pensions market in a bid to switch part of the burden of pension provision from the state to the private sector. This is essential if countries are to come to terms with the cost of state schemes as the number of elderly people claiming benefits rises and the number of workers contributing to the schemes falls.

The other point to note about an individual plan is that it may not provide the important fringe benefits that a good company scheme offers, such as death benefits and widows' and dependants' pensions. Most company schemes also offer good private medical and long-term disability insurance. If you have to go it alone, make sure your insurance policies cover these important requirements.

19.10   Offshore pensions

Owing to the inflexibility associated with some foreign pension schemes, many expatriates, and particularly those who are constantly on the move, prefer the idea of an offshore pension fund which can be built up from wherever the employment takes place.

Offshore pensions broadly divide into two categories, namely the employer-sponsored offshore trusts, and the individual plans sold by the offshore arms of UK and other European insurance companies.

19.10.1 Employer-sponsored offshore trust

By far the best arrangement is the employer-sponsored offshore trust. This type of arrangement is commonly used by the large multinationals which need to provide a top-quality pensions package to their expatriate executives.

Offshore pension trusts can be tailored to meet the specific needs of the employees. They can cater, for example, for an earlier retirement age than the company's main pension scheme—an essential feature for those expatriates who spend their working lives in a highly stressful or dangerous environment or in an unpleasant climate.

The trusts are established in a suitable offshore location. United Kingdom employers tend to prefer the Channel Islands, American companies opt for Bermuda and the Caribbean, German companies go for Liechtenstein or Luxembourg, while for historical reasons the Dutch prefer Curaçao.

Provided the offshore location offers a strong regulatory environment and the services necessary to operate a pension trust, few problems should arise. From the employee's point of view, however, it is essential to have a secure contract setting out the pension benefits in detail. This is important because a pension promise, which is simply a verbal agreement to the employee that the pension will be no less than that provided by the main company scheme, can prove worthless if the company is taken over or if the employee leaves under awkward circumstances.

19.10.2 Individual offshore plans

The scope for good quality offshore individual pension plans is limited, although for the UK expatriate there is a thriving market of offshore insurance companies, based in the Channel Islands and Isle of Man, that offer a range of financial products. Some of these are designed to mirror pension plans in the United Kingdom, but they should never be confused with the real article. The important point to remember with this type of policy is that it simply cannot mirror the tax advantages of an onshore, Revenue-approved UK pension plan, but some plans do offer limited tax advantages and can be transferred to a UK plan if the expatriate returns home.

There is not space here to undertake a detailed analysis of each product, but it is worth pointing out that many offshore plans used for the pensions market are based on ten-year maximum investment plans (MIP) and commit the individual to a long period of regular contributions. If an MIP is selected it is important to check what charges are imposed if, for example, the overseas secondment is terminated early.

Expatriates interested in an individual offshore plan suitable for retirement planning should consult a reputable firm of financial advisers specialising in expatriate tax and pension planning. A contact for offshore providers is given at the end of the chapter.

For many expatriates, particularly those on short-term secondment overseas, the most sensible route to retirement planning is to opt for a mixture of offshore investments which provide flexibility and good long-term growth prospects.

19.11   Transfers

So far we have dealt with current and future pension planning. But, it is equally important to consider the pension benefits built up before the individual goes overseas. There are several options for individuals who leave behind a preserved pension when they go overseas, but it must be stressed that the whole issue of pension transfers is fraught with difficulty and calls for the expertise of a professional tax or actuarial adviser.

Cash refund
Where membership of the UK company pension scheme was for less than two years, it is possible to get a cash refund of employee contributions less certain deductions for tax and back payments into Serps.

Preserved pension
In many cases the best option where the pension benefit is substantial is to leave it where it is and to draw a pension from this source in retirement. Before this decision can be made it is important to get a pensions expert to analyse what the former employer's scheme provides in the way of annual increases—both compulsory and discretionary—and dependants' benefits such as widows' and children's pensions.

A foreign company transfer
If the foreign employer has a pension scheme it is possible in certain circumstances to transfer the value of the UK scheme into the new scheme. This would need careful consideration to ensure that the benefits guar-

anteed in the new scheme were roughly equal to the benefits being given up in the old scheme. Transfers to foreign schemes are dealt with by the Pension Schemes Office and are permitted only in certain cases. This option is worth considering only where the employee intends to remain abroad and stay with the same company for a long period.

A UK personal pension or buy-out bond

If for some reason an expatriate does not want to leave their pension in a former employer's scheme it may be worth considering transferring the benefit out of the former employer's scheme and into a personal pension or buy-out bond, both of which are sold by insurance companies, although in the case of personal pensions other financial institutions such as unit trust groups, banks and building societies also offer products. In some cases such a transfer will yield better results, but it is essential that a pensions expert checks all other options first. This will require a detailed knowledge of the former employer's scheme.

Foreign individual plans

As mentioned above, a growing number of countries now offer an individual personal pension option. Transfers to individual plans overseas are rare, but in special circumstances can be authorised by the overseas branch of the Pension Schemes Office.

19.12   Retiring abroad

For many individuals the prospect of becoming expatriate does not arise until after retirement. In these circumstances pension planning centres around how to get your various pensions sent to your overseas address without incurring any double taxation penalties.

British state pensions can be claimed from anywhere in the world. However, the amount payable is frozen at the date the individual leaves the United Kingdom and cost-of-living increases are paid only if the individual retires to an EU country or to one of the countries with which the United Kingdom has a social security agreement which includes an uprating agreement (see Table **19.1**). This means that if you move to Australia or New Zealand, for example, you will not receive the annual increases. Without these increases the value of the pension will rapidly erode. The only good news is that if you subsequently return to the United Kingdom, your pension will be restored to its full current value.

Company pensions in the United Kingdom can be paid to virtually any address abroad with little difficulty. But to avoid the blow of double taxation it is necessary to obtain a declaration from the foreign tax authority stating that you are resident and being taxed on your worldwide income in that country. This must be sent as soon as possible to your UK tax inspector. Without this certificate the UK Inland Revenue will impose a withholding tax of 25 per cent on all pension payments, although this should be repaid once the certificate is through.

The same principles apply to private plans in the United Kingdom, including annuities purchased with retirement annuity pensions, the precursor to personal pensions, and personal plans.

Table 19.1   Countries with which the United Kingdom has a social security agreement to pay the state pension

Australia(1)	Gibraltar	Netherlands
Austria	Guernsey	New Zealand(1)
Barbados	Iceland	Norway
Belgium	Ireland	Philippines
Bermuda	Isle of Man	Portugal
Bosnia-Herzegovina(2)	Israel	Slovinia(2)
Canada(1)	Italy	Spain
Croatia(2)	Jamaica	Sweden
Cyprus	Jersey	Switzerland
Denmark	Luxembourg	Turkey
Finland	Macedonia(2)	USA
France	Malta	Yugoslavia (Serbia
Germany	Mauritius	and Montenegro)

(1)   No uprating agreement–pensions will be frozen if paid to these and any other country not included in the table.

(2)   The independent states of Bosnia-Herzegovina, Croatia, Macedonia and Slovinia have been formally recognised by the United Kingdom and all have confirmed to the UK government that they will honour the terms of all the treaties between the former Federal Republic of Yugoslavia and the United Kingdom including the social security agreement.

Table 19.2 State pension ages in the European Union

	Men	*Women*
Belgium(1)	65	65
Denmark(2)	67	67
France(3)	65	65
Germany(4)	65	65
Greece(5)	65	60/65
Ireland	65	65
Italy(6)	60	55
Luxembourg	65	65
Netherlands	65	65
Portugal(7)	65	62
Spain	65	65
UK(8)	65	60/65

Note: The ages shown assume the individual has completed the qualifying period of residence and/or contribution. In some countries earlier claims are possible.

(1) For Belgium, the full pension builds up over 45 years for men and 40 for women. A flexible age for retirement operates between 60 and 65.
(2) Partial and temporary retirement possible from age 60.
(3) Early retirement on reduced pension possible from age 60.
(4) Early retirement on full pension possible from age 63 but this will be phased out by 2011.
(5) For employees starting work after 1 January 1993, a common retirement age of 65 is applicable.
(6) For Italy, the pension ages shown are for the main system (INPS). Low retirement ages are being increased gradually to 65 (men) and 60 (women).
(7) A recent draft law proposed to raise the pension age for women to 65.
(8) Phased increase in the female retirement age to 65 to commence 2010.

Source: *Derived from statistics compiled by Sedgwick Noble Lowndes, R Watson & Sons and The Wyatt Company*

19.13 Useful addresses

The leaflets NI 106 *Pensioners or widows going abroad* and NI 38 *Social Security Abroad* may be obtained from local DSS offices.

For further information write to:

Department of Social Security
Overseas Benefits Directorate
Payments Group
Longbenton
Newcastle-upon-Tyne
NE98 1YX

Or telephone one of the following numbers:

(0191) 225 7341
(0191) 225 3002
(0191) 225 7431
(0191) 225 3310

State pensions forecast

To get an idea of the value of his future state pension, the expatriate should ask the local DSS for the pension forecast form BR 19.

If you have difficulty tracing your pension with a former employer contact:

The Occupational Pensions Board, Pension Schemes Registry
PO Box 1NN
Newcastle-upon-Tyne
NE99 1NN
Tel: (0191) 225 6393/6394

Pension complaints initially should be put in writing to the scheme manager, trustees or provider. The next step, if you are dissatisfied with the response, is to contact the Occupational Pensions Advisory Service (OPAS) preferably through the local Citizens Advice Bureau. OPAS can also be contacted direct at:

11 Belgrave Road
London
SW1V 1RB
Tel: (0171) 233 8080
Fax: (0171) 233 8016

For information on offshore products contact:

The Association of International Life Offices
Secretariat
PO Box 22
LS201
Sandweiler
Grand Duchy of Luxembourg
Tel: 00352 442659
Fax: 00352 442674

An independent survey of international life assurance products marketed via Jersey, Guernsey and the Isle of Man is available from consulting actuaries Bacon & Woodrow. The survey costs £250. For further information and to obtain a copy of the survey contact Ian Morris on the number given below or write to:

> Bacon & Woodrow
> Albert House
> South Esplanade
> St Peter Port
> Guernsey
> Channel Islands GY1 1AW
> Tel: 01481 728432
> Fax: 01481 724082

There is no specific organisation that list financial advisers who specialise in expatriate pensions but most firms of consulting actuaries would be able to give advice on this topic.

Contact:

> The Association of Consulting Actuaries (ACA)
> No 1 Wardrobe Place
> London EC4V 5AH
> Tel: (0171) 248 3163
> Fax: (0171) 236 1899

20 Coping with exchange rate movements

Howard Flight, Managing Director, Guinness Flight Global Asset Management Ltd

20.1 Exchange rates and cash: managed currency funds

Especially at times when equity markets have to be approached cautiously, many investors are concerned with managing liquid assets of one kind or another. International investors, including expatriates, must take particular account of the impact of exchange rate movements. But more and more investors are coming to realise that cash (liquidity) investment (in the form of bank deposits or so-called 'financial paper', ie readily negotiable financial instruments) on an international basis represents a major investment opportunity in its own right.

International investment in a managed spread of currencies is the logical approach for multicurrency cash investment, and the managed currency fund was pioneered for this objective by Guinness Flight in 1980. Investors buy shares or units in a fund whose liquid assets are invested in a managed spread normally of the three main currencies or currency blocs identified in the previous chapter, or their component currencies. The spread is changed over a period of time in accordance with the fund managers' assessment of expected exchange rate movements. For each particular currency, assets are held in a mixture of bank deposits, certificates of deposit, floating exchange rate notes and, in some cases where interest rates appear likely to fall, in fixed-interest securities. In broad terms, the investment strategy is to invest in a diversified portfolio of the currencies that are relatively undervalued in terms of economic fundamentals and entering, or soon to enter, bull market cycles, and to avoid undue exposure to currencies that are either in mature bull market cycles or in a phase of long-term declining trend.

There is no doubt that foreign exchange markets can be volatile. To hold cash in one currency only is, from an international perspective, a high-risk or speculative strategy. A diversified and properly managed invest-ment in currencies is the opposite of this—in the short term it will inevitably underperform the strongest currency, although outperforming all currencies over time.

Most managed currency funds (provided there is no element of gearing, whether directly or through unhedged exposure to currency futures) have shown themselves to be highly conservative and bearing a lower risk than either investment in a single specified currency or international invest-ment in equities or bonds. Equities carry higher risks than bonds; and bonds carry higher risks than cash.

20.2   Exchange rates and bonds

The market value of a particular bond is tied to the interest rate (and yield curve, or projection of interest rates over selected periods of time) of the currency in which it is denominated. When interest rates fall, the value of bonds rises, because a larger capital is now needed to yield the same return; and conversely, when interest rates rise, the value of bonds falls.

Under a regime of fixed exchange rates, the only scope for capital gains in bonds depends on the investor's ability to assess the future course of inter-est rates correctly. But under a system of floating exchange rates, a signifi-cant contribution to the total return, measured in the investor's own domestic currency, on investing in bonds internationally will depend on the extent to which the other currencies in which bonds are held either appreciate or depreciate. There are, besides, important links, in more than one context, between the respective movements of exchange rates and interest rates.

The main traditional relationship between exchange rates and bond markets has arisen where particular national bond markets have a large volume of foreign funds invested in them and are thus more influenced than other bond markets by the strength or weakness of the local cur-rency. The sterling gilt market has been a classic example of this, and the strength or weakness of sterling has heavily influenced this market and the interest rates of sterling-denominated bonds generally.

More recently, in 1994, bond prices declined and yields rose as heavily geared US hedge funds carrying significant exposure to bonds, unwound their leverage. Investors also increased their cash holdings in the light of an expected cyclical rise in US interest rates.

But a new and potentially more important contrary relationship than that determined by local currency strength or weakness has arisen. With interest rate differentials becoming a crucial factor in driving exchange rate movements among the three main currency blocs, there is an increasing tendency for bond markets and exchange rates to move automatically in opposite directions. This is in part because geographical currency groupings reduce the relative importance of wider international financing of bond issues, especially, for example, in the context of Europe.

Broadly speaking, as the market operates at present, if the state of the domestic economy (or group of economies) is likely to lead to lower interest rates, this will drive bond markets up, but it will tend to drive the exchange rate down. Conversely, where the prospective accelerating economic growth is expected to lead to higher interest rates and weaker bond markets, this will drive up the exchange rate.

20.3   Exchange rates and equity investment

Thanks to post-war developments in telecommunications and information technology, the world's main stock markets, like the foreign exchange markets, now operate globally, except in matters of administration. In this environment, exchange rate movements can mean the difference between profit and loss, or, in a stock market crash, the difference between a relatively small loss and a large one. Indeed, profitable international equity investment cannot be achieved unless the exchange rate factor is taken into account in the investor's calculations.

After the worldwide fall in stock markets in October 1987, US investors found that they had suffered less on their foreign investments measured in dollars than investors in other countries measuring their investments in their own currencies. Because the US dollar fell against the yen, the deutschemark and sterling, shares in the markets in Japan, Germany and the United Kingdom that had been bought with US dollars fell in value much less in dollar terms than in local currency market-value terms, to the extent that the dollar weakened against the currency in question.

Currency weakness is also generally good for the profits and share prices in their local currency terms of companies operating in international sectors (eg export-led sectors). The resulting equity gains, however, will naturally be reduced when measured in the currency of the foreign investor. The expected depreciation of the currencies in question must be included in calculations of comparative projected total investment returns.

For example, an investment in a US company in an international business sector, benefiting from future dollar weakness, may, let us say, be expected to show a 100 per cent return in dollar terms, thus attracting Japanese investors. But if the dollar depreciates by 25 per cent against the yen, the expected return in yen terms will be only 60 per cent. For equities, however, unlike cash and bonds, the positive impact (via profits) of currency depreciation on share prices is often greater for the foreign investor than the accompanying downwards adjustment due to the depreciation.

20.4   Exchange rates and day-to-day living expenses

A potential problem arises for the expatriate when his income and living expenses are in two distinct currency blocs, as might be the case, for example, for a retired United Nations official living in France and drawing a pension denominated in US dollars. If it is practical, the only route to protection here is to cover, by means of forward exchange contracts with the expatriate's bank, his known flow of income in the source currency into the currency of the country where he is living. If this is not a practical option, it may be prudent to keep a reasonable balance on deposit in the currency of the country of residence as a reserve to draw on when needed. This tactic can be particularly useful in dealing with temporary weakness in the source currency: the expatriate concerned can then postpone converting the income concerned until the currency is stronger.

21 Offshore financial centres

Peter Gartland, Editor, Offshore Alert

21.1 Introduction

As already explained at **1.2.6**, above, the term 'offshore' is not legally defined, but in the context of banking and insurance it has come to be applied to operations carried out in a jurisdiction at least one remove from the company, institution, or individual initiating or carrying out those operations. The term no doubt arose in the United Kingdom, and it implies an insular vantage point. But the United Kingdom is itself offshore to many individuals and companies not domiciled (though they may be resident) there; and the term is properly applied to a number of jurisdictions, such as Luxembourg or Liechtenstein that have no shores. If the term 'offshore' is not a legal one, still less is the expression 'tax haven', which is often applied to offshore centres. But this expression acknowledges the fact that the offshore centre in question does offer, and has been chosen because it offers tax mitigation opportunities to investors (and sometimes to borrowers). Just how many tax havens there are in various parts of the world depends on the definition of a tax haven, but even a conservative estimate might be as high as 40.

The mushrooming of offshore financial centres in recent years has come about for a number of reasons:

(1) the need of the local authorities to boost income because other sources are stagnant;
(2) the need to create employment opportunities for better educated workforces; or
(3) perhaps merely the desire to jump on what appears to be a successful bandwagon.

But in fairness it should be said that the regulators in most offshore financial centres (certainly the ones to be concentrated on in this chapter) go out of their way to try to ensure that only legitimate business is transacted by the banks, insurance companies, investment groups and trust managers established in their territory.

21.2   The Channel Islands and the Isle of Man

The British Isles offshore centres of the Channel Islands (Guernsey and Jersey) and the Isle of Man compete for business on a worldwide scale. Geographically close competitors are Dublin and landlocked Luxembourg. Slightly farther afield, Gibraltar, Cyprus and Malta vie for offshore business. On the other side of the Atlantic, Bermuda is an established offshore financial centre while, in the Caribbean, the British dependent territories of Cayman, Turks & Caicos, Anguilla, British Virgin Islands and Montserrat all have financial sectors. Cayman is easily the most developed and Montserrat is certainly the one with the most ground to make up following a series of banking scandals in the late 1980s. Elsewhere in the world there are offshore centres in the Bahamas, Barbados, the Cook Islands, Labuan (Malaysia), Madeira, Mauritius and Vanuatu, to name just a few.

From the point of view of a British expatriate, however, there is no financial service that cannot be found in the Channel Islands or the Isle of Man. We will be concentrating on these centres. In addition, we will also be looking at Luxembourg and Dublin because both these centres are increasingly important as locations for investment funds.

Jersey is the biggest and, thanks to Bergerac, the best known of the Channel Islands. Jersey's allegiance is to the British Crown, but the island makes its own laws and issues its own bank notes and coins. Guernsey is often thought of as just a smaller version of Jersey, and it is true that the two islands share several common features. Like its neighbour, Guernsey is responsible for making its own laws and issuing its own legal tender. Also like Jersey, Guernsey is effectively a member of the OECD on Britain's coat-tails and has designated territory status under the United Kingdom's financial services legislation. Designated territory status means that the United Kingdom has recognised that an offshore jurisdiction has equivalent investor protection legislation, including a compensation scheme in respect of funds designated under the FSA 1986, s 87. This equivalence makes it possible for such funds to be marketed in the United Kingdom.

The Isle of Man shares designated territory status with the Channel Islands. This status is at present under review by British Treasury officials to see if its terms need to be updated in the light of changes generally in the regulatory environment since its introduction in 1988. The Isle of Man has its own Parliament, sets its own income tax rates, and has long been a low-tax area enjoying total independence from the United Kingdom on matters of direct taxation. There is low corporate and personal tax, and no capital transfer or IHT.

All the major British banks have subsidiaries in one or more of the British offshore centres. They offer all the usual facilities that are available in the United Kingdom, such as cheque guarantee and credit cards, automatic cash dispenser facilities and regular statements, plus the benefit of interest paid gross. Multicurrency cheque accounts and a whole range of currency funds have become increasingly popular in recent years. Several banks in Jersey, Guernsey and the Isle of Man offer multicurrency accounts which can be opened with a minimum balance of, typically, around £2,000. The key features of such accounts include money market levels of interest in all major and other currencies, free cheques, standing orders and direct debits, easy currency switching at competitive interest rates and the ability to hold balances in a multitude of currencies. It is not just the specialist banks that provide non-sterling facilities. These are available also from the offshore subsidiaries of some clearing banks and building societies.

It is possible to access currency investments through a wide range of umbrella funds. Such funds typically offer money funds in US dollars, sterling, yen, Swiss francs and deutschemarks, all of which provide investors with access to income at wholesale interest rates through investing in a spread of short-term deposits, certificates of deposit and other negotiable money market instruments. Some umbrella funds also offer a managed currency fund, which aims to maximise the value of liquid assets through the management and diversification of currency exposure, see **21.1**, above. Umbrella funds are usually available either as distributing funds or on a roll-up basis. To qualify for distributor status under UK legislation, an offshore fund must distribute approximately 85 per cent of its income each year. Conversely, a roll-up fund, as its name suggests, is one in which the income accumulates inside the fund, with growth being reflected in the price per unit or per share.

Expatriates may also like to consider money funds which are also available in distributor or roll-up form. Money funds work like this: investors' money is pooled within the fund, and so qualifies for wholesale rates of interest available on the international money markets. These rates are often considerably higher than those available for smaller sums of money. Each currency is represented by its own class of share whose price will vary in line with underlying interest rates. A key point to remember is that investment in a managed share class or a currency other than the investor's own base currency is subject to exchange rate movements which can go up or down in relation to an investor's base currency.

As a guide, money funds are useful for investors who wish to hold cash deposits in a major, or even relatively minor, currency. Apart from their use as interest-bearing cash balances, they can be used to hold foreign currencies as an investment, for a business need, or simply to manage a holiday home. They can also act as a convenient parking place for money between equity investments. With managed money market currency funds or sub-funds of an umbrella, there is the prospect of added value if the managers get the timing on their currency switches right. If the investor's need is to deposit foreign currency cheques frequently and also to make payments in foreign currencies, he may be better served by using a multicurrency account on which he will receive interest paid without deduction of tax.

As can be seen, the range of banking services available to the expatriate is considerable. Many banks in the offshore centres also offer trust services. As an alternative to the banks, several building societies have set up offshore subsidiaries in recent years. The Isle of Man is unusual in that if offers a scheme to provide compensation to depositors of an amount up to £15,000 or the foreign currency equivalent in the event of the collapse of a bank or building society. The Isle of Man also differs from Jersey and Guernsey in that it has become a recognised centre for international life insurance.

21.3   Luxembourg and Dublin

Although Jersey, Guernsey and the Isle of Man are the offshore centres most often used by British expatriates, Luxembourg and Dublin are also important, especially as they are becoming more prominent in the fields of investment fund management and cross-border marketing of insurance and pension products.

Luxembourg was the first country in what is now the EU to implement the EC Directive on Ucits (see **17.3**) which allows open-ended collective investment funds authorised in one EU member state to be marketed freely, once they have been registered, in any other member state. At the same time as incorporating the Ucits Directive in its own legislation, Luxembourg also introduced legislation to embrace funds investing in assets other than transferable securities. What has given the investment fund sector in Luxembourg an enormous impetus, however, has been its benign tax regime: the funds themselves are subject only to a 0.06 per cent levy on their net assets, and for non-resident investors in them, there is no withholding tax on distributions and no tax on capital gains. Largely as a consequence of this regime, Luxembourg at present has, after France, the second largest investment fund industry in the EU, with the equivalent of over US$300 billion aggregate net assets. Over 60 per cent of these assets, however, are administered by banks and other financial institutions whose head offices are in other EU member states, and they are more often than not administering them on behalf of clients in their own country. German, Belgian and French banks, in particular, have a strong presence in Luxembourg and it is certain (although, naturally, no statistics are published on this point) that the greater part of the Luxembourg domiciled funds they are administering belongs to shareholders resident in those three countries. The UK presence in Luxembourg, on the other hand, is small, with only slightly more than 3 per cent of the fund industry's aggregate net assets.

Investment funds are not the only attraction of Luxembourg as a financial centre. For many of the wealthier internationally minded private investors an even greater attraction is the Luxembourg holding company. Shares in these companies may be registered in the holder's name, or be simply bearer shares, in which case they are anonymous. Another important advantage of these companies is that although quarterly returns must be filed for purposes of the low annual tax on issued capital that is payable, and an annual financial statement be submitted to the Luxembourg authorities, only a minimum amount of financial information has to be published. Apart from taking care of investments, the holding company can own and license trade marks and patents. The holding company pays no income taxes of any kind, but is excluded from Luxembourg's tax treaties with other countries, and so cannot claim relief for withholding taxes deducted at source on dividends and interest payments received in another jurisdiction.

In March 1987, the Irish government announced its intention to establish an International Financial Services Centre (IFSC) in Dublin, which would take advantage of a well-educated young workforce and various other favourable factors, to attract a wide range of operations by foreign institutions, including fund management and insurance, that would create employment opportunities for Irish citizens. To encourage the development of the centre, the government offers a number of incentives, including a favourable tax regime authorised by the European Commission. The first IFSC-licensed fund management company began operations in 1988. There are now over 60 fund management companies based in the

Centre, but only about 20 of these are running funds for the individual private investor. For such an investor, however, who is not resident in Ireland, distributions are free of Irish withholding tax, and there is in effect no capital gains tax payable. The funds themselves are also exempt from Irish capital gains and income tax.

The European Commission has confirmed that the concession whereby new licence holders in the IFSC are eligible for a corporation tax rate of 10 per cent, as opposed to the normal rate in Ireland of 40 per cent, is to be extended by six years, with the consequence that financial institutions obtaining licences before the end of 2000 will be subject to the low 10 per cent rate of corporation tax until 2005. A number of life assurance companies have chosen Dublin as their base from which to attack the European market, but as a rule they are regarding Germany as their premier market, followed by The Netherlands, France, Belgium and Italy.

Appendix I Checklists of do's and don'ts

Going abroad

One of the most daunting things about going abroad to work is gathering together all the information necessary. Obviously the intending expatriate needs full details of his contract, health, visa and permit requirements and many more. On the financial front, the following are some of the most important things to consider:

(1) *Do* bring your UK tax affairs up to date;
(2) *Do* submit a P 85 and claim any PAYE rebate if leaving part way through the tax year;
(3) *Do* inform the Department of Social Security, check if any contributions will be necessary and, if not, obtain an application form for voluntary contributions;
(4) *Do* make arrangements for offshore banking (including a current account for remaining UK commitments and a small amount in a deposit account);
(5) *Do* close any building society deposit accounts;
(6) *Do* inform any mortgagee that the mortgaged property is being left vacant, or if it is to be let, ask their permission;
(7) *Do* check the continuing validity of all protective insurances, both life and personal effects, property, etc;
(8) *Do* take legal advice on letting property;
(9) *Do* make or revise a will;
(10) *Do* review existing investments not already mentioned;
(11) *Do* consider comprehensive insurance protection while overseas;
(12) *Do* make use of duty-free facilities in purchasing a car or household appliances if appropriate;
(13) *Do* inform bankers, solicitors, accountants and other advisers of the new address;
(14) *Do not* leave everything to the last minute;
(15) *Do not* take on any new investment commitments just before leaving;

(16)   *Do not* forget that most countries are happy to let money in but may impose restrictions on taking it out again—check the rules;
(17)   *Do not* leave valuables at home;
(18)   *Do not* expect to have a large cash surplus, at least in the first few months.

While overseas

Given that earning and saving money is a prime motive in working abroad, many expatriates are very disappointed to find that after six months they have yet to amass a fortune. In retrospect it is hardly surprising. Even the fully furnished company house is usually missing much essential equipment, there can be a great deal of entertaining to be done either at home or at the club, the cost of living until experience of local produce and markets is gained is invariably high, and, after all, a new video and hi-fi are essential.

Usually after about six months, a regular savings or cash surplus pattern can be discerned and at that point some serious consideration can be given to investment.

(1)   *Do* invest surplus cash initially in a readily realisable form such as a very short-term bank deposit;
(2)   *Do* retain an adequate cash reserve;
(3)   *Do* wait until a regular pattern of surplus appears before entering into any major investment commitments;
(4)   *Do* examine all investment propositions very carefully;
(5)   *Do* seek independent advice on all financial matters;
(6)   *Do not* be tempted by tales of massive profits just waiting to be made, at least until a reasonably secure base has been built up;
(7)   *Do not* sign any investment document or part with cash as a result of a brief meeting with a salesman of whose credentials you are not absolutely certain;
(8)   *Do not* make any long-term commitments based on current earning capacity unless that capacity is extremely secure (for most expatriates, it is not);
(9)   *Do not* attempt to beat currency or tax regulations, as the penalties can be extremely severe;
(10)   *Do not* neglect to plan.

Coming home

One of the most vital occasions for tax and investment planning is in the months before returning to the United Kingdom. Much of what has been achieved in terms of savings and investment can be largely undone by a lack of forethought at this point. Amid the round of farewell parties, packing up and thinking of home, it is often very easy to forget to close a bank account or to realise accrued gains. The secret is to plan.

(1)   *Do* seek professional advice at least three months before the return date (or if the overseas period is unlikely to last, or to have lasted for at least three years, get advice in the tax year prior to return);
(2)   *Do* check any local requirements for tax clearance before the issue of exit visas;
(3)   *Do* check current exchange control regulations;
(4)   *Do* close all offshore deposit accounts (and in the tax year before return close any UK bank deposit accounts);
(5)   *Do* consider CGT and UK income tax liabilities on existing investments;
(6)   *Do* give notice to any tenants at home to quit;
(7)   *Do* read Chapter 12 again.

Appendix II   Tax tables

Income tax rates for 1995–96 and the previous four years

For 1991–92

Band of taxable income			
From	*To*	*Rate*	*Cumulative tax*
£	£	%	£
1	23,700	25	5,925
over	23,700	40	—

For 1992–93

1	2,000	20	400
2,001	23,700	25	5,825
over	23,700	40	—

For 1993–94

1	2,500	20	500
2,501	23,700	25	5,800
over	23,700	40	—

For 1994–95

1	3,000	20	600
3,001	23,700	25	5,775
over	23,700	40	—

For 1995–96

1	3,200	20	640
3,201	24,300	25	5,915
over	24,300	40	—

Income tax: Personal reliefs for 1995–96 and the previous four years

	1991–92	1992–93 and 1993–94	1994–95	1995–96
Personal (each) (s 257)	£3,295(1)	£3,445(3)	£3,445(3)	£3,525(3)
Married couple (s 257A)	£1,720	£1,720	£1,720(4)	£1,720(5)
(monthly reduction in year of marriage)	£143⅓	£143⅓	£143⅓	£143⅓

Age allowance

Reduced by £1 for every £2 income over	£13,500	£14,200	£14,200	£14,600

65 to 79 (to 1988–89)
or to 74 (from 1989–90) in year:

	1991–92	1992–93 and 1993–94	1994–95	1995–96
personal (each)	£4,020	£4,200	£4,200	£4,630
married couple	£2,355	£2,465	£2,665(4)	£2,995(5)
Maximum income—				
wife or single	£14,950	£15,710	£15,710	£16,810
husband	£16,220(2)	£17,200(2)	£17,600(2)	£19,360(2)

80 (to 1988–89) or 75
(from 1989–90) or over in year:

	1991–92	1992–93 and 1993–94	1994–95	1995–96
personal (each)	£4,180	£4,370	£4,370	£4,800
married couple	£2,395	£2,505	£2,705(4)	£3,035(5)
Maximum income—				
wife or single	£15,270	£16,050	£16,050	£17,150
husband	£16,620	£17,620	£18,020	£19,780

Additional relief for children (s 259)

	£1,720	£1,720	£1,720(4)	£1,720(5)

Widow's bereavement (s 262)

	£1,720	£1,720	£1,720(4)	£1,720(5)

Blind persons (each) (s 265)

£1,080	£1,080	£1,200	£1,200

(1)   Transitionally, for husband under 65 with wife at 5.4.90 born pre-6.4.25 £3,400; born pre-6.4.15 £3,540.
(2)   Different if wife in higher age bracket than husband.
(3)   Transitionally, for husband under 65 with wife at 5.4.90 born pre-6.4.15 £3,540.
(4)   Relief restricted to 20 per cent.
(5)   Relief restricted to 15 per cent.

Capital gains tax rates

Net gains added to income and taxed at income tax rates

	1991–92	1992–93 and 1993–94/1994–95	1995–96
Annual exemption (TCGA 1992, s 3)			
Individuals	£5,500	£5,800	£6,000
Most trusts	£2,750	£2,900	£3,000

Appendix III Useful addresses

Inland Revenue offices

Inland Revenue Headquarters
Somerset House
Strand
London WC2R 1LB

Tel: (0171) 438 6622

Inland Revenue Claims
  Branch
Foreign Division
1st Floor
St John's House
Merton Road
Bootle
Merseyside L69 9BL

Tel: (0151) 922 6363

Financial Intermediaries and
  Claims Office (FICO)
Fitzroy House
PO Box 46
Nottingham NG2 1BD

Tel: (0115) 974 2000

Inland Revenue Head
  Office (Public
  Departments)
Foreign Section
Ty-Glas
Llanishen
Cardiff CF4 5ZD

Tel: (01222) 753271

National Insurance

DHSS Overseas Branch
Newcastle-upon-Tyne
NE98 1YX

Tel: (0191) 213 5000

Investor protection: United Kingdom

Securities and Investments
   Board
Gavrelle House
2–14 Bunhill Row
London EC1Y 8RA

Tel: (0171) 638 1240

Investment Managers
   Regulatory
   Organisation (IMRO)
Broadwalk House
5 Appold Street
London EC2A 2LL

Tel: (0171) 628 6022

Personal Investment
   Authority
7th Floor
1 Canada Square
London E14 5AZ

Tel: (0171) 538 8860

The Securities and
   Futures Authority (SFA)
Cottons Centre
Cottons Lane
London SE1 2QB

Tel: (0171) 378 9000

Offshore centres: supervisory authorities

The Bahamas:
Office of the Registrar
   General
Rodney E Bain Building
Shirley & Parliament
   Streets
PO Box N-532
Nassau

Tel: 1 809 322 3316

Guernsey:
Guernsey Financial
   Services Commission
Valley House
Hirzel Street
St Peter Port

Tel: 44 481 712706

Isle of Man:
Financial Supervision
   Commission
PO Box 58
1–4 Goldie Terrace
Douglas

Tel: 44 624 62487

Jersey:
Economic Adviser's Office
Cyril Le Marquand House
The Parade
St Helier

Tel: 44 534 79111

Index

Accommodation
    available, 9
    furnished holiday lettings, 71–2
Addresses
    Inland Revenue offices, 223
    investor protection, 224
    National Insurance, 223
    offshore centres, 224
    pensions, 203–5
Administration of tax
    property in UK, 70–1
Agricultural property
    potentially exempt lifetime transfers, 93
    relief, IHT, 92
Airmen
    status of, 25–6
Annual allowances
    inheritance tax, 89–90
Appeal
    taxpayer's right of, 124
Apportionment of emoluments, 17–18
Armed forces
    status of, 25
Assets
    location of, IHT, 94
    more than one jurisdiction, in, 101–2
Assistance
    taxpayer's right to, 124
Available accommodation
    meaning, 9
Avoidance of tax
    higher rate liability, 63–4

Banks
    deposits
        interest, 49–51
        treatment of, 166–7
    interest from deposits, 49–51
    non-sterling bank accounts, 84–5

Banks—contd
    services for expatriates, 165–6
Bonds
    Bulldog, 170
    corporate, 172
    Eurobonds, 170–1
    exchange rates and, 208–9
    offshore single premium, 187, 188
    portfolio, 187, 189
Building societies
    deposits
        interest, 49–51
        treatment of, 166–7
Bulldog bonds, 170
Business
    double taxation agreement relating
        to, 140–1
    gains, 78–82
    sale of, 78–82
Business property
    potentially exempt lifetime transfer,
        93
    relief, IHT, 91–2

Capital gains tax
    business gains 78–82
    double taxation agreement, 141
    emigration, 78
    foreign taxes, 83
    gift from non-resident, 84
    husband and wife, 77
    non-resident, gift from, 84
    non-sterling bank accounts, 84–5
    offshore funds, 83–4
    principal private residence, 74–6
    property, 78
    rates, 222
    reinvestment relief, 82–3
    residence, 77

Capital gains tax—*contd*
  returning expatriate, 152–3
  sale of business, 78–82
  trusts, 83, 109–10
  UK investment managers, 85
Capitalisation of investments, 151
Cars
  value added tax, 119
Cash
  exchange rates and, 207–8
Categories of expatriate, 13–28
Certainty
  taxpayer's right to, 125
Channel Islands
  offshore financial centres, 212–14
Chargeable transfers
  inheritance tax, 88–9
Checklists of do's and don'ts
  coming home, 219
  going abroad, 217–18
  while overseas, 218
Choice, domicile of, 5–6
Collection of tax
  property in UK, 70–1
Collective investment vehicles
  generally, 177
  offshore funds. *See* Offshore funds
  UK investment trust, 177–9
  UK unit trust, 179
Coming home. *See* Returning
  expatriate
Confidentiality
  taxpayer's right to, 125
Contract
  life assurance, 186–7
Corporate bonds, 172
Corporate stocks
  interest, 53
Crown Servant
  status of, 24–5
Current year basis
  returning expatriate, taxation of,
    150–2

Debentures
  interest, 53
Deemed domicile
  meaning, 6
Dependence, domicile of, 5
Dependent personal services, 141–2
Deposits
  banks, 49–51, 166–7
  building societies, 49–51, 166–7
Direct investment in equities, 173–5

Dividends
  double taxation agreement relating
    to, 138–9
  paid by UK companies, 53–4
Domicile
  chart, 34–7
  choice, of, 5–6
  deemed, meaning, 6
  dependence, of, 5
  establishment of, 29
  guide to, 29–45
  meaning, 3–4
  non-UK domiciled spouse,
    IHT, 94–5
  origin, of, 4–5
  person not domiciled in UK, IHT, 93
Double taxation agreement
  businesses, 140–1
  capital gains, 141
  dependent personal services, 141–2
  dividends, 138–9
  entertainers, 142
  exchange of information, 144–5
  fiscal residence, 137–8
  income
    other, 144
    real property, from, 140
  independent personal services, 141
  inheritance tax, 145
  interest, treatment of, 53, 139
  mutual agreement procedure, 144
  non-discrimination, 144
  other income, 144
  pensions, 142–4
  personal services
    dependent, 141–2
    independent, 141
  real property, income from, 140
  royalties, 139–40
  sportsmen, 142
  students, 142
  teachers, 142
  treaty shopping, 146
  unilateral relief, 146
Dual residence
  meaning, 7–8
Dublin
  offshore financial centres, 214–16

Emigration
  capital gains tax, 78
  expatriate permanently emigrating,
    27–8
  meaning, 10

Emoluments
  apportionment of, 17–18
  foreign, 18
Employees
  pension planning for, 191–2
Employment
  income arising in UK, 57–8
Entertainer
  double taxation agreement relating to, 142
Equities
  direct investment in, 173–5
  exchange rates and equity investment, 209–10
  individual investors, 174–5
  useful publications, 173
Estate in course of administration
  income arising in UK, 62–3
Eurobonds, 170–1
European Union
  Multilateral Agreement, 194–5
  state pension ages in, 203
Evasion of tax
  returning expatriate, 153–4
Exchange of information, 144–5
Exchange rates
  bonds, and, 208–9
  cash, and, 207–8
  day-to-day living expenses, and, 210
  equity investment, and, 209–10
  managed currency funds, 207–8
Excise duties, 119
Excluded income
  meaning, 50–1
Expatriate
  categories of, 13–28
  family, 26–7
  long-term self-employed, 23–4
  meaning, 3
  permanently emigrating, 27–8
  remaining UK resident, 13–14
  retired, 28
  retiring abroad, 27–8
  returning. *See* Returning expatriate
  short-term self-employed, 22–3
  special status, with, 24
Expenses
  day-to-day living, exchange rates and, 210
  letting, associated with, 68
Extra-statutory concessions
  meaning, 2

Family
  dispositions for maintenance of, IHT, 91

Family—*contd*
  expatriate, 26–7
  home, IHT, 98–9
Final salary, 195–6
Finance Acts
  meaning, 2
Financial centres
  offshore, 211–16
Fiscal residence, 137–8
Fixed-interest securities
  British government stocks, 169–70
  Bulldog bonds, 170
  corporate bonds, 172
  Eurobonds, 170–1
Foreign emoluments
  nature of, 18
Foreign taxes
  capital gains tax, 83
Furnished holiday lettings
  income from, 71–2

Gifts
  marriage, in consideration of, IHT, 90–1
  non-resident, from, CGT, 84
Government
  service, occupational pensions in respect of, 143
  stocks
    generally, 169–70
    interest on, 51–3
Guide to domicile and residence, 29–45

Hearing
  taxpayer's right to be heard, 124
Higher rate liability
  avoidance of, 63–4
Holiday lettings
  furnished, 71–2
Husband and wife
  capital gains tax, 77
  non-UK domiciled spouse, IHT, 94–5
  transfers between spouses, IHT, 89

Incidence of inheritance tax, 103
Income
  arising in UK
    bank deposits, interest from, 49–51
    building society deposits, interest from, 49–51
    corporate stocks, interest from, 53
    debentures, interest from, 53
    dividends, 53–4
    employments, 57–8
    estate income, 62–3

Income—*contd*
  arising in UK—*contd*
    excluded income, 50–1
    generally, 47–8
    government stocks, interest
      from, 51–3
    higher rate liability, avoidance
      of, 63–4
    interest, 49–54
    life assurance policies, 54–6
    Lloyd's Underwriters, 64–5
    local authority stocks, interest
      from, 53
    maintenance payments, 61–2
    National Savings, 56
    patents, 61
    pensions, 56–7
    personal allowances, non-resident's
      entitlement to, 65–6
    professions, 58–61
    royalties, 61
    trades, 58–61
    trust income, 62–3
    UK schedular system of income
      tax, 48–9
  excluded, 50–1
  normal expenditure out of, IHT, 90
  real property, from, 140
  rental, 67–8
  unremittable overseas, 155
  worldwide, tax on, 149–50
Income tax
  higher rate liability, avoidance of, 63–4
  personal reliefs for 1995–96 and
    previous four years, 222
  rates for 1995–96 and previous four
    years, 221
  trusts, on, 107–9
  UK schedular system of income
    tax, 48–9
Independent personal services, 141,
Information
  exchange of, 144–5
  taxpayer's right to, 124
Inheritance tax
  agricultural property relief, 92
  annual allowances, 89–90
  assets, location of, 94
  business property relief, 91–2
  chargeable transfers, 88–9
  double taxation agreement, 145
  exemptions, 89
  family, disposition for maintenance
    of, 91

Inheritance tax—*contd*
  family home, 98–9
  generally, 87–8
  incidence of, 103
  income from property, 76
  insurance policies, 97–8
  location of assets, 94
  marriage, gifts in consideration of, 90–1
  non-UK domiciled spouse, 94–5
  normal expenditure out of income, 90
  other exempt transfers, 91
  persons not domiciled in UK, 93
  planning, 96–7
  potentially exempt transfers
    agricultural property, 93
    business property, 93
    generally, 89
  reliefs, 89
  settled property, 95–6
  spouses
    non-UK domiciled spouse, 94–5
    transfers between, 89
  trusts, on, 110–12
  written variations, 103–4
Inland Revenue
  addresses of offices, 223
Insurance policies. *See* Life assurance
Interest
  bank deposits, from, 49–51
  building society deposits, from, 49–51
  corporate stocks, from, 53
  debentures, from, 53
  double taxation agreements, 53, 139
  excluded income, 50–1
  government stocks, from, 51–3
  loan, property in UK, 68–9
  local authority stocks, from, 53
Investment trust
  nature of, 177–9
Investments
  capitalisation of, 151
  collective investment vehicles, 177–84
  constructing portfolio
    establishing objectives, 157–9
    generally, 157
    investor protection, 161–2
    method of, 162–4
    risks and rewards, 159–62
    rules of thumb, 160–1
  equities, direct investment in, 173–5
  guide to domicile and residence, use of,
    30–2
  offshore funds, *See* Offshore funds
  protection of investors, 161–2, 224

Investments—*contd*
  returning expatriate, 151, 154
  UK investment managers, CGT, 85
Isle of Man
  offshore financial centres, 212–14

Key terms and concepts, 1–11

Life assurance
  offshore single premium bonds, 187, 188–9
  policies
    generally, 185
    income arising in UK, 54–6
    inheritance tax, 97–8
    types of contract, 186–7
  portfolio bonds, 187, 189
  types of contract, 186–7
Living expenses
  day-to-day, exchange rates and, 210
Lloyd's Underwriters
  income arising in UK, 64–5
Loans
  property in UK, interest relating to, 68–9
Local authority
  service, occupational pensions in respect of, 143
  stocks, interest on, 53
Location of assets
  inheritance tax, 94
Long absence
  apportionment of emoluments, 17–18
  generally, 14–15
  qualifying periods, 15–17
Long-term working abroad
  non-resident, 21–2
  self-employed expatriate, 23–4
Luxembourg–
  offshore financial centres, 214–16

Maintenance
  family, of, dispositions for, IHT, 91
  payments
    post-15 March 1988 arrangements, 62
    pre-15 March 1988 arrangements, 61–2
Managed currency funds, 207–8
Marriage
  gifts in consideration of, IHT, 90–1
Money purchase, 196
Mortgage interest relief at source (MIRAS)
  expatriate letting property, 73–4

Mortgage interest relief at source (MIRAS)—*contd*
  expatriate not letting property, 72–3
  generally, 72
Mutual agreement procedure, 144

National Insurance
  addresses, 223
  returning expatriate, 155
National Savings
  income arising in UK, 56
Non-discrimination
  double taxation agreements, 144
Non-resident
  gifts from, CGT, 84
  long-term working abroad, 21–2
  offshore single premium bonds, UK taxation of, 188
  trusts, 112–16
  UK personal allowances, entitlement to, 65–6
Non-sterling bank accounts
  capital gains tax, 84–5
Normal expenditure out of income, 90

Obligations of taxpayer, 125–35
Occupational pensions
  government service, 143
  local authority service, 143
  not government, 143
  tax advantages, 195
Offshore
  addresses of centres, 224
  financial centres, 211–16
  meaning, 3
  pensions
    employer-sponsored offshore trust, 199
    generally, 198–9
    individual offshore plans, 199–200
  single premium bonds, 187, 188–9
Offshore funds
  advantages, 182–3
  capital gains tax, 83–4
  categories of, 181–2
  disadvantages, 183–4
  how to invest in, 184
  nature of, 179–81
Oil rig workers
  status of, 26
Old age pension, 143
Ordinary residence
  meaning, 10–11
Origin, domicile of, 4–5

Overseas income
  unremittable, 155

Patents
  income arising in UK, 61
Pensions
  buy-out bond, 201
  cash refund, 200
  double taxation agrement relating to,
    142–4
  employees, planning for, 191–2
  European Union
    Multilateral Agreement, 194–5
    state pension ages in, 203
  final salary, 195–6
  foreign company transfer, 200–1
  foreign individual plans, 201
  generally, 191
  income arising in UK, 56–7
  money purchase, 196
  occupational, 143, 195
  offshore
    employer-sponsored offshore trust, 199
    generally, 198–9
    individual offshore plans, 199–200
  old age, 143
  options abroad
    foreign employer's scheme, 197–8
    individual plans, 198
  personal, 144, 196–7, 201
  preserved pension, 200
  retention in home scheme, 195
  retiring abroad, 201–3
  social security agreement, 202
  transfers, 200–1
  UK state retirement, 143, 192–3
  useful addresses, 203–5
Personal allowances
  1995–96 and previous four years, 222
  non-resident's entitlement to, 65–6
Personal belongings
  importation of, 119–20
Personal pensions, 196–7, 201
Personal services
  dependent, 141–2
  independent, 141
Physical presence
  six-month rule, 8–9
  three-month rule, 9
Planning
  inheritance tax, 96–7
Portfolio bonds, 187, 189
Potentially exempt transfers
  agricultural property, 93

Potentially exempt transfers—*contd*
  business property, 93
  inheritance tax, 89
Principal private residence
  capital gains tax, 74–6
  inheritance tax, 98–9
Privacy
  taxpayer's right to, 125
Professions
  income arising in UK, 58–61
Property
  administration of tax, 70–1
  agricultural, 92, 93
  business, 91–2, 93
  capital gains tax, 74–6, 78
  collection of tax, 70–1
  furnished holiday lettings, 71–2
  inheritance tax, 76
  loan interest, 68–9
  mortgage interest relief at source
    (MIRAS)
    expatriate letting property, 73–4
    expatriate not letting property, 72–3
    generally, 72
  principal private residence, 74–6, 98–9
  rental income, 67–8
  self-assessment, 71
  settled, IHT, 95–6
  UK, tax aspects of, 67–76
  value added tax, 118–19
Protection of investors, 161–2, 224

Reinvestment relief
  capital gains tax, 82–3
Remittance basis
  taxation on, 148–9
Rental income
  property in UK, 67–8
Residence
  capital gains tax, 77
  chart, 38–9, 40–5
  dual, meaning, 7–8
  establishment of, 29
  fiscal, 137–8
  guide to, 29–45
  meaning, 7
  ordinary, meaning, 10–11
  summary, 10
  taxpayer's rights and obligations in
    country of, 123–35
  trusts, of, 105
Resident expatriate
  other reliefs, 19–21
  short-term working abroad, 13–14

Retention in home scheme, 195
Retirement
    expatriate retiring abroad, 27–8
    pensions. *See* Pensions
    retired expatriate, 28
Returning expatriate
    capital gains tax, 152–3
    checklist of do's and dont's, 219
    evasion, dangers of, 153–4
    generally, 147
    miscellaneous investments, 154
    National Insurance, 155
    other matters, 155–6
    tax liabilities on return
        current year basis, 150–2
        generally, 147–8
        remittance basis, 148–9
        worldwide income, tax on, 149–50
    unremittable overseas income, 155
Rights of taxpayer, 123–5
Royalties
    double taxation agreement relating
        to, 139–40
    non-resident, paid to, 61

Sale
    business, of, 78–82
Schedular system of income tax, 48–9
Seafarers
    status of, 25–6
Secrecy
    taxpayer's right to, 125
Securities
    fixed-interest, 169–72
Self-assessment
    income from property, 71
Self-employed
    expatriate
        long-term, 23–4
        short-term, 22–3
    pensions, 144
Settled property
    inheritance tax, 95–6
Short-term working abroad
    expatriate remains UK resident, 13–14
    self-employed expatriate, 22–3
Six-month rule
    physical presence, 8–9
Social security agreement
    state pensions, payment of, 202
Special status, expatriate with, 24
Sportsmen
    double taxation agreement relating
        to, 142

Spouses. *See* Husband and wife
Stamp duty, 120–1
Stocks
    corporate, 53
    government, 51–3, 169–70
    local authority, 53
Students
    double taxation agreement relating to, 142

Tax tables, 221–2
Tax year
    meaning, 3
Taxation
    guide to domicile and residence, use of,
        30–2
Tax Acts
    meaning, 2
Taxpayer
    appeal, right of, 124
    assistance, right to, 124
    certainty, right to, 125
    confidentiality, right to, 125
    correct amount of tax, right to pay no
        more than, 124
    hearing, right to, 124
    information, right to, 124
    obligations of, 125–35
    privacy, right to, 125
    residence, rights and obligations in
        country of, 123–35
    secrecy, right to, 125
Teachers
    double taxation agreement relating to, 142
Three-month rule
    physical presence, 9
Top-slicing relief, 188
Trades
    income arising in UK, 58–61
Treaty shopping, 146
Trusts
    capital gains tax, 83, 109–10
    created *inter vivos*, 107
    income arising in UK, 62–3
    income tax, 107–9
    inheritance tax, 110–12
    nature of, 104–5
    non-resident, 112–16
    residence of, 105
    resident, 105–7
    will trusts, 102–3

Unilateral relief, 146
Unit trust
    nature of, 179

United Kingdom
  establishment of, 2
  Finance Acts, 2
  income arising in. *See* Income
  meaning, 2
  property. *See* property
  schedular system of income tax, 48–9
  tax year, 3
  Taxes Acts, 2
Unremittable overseas income, 155

Value added tax
  cars, on, 119
  exemptions, 117–18
  generally, 117
  property, on, 118–19
  standard rate, 117

Value added tax—*contd*
  zero-rating, 117–18

Wife. *See* Husband and wife
Wills
  more than one jurisdiction, in, 101–2
  trusts, 102–3
  written variations, 103–4
Working abroad
  long-term, 21–2
  meaning, 9–10
  short-term, 13–14
Worldwide income
  returning expatriate, 149–50
Written variations, 103–4

Zero-rating, 117–8